W9-CEZ-062

ATLANTA

TRAY BUTLER

Contents

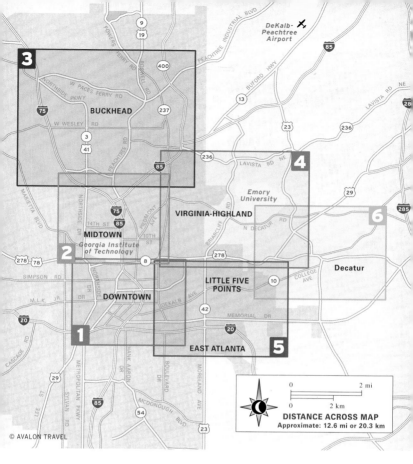

Maps

SEE MAP 2

SIGHTS

2 NATIONAL CENTER FOR CIVIL AND HUMAN RIGHTS
3 GEORGIA AQUARIUM
4 WORLD OF COCA-COLA
12 CENTENNIAL OLYMPIC PARK
13 COLLEGE FOOTBALL HALL OF FAME AND FAN EXPERIENCE
18 INSIDE CNN TOUR
21 SKYVIEW ATLANTA
36 MARTIN LUTHER KING JR. NATIONAL HISTORIC SITE
41 UNDERGROUND ATLANTA
42 GEORGIA CAPITOL MUSEUM
44 OAKLAND CEMETERY
57 ZOO ATLANTA

RESTAURANTS

20 THRIVE
23 TED'S MONTANA GRILL
25 SLICE DOWNTOWN
28 SUN DIAL RESTAURANT, BAR & VIEW
30 SWEET GEORGIA'S JUKE JOINT
35 NONI'S BAR AND DELI
39 THE SOUND TABLE
43 DADDY D'Z
45 RIA'S BLUEBIRD
46 SIX FEET UNDER
48 PASCHAL'S
50 NO MAS! CANTINA
53 SOUL VEGETARIAN
56 GRANT CENTRAL PIZZA AND PASTA

NIGHTLIFE

7 MAX LAGER'S AMERICAN GRILL AND BREWERY
10 TRADER VIC'S
26 SIDEBAR ATLANTA
37 SISTER LOUISA'S CHURCH OF THE LIVING ROOM & PING PONG EMPORIUM
38 JOYSTICK GAMEBAR

ARTS AND CULTURE

5 IMAGINE IT! THE CHILDREN'S MUSEUM OF ATLANTA
16 PHILIPS ARENA
22 TABERNACLE
27 THEATRICAL OUTFIT
32 AGATHA'S: A TASTE OF MYSTERY
33 THE APEX MUSEUM
40 EYEDRUM ART AND MUSIC GALLERY
47 CLARK ATLANTA UNIVERSITY ART GALLERIES
49 MARCIA WOOD GALLERY
51 SPELMAN COLLEGE MUSEUM OF FINE ART
52 WREN'S NEST HOUSE MUSEUM

SPORTS AND ACTIVITIES

15 ATLANTA FALCONS
17 ATLANTA HAWKS
24 ATL CRUZERS
54 ATLANTA BRAVES
55 ATLANTA PRESERVATION CENTER GUIDED WALKING TOURS

DISTANCE ACROSS MAP
Approximate: 4.1 mi or 6.6 km

0   500 yds
0   500 m

National Center
For Civil and
Human Rights

Civic
Center

RALPH MCGILL BLVD NE

OLD FOURTH

WARD

WABASH AVE NE

EAST AVE NE

SIMPSON ST NW

BAKER ST NW

World of
Coca-Cola

HARRIS ST NW

Centennial
Olympic Park

Peachtree
Center

FREEDOM PKWY

IRWIN ST NE

Martin Luther King Jr.
National Historic Site

SWEET
AUBURN

OLD WHEAT ST NE

AUBURN AVE NE

AUBURN AVE NE

EDGEWOOD AVE NE

EDGEWOOD AVE SE

CHAMBERLAIN

DECATUR ST

Five
Points

Underground
Atlanta

Georgia
State

Georgia
State
Capitol

Georgia
Capitol Museum

King
Memorial

CABBAGETOWN

Oakland
Cemetery

MEMORIAL DR SW

MEMORIAL DR SE

WOODWARD AVE SE

BRYAN ST SE

BRYAN ST SE

FULTON ST SW

FULTON ST

GLENWOOD AVE SE

SEE MAP 5

SYDNEY ST SE
ST PAUL SE

ORLEANS ST

MILLEDGE AVE

GRANT
PARK

Grant

Park

Turner
Field

CHEROKEE PL SE

GEORGIA AVE SE

Zoo Atlanta

ATLANTA AVE SE

© AVALON TRAVEL

🛍 SHOPS

34 SWEET AUBURN CURB MARKET

🅗 HOTELS

1   TWELVE HOTEL
    CENTENNIAL PARK
6   ALOFT ATLANTA
    DOWNTOWN
8   HYATT REGENCY
    ATLANTA
9   ATLANTA MARRIOTT
    MARQUIS
11 EMBASSY SUITES
    ATLANTA AT
    CENTENNIAL
    OLYMPIC PARK

14 OMNI HOTEL
    AT CNN CENTER
19 GLENN HOTEL
29 WESTIN
    PEACHTREE PLAZA
31 ELLIS HOTEL
58 SOCIAL GOAT
    BED AND BREAKFAST

❂ SIGHTS

30	HIGH MUSEUM OF ART	71	ATLANTA
45	MARGARET MITCHELL		BOTANICAL GARDEN
	HOUSE AND MUSEUM	81	PIEDMONT PARK
63	FOX THEATRE		

ℛ RESTAURANTS

2	BACCHANALIA	41	EINSTEIN'S
3	JCT KITCHEN & BAR	43	HENRY'S
9	COOKS & SOLDIERS		MIDTOWN TAVERN
10	YEAH! BURGER	46	EMPIRE STATE SOUTH
11	WEST EGG CAFÉ	52	ECCO
13	MILLER UNION	53	THE LAWRENCE
16	THE OPTIMIST	56	TAKOREA
17	OCTANE COFFEE	61	THE VARSITY
19	ANTICO PIZZA	67	GLADYS KNIGHT &
	NAPOLETANA		RON WINANS
27	NAN THAI FINE DINING		CHICKEN AND WAFFLES
31	TABLE 1280	69	MARY MAC'S
36	SOUTH CITY KITCHEN		TEA ROOM
38	PASTA DA PULCINELLA	75	VARUNI NAPOLI
40	STK	84	APRÈS DIEM

◐ NIGHTLIFE

7	ORMSBY'S	55	HALO LOUNGE
12	NORTHSIDE TAVERN	60	APACHE CAFÉ
21	LOBBY AT TWELVE	64	CHURCHILL GROUNDS
37	OPERA	77	AMSTERDAM CAFÉ
47	TEN ATLANTA	78	LOCA LUNA
48	G'S MIDTOWN	79	RED LIGHT CAFÉ
49	BLAKE'S ON THE PARK	82	PARK TAVERN

SEE MAP 3

WEST MIDTOWN

ATLANTIC STATION

WESTSIDE

❸ SHOPS

4	ANN MASHBURN	57	LOOK YOUNG ATLANTA
5	SID MASHBURN	70	GREEN MARKET FOR
6	STAR PROVISIONS		PIEDMONT PARK
8	SEED FACTORY	72	BOY NEXT DOOR
23	FAB'RIK	73	INTAGLIA HOME
44	BLUE MEDSPA		COLLECTION
50	HELMET HAIRWORX	74	PHIDIPPIDES
		76	PIEDMONT BARK

Ⓗ HOTELS

22	TWELVE HOTEL	58	SHELLMONT INN
	ATLANTIC STATION	59	GEORGIA TECH HOTEL
28	ARTMORE HOTEL		AND CONFERENCE
	ATLANTA		CENTER
34	W ATLANTA MIDTOWN	62	CROWNE PLAZA
35	FOUR SEASONS HOTEL		ATLANTA MIDTOWN
42	LOEWS ATLANTA	65	HOTEL INDIGO
	HOTEL		ATLANTA MIDTOWN
51	STONEHURST PLACE	66	THE GEORGIAN
54	RENAISSANCE		TERRACE
	ATLANTA MIDTOWN		
	HOTEL		

BANKHEAD AVE NW

© AVALON TRAVEL

Ⓖ ARTS AND CULTURE

1 THE GOAT FARM ARTS CENTER
14 KAI LIN ART
15 ACTOR'S EXPRESS
18 THE ATLANTA CONTEMPORARY ART CENTER
20 THE MILLENNIUM GATE
24 RHODES HALL
25 WILLIAM BREMAN JEWISH HERITAGE MUSEUM
26 CENTER FOR PUPPETRY ARTS
29 MUSEUM OF DESIGN ATLANTA
32 ALLIANCE THEATRE
33 ATLANTA SYMPHONY ORCHESTRA
68 NEW AMERICAN SHAKESPEARE TAVERN
85 MIDTOWN ART CINEMA

Ⓐ SPORTS AND ACTIVITIES

39 SKATE ESCAPE
80 URBAN BODY FITNESS
83 ATLANTA BELTLINE EASTSIDE TRAIL

SEE MAP 3

SEE MAP 4

MORNINGSIDE DR

CUMBERLAND RD NE

BEVERLY RD NE

THE PRADO NE

17TH ST NE

ANSLEY PARK

Eubanks Park

W PEACHTREE ST

High Museum of Art

Winn Park

Arts Center

Atlanta Botanical Garden

Piedmont

AMSTERDAM AVE NE

ORME CIR NE

PARK DR NE

VIRGINIA-HIGHLAND

Piedmont Park

Piedmont Lake

Park

CRESTHILL AVE NE

SPRING ST NW

WILLIAMS ST NW

14TH ST NE

13TH ST NE

12TH ST NW

Margaret Mitchell House and Museum

10TH ST NW

10TH ST NE

VIRGINIA AVE NE

PEACHTREE PL NE

Midtown

9TH ST NE

8TH ST NE

MIDTOWN

7TH ST NE

JUNIPER ST

6TH ST NE

PIEDMONT AVE NE

DURANT PL NE

ARGONNE AVE NE

PENN AVE NE

CHARLES ALLEN DR NE

MEADOW DR NE

MONROE DR NE

5TH ST NE

5TH ST NW

CYPRESS ST NE

4TH ST NE

3RD ST NW

3RD ST NE

SPRING ST

PONCE DE LEON AVE NE

Fox Theatre

North Avenue

NORTH AVE

SEE MAP 1

0   500 yds

0   500 m

DISTANCE ACROSS MAP
Approximate: 3.4 mi or 5.5 km

KINGSWOOD

WEST PACES FERRY/
NORTHSIDE

Georgia
Governor's
Mansion

WYNGATE

DISTANCE ACROSS MAP
Approximate: 5.6 mi or 9.1 km

Georgia
Memorial
Park

COLLIER
HILLS

Bobby Jones
Golf Course

SEE MAP 2

● SIGHTS
2 GEORGIA GOVERNOR'S
MANSION

29 ATLANTA
HISTORY CENTER

● RESTAURANTS
1 OK CAFE
14 RU SAN'S BUCKHEAD
AT TOWER PLACE
18 BONE'S
20 FOGO DE CHÃO
CHURRASCARIA
21 OCEAN PRIME
22 ARIA
23 SOUPER JENNY
30 CHOPS LOBSTER BAR
35 ROASTERS

40 GEORGIA GRILLE
41 RESTAURANT EUGENE
46 CAFE SUNFLOWER
47 WATERSHED
ON PEACHTREE
48 R. THOMAS
DELUXE GRILL
51 FAT MATT'S RIB SHACK
52 THE COLONNADE
54 TAQUERIA DEL SOL

● NIGHTLIFE
4 THE IVY BUCKHEAD
5 THE TAVERN AT PHIPPS
19 HAVANA CLUB
24 PROHIBITION

32 FADÓ IRISH PUB
37 TONGUE & GROOVE
38 GOLD ROOM
53 JUNGLE ATLANTA

● ARTS AND CULTURE
26 BUCKHEAD THEATRE
34 THE BILL LOWE
GALLERY

44 MUSEUM OF
CONTEMPORARY ART
OF GEORGIA
45 TULA ART CENTER

● SPORTS AND ACTIVITIES
6 LEGOLAND
DISCOVERY CENTER
42 BOBBY JONES
GOLF COURSE

43 BITSY GRANT
TENNIS CENTER
50 MIDTOWN BOWL

● SHOPS
3 GLOWDRY
7 JEFFREY ATLANTA
8 PHIPPS PLAZA
12 LENOX SQUARE MALL
13 ONA ATLANTA
15 BINDERS ART SUPPLIES
AND FRAMES
25 ONWARD RESERVE
27 MODA404

28 JONATHAN ADLER
31 SUGARCOAT
33 OXFORD
COMICS & GAMES
36 BELVEDERE
FURNITURE, LIGHTING
& DECORATIONS
39 RICHARD'S
VARIETY STORE
49 SAM FLAX ATLANTA

● HOTELS
9 RITZ-CARLTON
BUCKHEAD
10 MANDARIN ORIENTAL,
ATLANTA
11 WESTIN BUCKHEAD
ATLANTA

16 GRAND HYATT
ATLANTA
17 INTERCONTINENTAL
BUCKHEAD

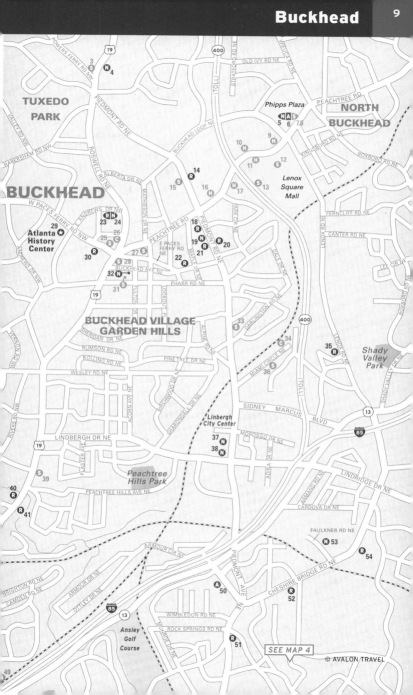

MORNINGSIDE

1 Ⓐ

Morningside
Nature Preserve

SEE MAP 3

WILDWOOD RD NE

Lenox-
Wildwood
Park

8 Ⓡ
9 Ⓢ

Ⓢ 10

VIRGINIA-
HIGHLAND

SEE MAP 2

Ⓗ 11

AMSTERDAM AVE NE

12 Ⓢ

Orme
Park

GLEN ARDEN WAY

LOS ANGELES
AVE

13 Ⓢ
14 Ⓢ
15 Ⓡ Ⓝ 16

Ⓡ Ⓡ
17　18

19 Ⓢ

HIGHLAND VIEW NE

DREWRY ST NE

20 Ⓝ
21 Ⓝ
22 Ⓝ
23 Ⓢ
24
25 Ⓡ
26

27 Ⓡ
28 Ⓢ
Ⓝ 29

Ⓝ 30

SEE MAP 1

Ⓝ 31

32 Ⓝ Ⓡ 33

34 Ⓒ Ⓝ 35

Springdale
Park

278

PONCEY-HIGHLAND

© AVALON TRAVEL

PONCEY-HIGHLAND

NORTH AVE NE

NORTH AVE NE

LITTLE
FIVE POINTS

DRUID PL NE

MORGAN ST NE

DALLAS ST NE

RANKIN ST NE

ANGIER AVE

WABASH AVE NE

RALPH MCGILL BLVD NE

EAST AVE NE

Jimmy Carter
Presidential
Library and
Museum

OLD FOURTH
WARD

FREEDOM PKWY NE

HIGHLAND AVE NE

INMAN
PARK

EUCLID AVE NE

AUSTIN AVE NE

ELMIRA PL NE

JOSEPHINE ST NE

ALTA AVE NE

HARALSON
AVE

CAROLINE ST NE

Spring-
dale
Park

Inman
Park

SANDERSON ST

GLEN IRIS DR NE

HOWELL ST NE

IRWIN ST NE

AUBURN AVE NE

DIXIE AVE NE

HARDEE ST NE

EDGEWOOD AVE NE

EDGEWOOD AVE SE

DANIEL ST SE

DECATUR ST SE

WYLIE ST SE

CABBAGETOWN

MANIGAULT ST SE

KIRKWOOD AVE SE

MAULDIN ST SE

Historic
Oakland
Cemetery

MEMORIAL DR SE

SEE MAP 1

WOODWARD AVE SE

0   500 yds

0   500 m

DISTANCE ACROSS MAP
Approximate: 4 mi or 6.4 km

FAITH AVE SE

SANDERS AVE SE

FLAT SHOALS AVE SE

METROPOLITAN AVE SE

GLENWOOD AVE SE

GARRETT ST

Woodland
Garden
Park

EAST
ATLANTA

PORTLAND AVE SE

© AVALON TRAVEL

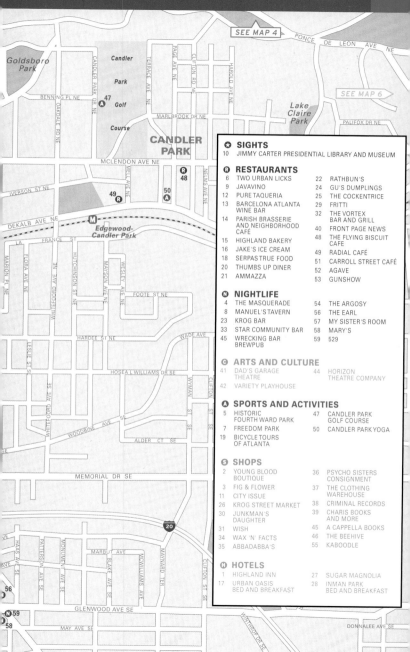

☼ SIGHTS
10 JIMMY CARTER PRESIDENTIAL LIBRARY AND MUSEUM

℞ RESTAURANTS
6 TWO URBAN LICKS
9 JAVAVINO
12 PURE TAQUERIA
13 BARCELONA ATLANTA WINE BAR
14 PARISH BRASSERIE AND NEIGHBORHOOD CAFÉ
15 HIGHLAND BAKERY
16 JAKE'S ICE CREAM
18 SERPAS TRUE FOOD
20 THUMBS UP DINER
21 AMMAZZA

22 RATHBUN'S
24 GU'S DUMPLINGS
25 THE COCKENTRICE
29 FRITTI
32 THE VORTEX BAR AND GRILL
40 FRONT PAGE NEWS
48 THE FLYING BISCUIT CAFE
49 RADIAL CAFÉ
51 CARROLL STREET CAFÉ
52 AGAVE
53 GUNSHOW

◑ NIGHTLIFE
4 THE MASQUERADE
8 MANUEL'S TAVERN
23 KROG BAR
33 STAR COMMUNITY BAR
45 WRECKING BAR BREWPUB

54 THE ARGOSY
56 THE EARL
57 MY SISTER'S ROOM
58 MARY'S
59 529

◉ ARTS AND CULTURE
41 DAD'S GARAGE THEATRE
42 VARIETY PLAYHOUSE

44 HORIZON THEATRE COMPANY

◎ SPORTS AND ACTIVITIES
5 HISTORIC FOURTH WARD PARK
7 FREEDOM PARK
19 BICYCLE TOURS OF ATLANTA

47 CANDLER PARK GOLF COURSE
50 CANDLER PARK YOGA

◉ SHOPS
2 YOUNG BLOOD BOUTIQUE
3 FIG & FLOWER
11 CITY ISSUE
26 KROG STREET MARKET
30 JUNKMAN'S DAUGHTER
31 WISH
34 WAX 'N' FACTS
35 ABBADABBA'S

36 PSYCHO SISTERS CONSIGNMENT
37 THE CLOTHING WAREHOUSE
38 CRIMINAL RECORDS
39 CHARIS BOOKS AND MORE
45 A CAPPELLA BOOKS
46 THE BEEHIVE
55 KABOODLE

◓ HOTELS
1 HIGHLAND INN
17 URBAN OASIS BED AND BREAKFAST

27 SUGAR MAGNOLIA
28 INMAN PARK BED AND BREAKFAST

SEE MAP 4

SEE MAP 5

OAKLAND ST

FAIRVIEW

MONTGOMERY ST

MERRILL AVE

SCOTT BLVD

WOODLAWN AVE

CLARION AVE

NELSON FERRY RD

PINETREE DR

WATERS ST

TRINITY PL

78

W PONCE DE LEON AVE NE

OAKLAND RD

UPLAND RD

MELROSE AVE

DREXEL AVE

LANSDOWNE AVE

ADELE ST

HIBERNIA AVE

HOWARD AVE

W COLLEGE AVE

JEFFERSON PL

OLYMPIC PL

CAMBRIDGE AVE

FIELD AVE

M East Lake

278

COLLEGE AVE NE

MURRAY HILL AVE NE

SISSON AVE NE

LELAND TER NE

WISTERIA WAY NE

WINTER AVE NE

2ND AVE

3RD AVE

LEYDEN ST

MEAD RD

LAKE DR

Oakhurst Park

OAKHURST

3

16

17

18

© AVALON TRAVEL

Decatur
Cemetery

W PONCE DE LEON AVE

E PONCE DE LEON AVE

E COURT SQ

SWANTON WAY

SYCAMORE ST

ROBIN ST

E COLLEGE AVE

To Mileybright
Farmhouse
Bed & Breakfast

DECATUR

Agnes

Scott

College

DOUGHERTY ST

HANCOCK ST

DAVIS ST

OAKVIEW RD

GREEN

KIRK RD

BENSON ST

HILL ST

McKoy
Park

R RESTAURANTS

3	FARM BURGER	12	THE IBERIAN PIG
5	BRICK STORE PUB	13	CAKES & ALE
6	SWEET MELISSA'S	16	SUN IN MY BELLY
10	LEON'S FULL SERVICE	17	MATADOR MEXICAN CANTINA
11	JAVA MONKEY	18	UNIVERSAL JOINT

N NIGHTLIFE
14 EDDIE'S ATTIC

A SPORTS AND ACTIVITIES
7 DECATUR GHOST TOUR

S SHOPS

| 2 | WILD OATS AND BILLY GOATS | 8 | LITTLE SHOP OF STORIES |
| 4 | HELIOTROPE | 9 | SALON RED |

H HOTELS

| 1 | COURTYARD ATLANTA DECATUR | 15 | MILEYBRIGHT FARMHOUSE BED & BREAKFAST |

0   300 yds

0   300 m

DISTANCE ACROSS MAP
Approximate: 3.4 mi or 5.5 km

© AVALON TRAVEL

DISTANCE ACROSS MAP
Approximate: 28 mi or 43 km

0
0
2 km
2 mi

Adamsville

Fulton County Airport

Union City

Cascade Heights

College Park

Hartsfield-Jackson Atlanta International Airport

Rockdale

Adams Park

MARIETTA BLVD

Georgia Institute of Technology

ATLANTA

West End

LAKEWOOD AVE

Riverdale

Forest Park

MCDONOUGH BLVD

Conley

MORELAND AVE

Eastland Heights

Thomasville

Emory University

DEKALB

DECATUR RD

Decatur

Fort Gillem

FOREST PKWY

Lake City

Clayton State University

Stone Mountain

STONE MOUNTAIN

HALL

R RESTAURANTS
6 THE SWALLOW AT THE HOLLOW
10 MCKENDRICK'S STEAK HOUSE
13 SOUTHBOUND
15 HORSERADISH GRILL
20 OLD VININGS INN
21 CANOE
24 NUEVO LAREDO CANTINA
32 ONE FLEW SOUTH

N NIGHTLIFE
12 5 SEASONS BREWING

A ARTS AND CULTURE
1 ZUCKERMAN MUSEUM OF ART
3 MARIETTA/COBB MUSEUM OF ART
4 MARIETTA GONE WITH THE WIND MUSEUM: SCARLETT ON THE SQUARE
14 CINEBISTRO
16 CHASTAIN PARK AMPHITHEATER
19 COBB ENERGY PERFORMING ARTS CENTRE
23 ATLANTA OPERA
25 ATLANTA BALLET
29 STARLIGHT SIX DRIVE-IN
30 AARON'S AMPHITHEATRE AT LAKEWOOD
31 DELTA FLIGHT MUSEUM
33 SPIVEY HALL

S SPORTS AND ACTIVITIES
5 SIX FLAGS WHITE WATER
7 CHATTAHOOCHEE RIVER NATIONAL RECREATION AREA
8 HIGH COUNTRY OUTFITTERS
9 ATLANTA LAWN TENNIS ASSOCIATION (ALTA)
17 CHASTAIN PARK
18 CHASTAIN PARK TRAIL
22 ATHLETIC CLUB NORTHEAST
26 SILVER COMET TRAIL
27 SILVER COMET CYCLES
28 SIX FLAGS OVER GEORGIA

H HOTELS
2 STANLEY HOUSE INN
11 LE MERIDIEN ATLANTA PERIMETER

DISCOVER
Atlanta

In the capital of the New South, the key word is "new." Signs of renewal are everywhere. Electric-blue streetcars ferry passengers to new multimillion-dollar museums downtown. You can almost smell the paint drying on mixed-use developments from Inman Park to Buckhead. Conversations turn to news of film studios breaking ground or the forthcoming sports arenas.

Building booms have been all the rage here since the Reconstruction. Atlanta's chosen mascot, a phoenix rising from flames, commemorates its Civil War torching and comeback as an engine of industry. Dubbed the City of Trees, Atlanta has felt more like a city of cranes since hosting the 1996 Olympic Games. Shiny glass skyscrapers keep popping up like clockwork.

The reputation for boosterism and unchecked sprawl might imply a fast-paced commuter culture. In truth, the quality of life in this network of diverse neighborhoods tends to be relaxed and gracious (though all bets are off during rush hour).

Many small-town Southern charms remain: festivals celebrating barbecue and dogwood blossoms, pitchers of sweet tea on restaurant patios, and the famous hospitality. Almost 40 million visitors come here annually—even more since the ATL emerged as a hip-hop powerhouse in the mid-2000s. The buzz these days is less Dirty South and more Hollywood South, all eyes on the thriving film industry.

Beyond the stadiums and studios, you can detect a quieter resurgence underway. Urbanist marketplaces fill once-dilapidated factories. Indie arts groups stage performances and paint murals in forgotten buildings. Biggest of all, the Atlanta BeltLine keeps gaining steam, redeveloping an abandoned railway corridor into vibrant public space. Maybe even future-focused Atlanta is learning how to feather its nest without incinerating the past.

Clockwise from top left: an Olympic torch-shaped lamppost, Centennial Olympic Park; Fox Theatre; Lasershow Spectacular at Stone Mountain; view of Atlanta's skyline from Centennial Olympic Park.

Georgia Aquarium

Planning Your Trip

Where to Go

Downtown

Many first-time travelers to Atlanta never venture beyond Downtown—and who can blame them? In the dense, pedestrian-friendly business district, several of the city's largest high-rise hotels sit within four or five blocks of attractions including **CNN Center,** the **Georgia Aquarium,** and the **World of Coca-Cola.** Heavy on conventioneers and commuters but light on locals, Downtown becomes a ghost town after dark. Check out the bars and restaurants of **Edgewood Avenue** or **Cabbagetown** for evening entertainment. Better yet, go farther afield to get a real taste of Atlanta's idiosyncratic neighborhoods.

Midtown

With a critical mass of landmarks like the **High Museum of Art** and the **Fox Theatre, Midtown** is known as Atlanta's home of high culture. It's also a popular recreation destination, whether for sunny afternoons in **Piedmont Park** or evenings on the **Midtown Mile** (Peachtree Street south of 15th Street). **Atlantic Station,** a self-contained retail and entertainment complex, attracts a busy college scene on weekend nights. The constellation of nightspots around 10th Street and Piedmont Avenue remains the Southeast's most vivacious gayborhood. The ongoing evolution of **West Midtown** features trendy shops and swanky dining in refurbished warehouses.

Buckhead

An old joke calls Buckhead the place where old money lives and new money parties. The late-night mischief lives on in the **East Andrews Drive bar** district, as rowdy as it is resilient. But the real allure of Buckhead lies in its resplendent **Southern estates (including the Georgia Governor's Mansion)**, high-end fashion boutiques in **Buckhead Atlanta**, and the charming **Atlanta History Center.** Farther north, **Lenox Square Mall** qualifies as more than just a shopping center due to its longstanding Independence Day and Christmas events.

Virginia-Highland

The tree-lined avenues of Virginia-Highland may be quaint and homey, but the **clusters of shops** along **North Highland Avenue** are the real jewels in the neighborhood's crown. It's a hodgepodge of casual restaurants, yuppie pubs, and clothing shops. Nearby **Emory University** features the prestigious **Michael C. Carlos Museum,** notable for rare Egyptian artifacts. Younger kids may prefer the massive dinosaur skeletons and IMAX theater at **Fernbank Museum of Natural History.**

Little Five Points and East Atlanta

For decades, Little Five Points has been a fertile oasis of **all things alternative**, dotted with dive bars, tattoo parlors, and thrift stores. Its more refined, yet still free-spirited, older sister **Inman Park** boasts Atlanta's most postcard-ready assortment of Queen Anne and Romanesque homes and a not-to-be missed spring festival. The **Old Fourth Ward,** once a sleepy backlot, has become scenester central with its crowded restaurant patios on Highland Avenue and the booming Edgewood nightlife corridor. The vibe gets grungier in East Atlanta, worth the trek for the indie clubs or the offbeat **East Atlanta Strut** each fall.

Decatur

Though technically older than Atlanta, the city of Decatur has matured with a unique, independent personality. The tight-knit community located 15 minutes east of Downtown is best known for its **annual book festival**

High Museum of Art

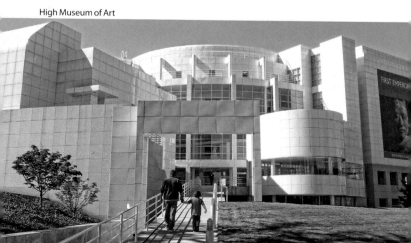

and **gorgeous town square,** as well as urbane restaurants, coffee shops, and bookstores. Local haunt **Eddie's Attic** is one of the region's most well-respected acoustic music venues. Close by, tiny **Oakhurst** gets props for the easygoing gastropubs.

Greater Atlanta

Atlanta's expansive metropolitan region touches 31 counties and covers more than 8,300 square miles (roughly the size of New Jersey). The town of **Marietta,** half an hour northwest of Downtown, has done a fine job of preserving a handful of important Civil War sites and the old-fashioned business district. The same holds true for neighboring **Roswell,** where the historical eye candy includes antebellum mansions and picturesque mill ruins. **Sandy Springs,** an affluent commercial crossroads and bedroom community, became a city in 2005 after a long tug-of-war with Atlanta.

When to Go

Atlanta's **temperate climate** allows a tourism season that lasts virtually all year. **Spring** arrives early, with short sleeves comfortable sometimes by **March** (also the start of Georgia's three-month tornado season). **April** and **May** bring in a phenomenal fit of **blossoms,** along with popular **events** like the Atlanta Dogwood Festival. **Summer's** warmth lingers into **autumn,** with beautiful breezy days common in October. **Winters** tend to be mild with very little snow and rare bouts of freezing rain. Temperatures can dip below freezing in December or January, but cold snaps don't usually stick. Visitors should proceed with caution before booking a trip in late **July** or **August.** The double punch of temperatures in the 90s and Georgia's infamous **humidity** can make outside activities miserable. No wonder Atlantans tend to spend the dog days of summer indoors.

Four Seasons, by sculptor Philip Haas, in the Atlanta Botanical Garden

Ebenezer Baptist Church

The Three-Day Best of Atlanta

A visit to Atlanta could easily last a week a longer, with mornings exploring museums and historic sites, easygoing afternoons sampling patio culture, and nights at any number of theaters or clubs. If your schedule is tight, you can squeeze many of the highlights into a few days. This itinerary requires a good deal of walking and a couple of drives or taxi rides. Stay in Downtown or Midtown for the easiest commute.

Day 1

▶ Begin with breakfast at **Thumbs Up Diner** on Edgewood Avenue. Don't linger too long over your Skillet Heap: You'll want to arrive early at the **Martin Luther King Jr. National Historic Site.** Tickets to tour the late civil rights leader's **birth home** are free and available at the visitors center starting at 9am, but they tend to be snapped up quickly. Taking in the site's various exhibitions and properties, including historic **Ebenezer Baptist Church,** will require 2-3 hours.

▶ For lunch, head a few blocks west to **Sweet Auburn Curb Market,** a retro food court with deep Downtown roots.

▶ Hop on the **Atlanta Streetcar** ($1 for a one-way trip) and ride to **Centennial Olympic Park.** Stop by the Fountain of Rings and the monuments to Olympic athletes, but be sure to plan ahead to enjoy at least a couple of the big attractions, which typically close at 5pm. The **National Center for Civil and Human Rights** and the **Inside CNN Tour** each take an hour or more; budget 2-3 hours for the **Georgia Aquarium,** the **World of Coca-Cola,** or the **College Football Hall of Fame.** Purchase tickets online to save time.

Backcountry Starters

A trip to **Empire State South** feels like visiting some eccentric cousin's middle-Georgia hunting lodge. The ever-changing menu of Southern staples puts a modern spin on "the beautiful foods of the region." You may not consider pimento cheese and bacon marmalade served in a Mason jar *beautiful*, but it's a scrumptious delicacy. Ditto for the boiled peanuts.

It's tough to choose just one starter from the creative menu at **Sweet Georgia's Juke Joint,** featuring a mélange of flavors from Mississippi bayou country (crispy crawfish tails, freshwater rock shrimp) and more local fare (crispy Vidalia onions, fried okra). Who said you had to order only one?

Fancy and Fried

Thanks to Fannie Flagg, fried green tomatoes are synonymous with Southern cooking. No place in town prepares them better than **South City Kitchen,** a Midtown institution delivering Southern with an upscale twist. The fried green tomatoes arrive with goat cheese and sweet red-pepper coulis. The fried wild Tennessee catfish is also a treat.

Watershed on Peachtree bears little resemblance to the restaurant's original Decatur incarnation, but its much-loved Southern fried chicken remains a major draw. Deemed the best fried chicken in the United States by *Food & Wine,* the crispy delicacy is cooked in ham hock-flavored fry fat yet comes out far less crunchy than you may expect. It's only served on Wednesdays and often out sells early in the evening.

Another popular destination for Southern farmstead cooking in a refined setting, **JCT Kitchen & Bar** goes for a more traditional approach with its crunchy finger-lickin' fried chicken, a gut-busting delight that comes with a hearty bacon macaroni and seasonal veggies.

Soul Standards

Paschal's is a bona fide culinary landmark, known as a meeting spot for civil rights leaders and power elite since the late 1940s. It's also a great place to

▶ Grab a pre-dinner cocktail at the **Sun Dial Restaurant,** a rotating lounge perched 723 feet above the city. The sunset views are worth the climb.

▶ Make dinner reservations at one of the many buzz-worthy restaurants in West Midtown, such as **Miller Union.** For more affordable, family-style dining, get in line at **Antico Pizza Napoletana.** Afterwards, treat yourself to a cupcake at **Star Provisions.**

Day 2

▶ Order a healthy breakfast at **R. Thomas Deluxe Grill,** a colorful local favorite since 1985, then immerse yourself in Southern culture at the **Atlanta History Center** in Buckhead. Don't miss the splendid **Swan House,** which gives a peek into how upper-crust Atlantans lived in the Jazz Age.

JCT Kitchen & Bar

discover soul food classics such as collard greens, black-eyed peas, steamed cabbage, candied yams, and grits.

Gladys Knight's Chicken and Waffles delivers on the classic brunch combination that its name promises, as well as traditional favorites like braised oxtail. Another standout: deep-fried salmon croquettes served with cinnamon raisin toast soaked in Georgia peach butter.

For clever updates on homespun classics, head to **Soul Vegetarian** and try the vegan barbecue Kalebone or country-fried tofu. Almost everything is vegetarian- or vegan-friendly and served without trans fats or preservatives. It's soul food sans guilt.

▶ If you can resist perusing the shops at **Buckhead Atlanta,** head to Midtown and snag an outdoor table at **The Lawrence.** After lunch, spend the afternoon exploring the **High Museum of Art** or one of the neighboring cultural sites, such as the **Center for Puppetry Arts** or the **Museum of Design Atlanta.** Save time for a quick tour of the **Margaret Mitchell House and Museum,** birthplace of *Gone With the Wind.*

▶ Midtown has no lack of affordable dinner options on Peachtree Street's **Midtown Mile** or nearby Crescent Avenue, but die-hard foodies may want to venture back to Buckhead for **Restaurant Eugene.** With a little planning, you can score tickets to a play at the **Alliance Theatre** or a performance at the **Fox Theatre,** an eye-popping 1920s movie palace that hosts touring Broadway musicals and concerts.

Swan House

▶ After dinner, travel to Virginia-Highland for a sample platter of casual nightlife (including landmarks **Atkins Park** and **Dark Horse Tavern**).

Day 3

▶ Eat a down-home breakfast at **Mary Mac's Tea Room,** then head into **Piedmont Park.** (If possible, time your visit to see the **Green Market,** open Saturday mornings March through December). Plant lovers may want to stroll the quiet grounds of the **Atlanta Botanical Garden** for hours, but remember to pace yourself for the hike ahead.

▶ Look for signs to the **Atlanta BeltLine Eastside Trail** at the corner of Monroe Drive and 10th Street. Follow the BeltLine south, stopping for lunch at **Two Urban Licks.**

the Martin Luther King Jr. National Historic Site

Atlanta has been called "the crown jewel in the story of black America" for good reason.

The city's distinction as a crossroads for equal opportunity dates back generations, due in no small part to the concentration of historically black colleges (the largest in the country) and long legacy of African American entrepreneurship and innovation. This unique heritage is also a major draw for tourism. Almost a million people annually visit the burial site of Martin Luther King Jr. and his wife, Coretta. Each January, the King Center for Nonviolent Social Change and nearby Ebenezer Baptist Church host a full week of programming leading up to the federal MLK holiday and remain busy during February's observance of Black History Month. The **National Black Arts Festival,** founded in 1987, has expanded beyond its traditional July programming to produce educational and cultural events year-round. No matter what the calendar says, it's always Black History Month in Atlanta.

National Center for Civil and Human Rights

The latest addition to the growing tourist district surrounding Centennial Olympic Park, the National Center for Civil and Human Rights serves as an worthy complement to the Martin Luther King Jr. National Historic Site. Interactive exhibitions help to place King's life and the struggles of the 1960s in a global context.

The Atlanta University Center

Although the West End campuses of Atlanta's historically black universities (including Spelman, Morehouse, and Morris Brown colleges) aren't necessarily a must-see attraction, they do include a few gems for art lovers and African American history buffs. **Clark Atlanta University Art Galleries** (223 James P Brawley Dr., Tues.-Fri. 11am-5pm, free) features ambitious murals by Hale Woodruff and more than 600 works from the school's historical collection of sculpture and paintings. Close by, the **Spelman College Museum of Fine Art** features works by and about women of the African diaspora.

High Museum of Art

The first general museum in North America to have a full-time curator dedicated to folk art, the High Museum of Art pays special tribute to Georgia native Nellie Mae Rowe. *At Night Things Come to Me,* on permanent display in the Nellie Mae Rowe Room, gives a peek at the colorful "haints" and "varmints" from African American folklore that often surface in the self-taught artist's drawings and mixed-media sculpture. The outstanding folk art collection includes noteworthy works by Thornton Dial, Ulysses Davis, Sam Doyle, and others.

Sweet Auburn Historic District

Designated as a National Historic Landmark in 1976, the Sweet Auburn Historic District stretches from Courtland Street to the Downtown Connector. The six-square-block area was once an essential enclave for the city's African American movers and shakers. Atlanta's first black-owned office building rose here, as did the city's first black-owned newspaper. The Royal Peacock Club hosted acts like Ray Charles, James Brown, and Aretha Franklin.

The **APEX Museum** includes historical information about Atlanta's African American pioneers and the neighborhood's role in civil rights history.

Atlanta BeltLine Eastside Trail

▶ Even with pauses to take in the **Historic Fourth Ward skate park,** you should reach Bernina Avenue in under an hour. Turn left onto the Freedom Park Trail in **Freedom Park** and proceed to the **Jimmy Carter Presidential Library and Museum.** Touring the site will take 1-2 hours.

▶ For a more adventurous itinerary, keep following the BeltLine until the trail ends near Irwin Street. Pass through Krog Street Tunnel, a famous canvas for street art, and weave through the narrow streets of **Cabbagetown** into the historic **Oakland Cemetery.** Plan ahead to catch a guided tour of the evocative Victorian graveyard or download the self-guided tour (www.oaklandcemetery.com).

▶ Eat dinner at **Barcelona Atlanta Wine Bar** or one of the many buzz-worthy restaurants in the Old Fourth Ward along **Highland Avenue** (starting at Elizabeth Street). **Krog Street Market,** a few blocks south, is also worth a look. End the day with an irresistible scoop of Chocolate Slap Yo Mama at **Jake's Ice Cream.** After all the miles you've covered in Atlanta, you deserve it.

Sights

Highlights

★ **Best Animal Life:** The largest indoor aquarium in the world, with 10 million gallons of water and more than 100,000 animals, the **Georgia Aquarium** is the only place outside of Asia that displays whale sharks (page 35).

★ **Best Behind-the-Scenes Tour:** Spend an hour exploring one of the world's most influential news organizations at the **Inside CNN Tour.** The interactive tour gives a thrilling backstage view of live television news in the making (page 37).

★ **Best Monument:** Hordes of travelers each year come to the **Martin Luther King Jr. National Historic Site,** a fitting tribute to the civil rights leader. The site includes a must-see visitors center and museum surrounded by other spots dear to the life of the famous Atlantan (page 38).

★ **Most Striking New Attraction:** The long-planned **National Center for Civil and Human Rights** adds a noticeable gravitas and architectural sparkle to Centennial Olympic Park. The $68 million museum chronicles the worldwide struggle for social justice and equality (page 39).

★ **Best Hidden Gem:** The quiet **Atlanta Botanical Garden** offers 30 acres of verdant splendor. Don't miss the lovely Fuqua Conservatory, which features the largest collection of orchid species on permanent display in the country (page 45).

★ **Most Beautiful Theater:** Built in 1929 as both a lavish movie palace and Shriners mosque, the fabulous **Fox Theatre** today hosts a lively mix of touring Broadway musicals, concerts, and a sold-out summer film series (page 45).

★ **Best Art Museum:** The **High Museum of Art** has grown into a magnificent cultural campus designed by star architects Renzo Piano and Richard Meier (page 46).

★ **Best Park:** Sometimes compared to New York City's Central Park, the 189-acre **Piedmont Park** in Midtown is one of the city's favorite recreation spots, home to dozens of events throughout the year and a seductive natural oasis in the middle of the metropolis (page 48).

★ **Best History Lesson:** Tucked in a pocket of Buckhead famous for over-the-top mansions, the extensive **Atlanta History Center** tells the story of the city from antiquity through the modern era. Its grounds include the graceful Swan House, a restored Jazz Age gem (page 50).

When the time came to observe the 150th anniversary of the Battle of Atlanta, one of the most pivotal skirmishes ever fought on American soil, the city rose to the occasion with customary gusto and no small amount of wit. The obligatory Civil War reenactments and lectures about the Confederate legacy were complemented with banjo and bagpipe performances, whiskey tastings, ghost tours, dance recitals, gala dinners, a 5K fun run, and an offbeat production of Carol Burnett's "Went With the Wind." Rather than mourning the devastation of July 1864, modern Atlanta turned the occasion into a citywide celebration that lasted all summer.

This can-do spirit is part of Atlanta's DNA, a powerful bonding agent that connects two of the city's chief preoccupations: movement and money. Founded as a railroad terminus in 1847, the rural outpost with no natural boundaries made its name as a crossroads for business. The town's love affair with transportation blossomed in the 20th century as civic boosters helped create a major hub for air travel. Today, Hartsfield-Jackson Atlanta International Airport is one of the busiest in the world. Three major interstates converge in the beating heart of Downtown—though as a commuter who's ever spent a sweaty afternoon stuck on the Connector can attest, that's not always a good thing.

On the commercial side, the city has been known for years as a haven for conventions, many of which take place in and around the Georgia World Congress Center. The past two decades have seen a rise in visitors traveling to Atlanta not for business but for pleasure, lured by the agreeable climate and lively local culture. As a legacy of the 1996 Olympic Games,

Previous: Centennial Olympic Park; Zoo Atlanta.

Downtown has polished its image with a growing campus of attractions around Centennial Olympic Park, including the World of Coca-Cola museum, CNN Center, and the world's largest indoor aquarium. New electric streetcars, launched in late 2014, connect the tourist district with the Martin Luther King Jr. National Historic Site and Sweet Auburn.

Though it's possible to spend days in Atlanta without leaving the urban grid of Downtown, which includes many of the most famous sights, any serious explorer should make it a priority to sample other neighborhoods. Midtown in particular has benefited from an influx of development since the late 1990s. Its crown jewel is still the stunning High Museum of Art, but the neighborhood doesn't hurt for prestigious landmarks, such as the Woodruff Arts Center (which includes the Alliance Theatre and the Atlanta Symphony Orchestra) and the majestic Fox Theatre. Piedmont Park remains a major draw, as does the recently expanded Atlanta Botanical Garden.

Atlanta's other key sights tend to be more scattered, with no one neighborhood offering the same concentration of headliners as Downtown or Midtown. The exception here is the Atlanta History Center in Buckhead, which includes an unrivaled collection of local artifacts and an assortment of notable buildings, or the fascinating Jimmy Carter Presidential Library and Museum near Little Five Points. To get the best handle on Georgia's capital city, be prepared to cover a lot of ground and zigzag between several spread-out neighborhoods even in the course of a day. Atlanta, the restless Southern mecca, is worth the commute.

Downtown   Map 1

CENTENNIAL OLYMPIC PARK

Newcomers to Atlanta tend to flock to Centennial Olympic Park as a starting point for sightseeing, which isn't a bad strategy. The 21-acre park was built to accommodate 1996's Centennial Olympic Village. It's since become a well-groomed green space in the thick of the tourist sector, with easy access to the World of Coca-Cola, the Georgia Aquarium, the National Center for Civil and Human Rights, CNN Center, Philips Arena, and the Georgia World Congress Center.

The park features several monuments dedicated to Olympic ideals as well as a memorial to the two people killed during the 1996 bombing. The playful **Fountain of Rings** blasts jets of water into the air from the central plaza. The fountain overflows with toddlers during warm months, and the plaza is cleared a few times a day for synchronized water-dancing shows, complete with music and lighting effects. December finds the park's towering Olympic torch-shaped lampposts dripping with strings of lights and decorations for the holiday season. An outdoor ice skating rink operates in the park from November through early January, running on roughly the same schedule as the annual Holiday in Lights celebration, which covers the grounds in eye-popping decorations.

It may be one of the city's grandest public spaces, but Centennial

Above: College Football Hall of Fame. **Below:** the Georgia Aquarium.

Olympic Park has never quite won over locals. Like much of Downtown, the park draws a share of homeless people, including a few aggressive panhandlers. A visible police presence and the private Downtown Ambassador Force help keep the area safe.

MAP 1: Centennial Olympic Park Dr. and Luckie St., 404/222-7275, www.centennialpark. com; daily 7am-11pm; free

COLLEGE FOOTBALL HALL OF FAME AND FAN EXPERIENCE

"In the South," legendary coach Marino Casem once observed, "college football is a religion, and every Saturday is a holy day." An outing to Downtown's impressive new sports museum, which opened in 2014, drives the point home. The sparkling, $68.5 million shrine honors the pastime's greatest champions with reverence and fervor. If college football really is a religion, this high-tech temple does a reverent job of celebrating its most colorful traditions and passions.

The tunnel-like ingress to the 94,000-square-foot museum echoes the experience of players entering a stadium. Guests register an all-access "pass" and choose their favorite college team. The selection follows visitors from room to room, with interactive exhibitions that come to life spouting bits of team trivia. Diehard fans could spend hours poking through the touch-screen "augmented reality" displays in the Hall of Fame. Downstairs, fantasy footballers of all ages have a chance to kick, toss, and tackle on a 45-yard indoor field.

Chick-fil-A and other corporate sponsors make their presence unavoidable throughout the exhibitions, but the shills never drain the College Football Hall of Fame's obvious adrenaline. For Centennial Olympic Park's expanding tourism quarter, the inspired addition is nothing short of a touchdown.

MAP 1: 250 Marietta St. NW, 404/880-4800, www.cfbhall.com; Sun.-Fri. 10am-5pm, Sat. 9am-6pm; $20 adult, $17 child, $18 senior

Save Money with CityPass

If you're planning to hit several of the city's busiest tourist spots, CityPass can be a real bargain. The pocket-size booklet includes admission to the Georgia Aquarium, the World of Coca-Cola, the Inside CNN Tour, and two additional "option tickets." (Visitors choose either the Fernbank Museum of Natural History or the High Museum of Art, and Zoo Atlanta or the Atlanta History Center.) The pass is valid for nine days starting on the first day the booklet is used. Passholders can skip the lines at some attractions, and the booklet also contains site information, directions, best times to visit, maps, and suggestions for shopping and eating. The cost, including tax, is $75 (a $130 value) for adults and $60 for kids. Purchase passes online (www.citypass.com/atlanta) or at the ticket offices of any of the participating attractions.

Walking with Oakland's Ghosts

Who wants to spend an afternoon hunched over tombstones in a spooky antebellum graveyard?

Apparently, lots of people. Guided tours of Oakland Cemetery bring in around 12,000 visitors annually. Memorials to famous Atlanta residents add eerie star power to the cemetery's **Sights, Symbols, and Stories Tour**, a 90-minute overview of the cemetery (Dec.-Mar. Sat.-Sun. 2pm, Apr.-Nov. 10am, 2pm, and 4pm; adults $10, students $5, seniors $5). Throughout the year, the Historic Oakland Foundation also offers more than a dozen specialty tours on topics ranging from love stories to Victorian symbolism. (For a schedule, see www.oaklandcemetery.com.)

Although there's no comparison to a living, breathing docent to usher you around the immense grounds, visitors itching to wander at their own pace can download two self-guided walks. The handy Oakland Cemetery Audio Tours app (free via iTunes) includes **African American Voices** and **Timeless Gardens;** both take around two hours to finish.

★ GEORGIA AQUARIUM

Leave it to go-getting Atlanta, stranded 250 miles from the ocean, to overcompensate for being landlocked by building one of the most ambitious fish tanks in the country. The Georgia Aquarium came about through an extraordinary $250 million gift to the city from Bernie Marcus, cofounder of Atlanta-based Home Depot, who envisioned a world-class aquarium like those he had visited elsewhere. The dream became a reality in 2005.

The aquarium now draws 2.2 million visitors each year. Its star residents include four fully grown whale sharks, the largest fish in the world. The aquarium boasts being the only facility outside of Asia featuring whale sharks, which can be surveyed from below via an always-crowded underwater viewing tunnel with a moving sidewalk. The graceful, alien-faced beluga whales also draw big crowds, as do the frisky southern sea otters.

A 2010 renovation introduced an unusual dolphin attraction, featuring a show that incorporates costumed actors, musical theater, lighting effects, and a spirited cast of bottlenose dolphins. The 25-minute production can be a convoluted affair, but toddlers will probably love it.

Adventurous guests can grope squishy stingrays and tickle horseshoe crabs in the touch pools; *really* adventurous guests can pay $235 to reserve one of the limited daily spots to scuba dive among the whale sharks and manta rays. The aquarium also offers an exclusive Behind the Seas Tour, which explains how the staff cares for the animals. The tour costs $48 (above normal admission) and departs hourly 11am-4pm daily.

MAP 1: 225 Baker St. NW, 404/581-4000, www.georgiaaquarium.org; Sun.-Fri. 10am-5pm, Sat. 9am-6pm, variable hours during holidays and special events; $32-36 adult, $26-30 child, $28-32 senior, higher prices Fri.-Sun. and in summer

Clockwise from top left: World of Coca-Cola; CNN Center; Martin Luther King Jr. National Historical Site.

Completed in 1889, the regal Georgia State Capitol is one of Atlanta's most recognizable landmarks. Its noble 75-foot dome is plated in Georgia gold, which was mined in Dahlonega. Its neoclassical structural style is said to mimic the U.S. Capitol in Washington, D.C. The vital nerve center of the state's government operates here, including the governor's office and both chambers of the General Assembly. The Georgia Capitol Museum, founded in 1895, features exhibitions detailing the cultural heritage of Georgia, including artifacts from the state's earliest history, Native American exhibitions, portraits of famous Georgians, and a discussion about the construction of the building itself.

No visit to the capitol should end with the museum alone. Check out the Georgia Capitol Flag collection housed in the Hall of Valor on the first floor, and take some time to admire the works of art inside the high Victorian rotunda. Free guided tours are available year-round (Jan.-Mar. Mon.-Fri. 10am, 10:30am, 11am, and 11:30am; Apr.-Dec. Mon.-Fri. 9:30am, 10:30am, and 11:30am); groups of more than nine require advance reservations. It's possible to see the Georgia General Assembly during their annual session, which begins the second Monday in January and continues for 40 working days.

MAP 1: 2 Martin Luther King Dr. NW, Ste. 820, 404/656-2846, www.sos.georgia.gov/state_capitol; Mon.-Fri. 8am-5pm; free

★ INSIDE CNN TOUR

Blame the 24-hour news cycle on Atlanta's own Ted Turner, who launched the Cable News Network in 1980 and forever changed the pace and character of broadcast journalism. Though many of CNN's banner shows and personalities operate out of New York or Washington, D.C., Atlanta's **CNN Center** remains the company's largest news bureau and home to its sister network, HLN (formerly CNN Headline News).

The Inside CNN Tour takes visitors on a behind-the-scenes journey through the newsrooms of CNN and CNN International. Guests start by ascending what's billed as the world's longest freestanding escalator and begin the tour with an interactive exhibit detailing CNN's founding and early history. A viewing chamber gives an overhead look at reporters and anchors in action, along with an absorbing narrative on how live news programs come together in real time. Diehard news junkies might want to spring for the $35 VIP tour (Mon.-Sat. 9:30am, 11:30am, 1:30pm, and 3:30pm), a more immersive version of the regular tour that also ventures inside the actual HLN Control Room and HD Studio 7. Another option: The Morning Express with Robin Meade Tour ($49; Thurs. 8:30am) goes backstage at HLN's Studio H and leaves guests with a keepsake travel mug.

Once the tour is over, mill around CNN Center for the many souvenir shops and the large mall-style food court. The building connects to the Omni Hotel, Philips Arena, and the CNN Center MARTA station.

MAP 1: 190 Marietta St. NW, 404/827-2300, www.cnn.com/studiotour; daily 9am-5pm; $16 adult, $13 child, $15 senior

SIGHTS DOWNTOWN

Martin Luther King Jr.'s Atlanta

The King Birth Home on Auburn Avenue

Almost a million people make the pilgrimage to Atlanta each year to pay tribute to the legacy of Martin Luther King Jr. Since 1980, the National Park Service has maintained the Martin Luther King Jr. National Historic Site, which includes the graves of King and his wife, the historic Ebenezer Baptist Church, the King Birth Home, and Historic Fire Station No. 6.

★ MARTIN LUTHER KING JR. NATIONAL HISTORIC SITE

More than just a memorial to a man who changed the course of the 20th century, the Martin Luther King Jr. National Historic Site provides a thorough and poignant history lesson on the civil rights movement. A vast preservation district administered by the National Park Service surrounds the **King Birth Home, Ebenezer Baptist Church,** the **King Center,** and the tombs of King and his wife, Coretta Scott King. The site borders the Sweet Auburn Historic District, a once-vital African American neighborhood that's begun to experience noticeable new life and gentrification.

Any outing should start at the National Park Service visitors center, which offers a series of engaging and interactive exhibits on King's life and a stark retelling of the history of racial segregation in America. On display is the wooden mule wagon that carried King's body during his 1968 funeral procession, with extensive photography from the turbulent era. Temporary exhibitions relate to social justice. The large, free visitors parking lot is accessible from John Wesley Dobbs Avenue.

MAP 1: 450 Auburn Ave. NE, 404/331-5190, www.nps.gov/malu; daily 9am-5pm; free

The King Birth Home

Built in 1895, this Queen Anne-style dwelling housed several generations of the King family. For the first dozen years of his life, Martin Luther King Jr. shared the house with his grandparents, parents, brother, sisters, a great aunt, and an uncle. The King Birth Home (501 Auburn Ave., 404/331-6922, www.nps.gov/malu, daily 10am-5pm) has been refurbished to reflect the aesthetics of the 1930s. Visitors who want to tour the King Birth Home should plan to arrive early to collect tickets at the National Park Service Visitor Center (450 Auburn Ave., daily 9am-5pm; tours are free but typically fill up fast because they're limited to 15 people). The half-hour tours are led by park rangers.

Historic Fire Station No. 6

Atlanta's oldest standing fire station was built in 1894 and served the Sweet Auburn neighborhood until 1991. It underwent a thorough renovation in 1995, and today the two-story redbrick Romanesque Revival building houses a museum (39 Boulevard, 404/331-5190, www.nps.gov/malu, daily 10am-5pm, free) detailing the desegregation of Atlanta's fire department and features a 1927 American LaFrance fire engine. Two of the original brass sliding poles also remain.

Ebenezer Baptist Church

Martin Luther King Jr.'s father and grandfather presided at this landmark (407 Auburn Ave., 404/688-7300, www.historicebenezer.org, Mon.-Sat. 10am-5pm), which was built in 1922. King was baptized at Ebenezer as a child and ordained at the age of 19. His funeral was held here in 1968. In 1974, violence erupted in the church when a gunman shot and killed King's mother, Alberta Christine Williams King, along with another deacon. The church's congregation moved in 1999 to the massive Horizon Sanctuary across the street. Plan to spend 20-30 minutes sitting in the sanctuary, where recordings of King's sermons play on repeat.

★ NATIONAL CENTER FOR CIVIL AND HUMAN RIGHTS

Given the enduring—and deserved—popularity of the Martin Luther King Jr. National Historic Site, the arrival of another Downtown civil rights museum may seem excessive. The new National Center for Civil and Human Rights quickly puts any such doubts to rest. Designed by architect Phil Freelon, the handsome building's curvy wood-toned exterior is said to evoke a pair of hands cupped around a precious cargo, an appropriate image for this important cultural institution.

Opened in 2014, the 42,000-square-foot museum documents the legacy of King and many other civil rights leaders. Well-designed exhibitions revisit the fight for equality from the 1950s through today. A replica lunch counter lets visitors experience threats and slurs similar to those heard during historic sit-in protests.

Overlaps with the King historic site are inevitable but handled with admirable care, especially in the poignant reflection on his assassination day. The center displays King's personal belongings and manuscripts, rotating from an assortment of 50,000 items from the permanent collection.

Other interactive displays succeed in placing the American fight for equality within the greater framework of human rights around the world.

MAP 1: 100 Ivan Allen Jr. Blvd. NW, 678/999-8990, www.civilandhumanrights.org; Tues.-Sat. 10am-5pm, Sun. noon-5pm; $15 adult, $10 child, $13 senior

OAKLAND CEMETERY

Although it sits just a stone's throw from Downtown, Oakland Cemetery feels like a hundred years away from the buzz of the capital. This rambling 88-acre graveyard is one of the few sites in the city dating from before the Civil War. Founded in 1850, it was the spot from which Confederate general John B. Hood watched the Battle of Atlanta, and where nearly 7,000 Confederate—and Union—soldiers are buried today.

Famous Atlantans, including *Gone With the Wind* author Margaret Mitchell, golf champion Bobby Jones, and former Atlanta mayor Maynard Jackson, are buried in Oakland Cemetery. The graveyard contains sections devoted to Jewish, black, and pauper graves, which were separated from other areas. Despite its macabre ambience, the cemetery today is a frequent destination not only for history buffs, but also for joggers, dog-walkers, and picnickers needing a breather from the commotion of the city. Don't miss the fun slate of Halloween-themed activities or the lineup of guided walking tours. The visitors center and museum shop, located in the Bell Tower (Mon.-Fri. 9am-5pm, Sat.-Sun. 9am-dusk) deserves a look for its macabre souvenirs.

MAP 1: 248 Oakland Ave. SE, 404/688-2107, www.oaklandcemetery.com; daily 8am-8pm; free

SKYVIEW ATLANTA

"You can see Atlanta from here," declares the tagline of this high-profile carnival ride—a claim that's *sort of* true. The Ferris wheel lifts riders 200 feet above Centennial Olympic Park, offering rooftop views of adjacent destinations like the Georgia Aquarium, the Tabernacle, and the World of Coca-Cola. But the London Eye, it ain't. The proximity to other attractions makes sense, perhaps, but the 20-story climb can't exactly compete with nearby skyscrapers that double or even triple its height.

Quibbles over the vista have a way of disappearing after dark, when SkyView is at its finest (and the lines are usually shortest). The ride sparkles like a giant neon kaleidoscope at night and brings a fun, amusement-park vibe to the tourist quarter. Each "flight" involves four rotations of the slow-moving wheel. Its 42 climate-controlled gondolas are comfy and private, making SkyView a popular date-night destination. Big spenders can upgrade to a VIP gondola ($50 per ticket), featuring leather seats, glass floors, and room enough for five. Add in a couple of the adult beverages sold in the ticket queue and you just might have a party, no skyline necessary.

MAP 1: 168 Luckie St. NW, 678/949-9023, www.skyviewatlanta.com; Mon.-Thurs. noon-11pm, Fri. 10am-midnight, Sun. 10am-11pm; $14 adult, $9 child, $13 senior

Clockwise from top left: SkyView Atlanta; Oakland Cemetery; the National Center for Civil and Human Rights.

All Aboard the Atlanta Streetcar

The new **Atlanta Streetcar** (http://streetcar.atlantaga.gov, Mon.-Thurs. 6am-11pm, Fri. 6am-1am, Sat. 8:30am-1am, Sun. 9am to 11pm) began service in 2014 after construction delays and no lack of local skepticism. "It's fun, it's sleek," an Atlanta Journal-Constitution op-ed asked before the opening, "but is it useful?"

For sightseers taking in the city's most famous attractions, the answer is an obvious "yes." The 2.7-mile Downtown Loop connects Centennial Olympic Park (including the Georgia Aquarium, the World of Coca-Cola, and CNN Center) with Sweet Auburn and the Martin Luther King Jr. Historic Site. It also serves the Peachtree Center MARTA Station and several of the convention district's major hotels.

Atlanta scrapped a previous streetcar line in 1949. Like the trolleys of yesteryear, the new electrically powered vehicles run on rails and share lanes with other traffic. Each 80-foot tram carries up to 60 commuters between a dozen stops. The 15-minute wait time can be irksome, but there's no arguing with the cost ($1 adult, $3 one-day pass) or the thrill of escaping hot and noisy sidewalks for a calm, air-controlled lift.

Typical of any major public works project in the ATL, the $98 million streetcar initiative remains controversial. Critics have dismissed it as an expensive gimmick that doesn't help regional traffic woes. Advocates say the network has spurred investment in once-shunned neighborhoods, such as the undeniable gentrification of Edgewood Avenue.

More than 100,000 passengers caught a ride on the streetcar during its first three months of operation. Atlanta mayor Kasim Reed, a major proponent, has worked to persuade disbelievers and boost ridership by waiving fares and laying out an ambitious vision for the network. Future phases would extend service from the West End to Buckhead and link up with the Atlanta BeltLine—lofty plans that may become reality if the streetcar can win over tourists and locals alike.

UNDERGROUND ATLANTA

The number of incarnations we've seen of Underground Atlanta is getting to be ridiculous. The bizarre, subterranean entertainment district was born by accident in the 1920s when the city built a system of viaducts to raise traffic flow above its tangled railroad tracks. Businesses moved up to the higher floors, leaving their former storefronts below for storage—or use as speakeasies during Prohibition. In the late 1960s, the abandoned five-block area below Alabama Street was rediscovered and gained new life as a historic site and groovy nightlife district.

The experiment didn't last. By the early 1980s Underground was again shuttered. It sprang to life once more in 1989 as a far more sanitized shopping mall aimed at tourists. The 1990 arrival of the World of Coca-Cola next door increased the site's foot traffic, though it was filled with suburban-style chain stores and souvenir stands. By the end of the decade it had again fallen into financial turmoil. The past few years have seen various efforts to reboot the concept, but so far no single concept has hit a home run. The departure of the World of Coca-Cola for Centennial Olympic Park hasn't helped.

Underground still draws its biggest crowd on New Year's Eve as thousands of revelers fill the main plaza to watch the annual Peach Drop. Explorers with time to kill downtown might take a fast stroll through Underground, but a better taste of Atlanta architecture from yesteryear is a few blocks north in the Fairlie-Poplar Historic District.

MAP 1: 50 Upper Alabama St., 404/523-2311, www.underground-atlanta.com; Mon.-Thurs. 10am-8pm, Fri.-Sat. 10am-9pm, Sun. noon-6pm, bar and restaurant hours vary; free

WORLD OF COCA-COLA

There's something very Willy Wonka about the World of Coca-Cola. The soft-drink giant's museum-meets-infomercial lures visitors into a candy-coated, sometimes surreal otherworld where the docents are called "ambassadors" and vintage advertisements are labeled "artifacts." After 17 years at Underground Atlanta, the museum relocated in 2007 to a fancy $96 million facility next to the Georgia Aquarium and within deliberate eyeshot of Coca-Cola's global headquarters.

Visitors begin with a quick (and mandatory) *Moments of Happiness* film, and then they're shepherded into the museum's light-filled atrium, where they can choose exhibitions ranging from a 4-D theater (a 3-D movie with moving seats) to an exhaustive collection of memorabilia. A bank-sized vault holds the cola's original secret formula, which was moved to the premises in 2011, as well as an amusing, family-friendly history lesson in how this pharmaceutical concoction came to rule the world.

Costumed mascots give guests a chance to have photos taken with polar bears and other familiar Coke characters. A working production line offers a behind-the-scenes peek at how glass bottling plants work; guests are later given free eight-ounce bottles of Coke filled on-site. Though the experience can feel like a long and relentless commercial, the World of Coca-Cola does have moments of happiness even for skeptics. One gallery features cola-inspired paintings and sculptures by Georgia artists Howard Finster and Steve Penley. The tour ends with a tasting room, where caffeinated guests can sample exotic beverage brands from five continents. Now there's a pause that refreshes.

MAP 1: 121 Baker St. NW, 404/676-5151, www.worldofcoca-cola.com; Sun.-Thurs. 10am-5pm, Fri.-Sat. 9am-5pm; $16 adult, $12 child, $14 senior, $10 parking; MARTA: Peachtree Center or CNN Center

ZOO ATLANTA

With a history in Grant Park dating all the way back to 1889, Zoo Atlanta has long been one of the city's trademark attractions, adored by schoolchildren for generations and endured by just as many adults. After an ugly period during the 1980s when the facility lost national accreditation due to substandard animal housing, the zoo bounced back with a sweeping renovation. Most of the more than 1,000 animals roam freely in lush, naturalistic habitats, no longer confined to cramped glass cages or dirty cement ditches.

Zoo Atlanta was synonymous for decades with its mascot, Willie B.,

Top 10 for Kids

- Get soaked in the Fountain of Rings at **Centennial Olympic Park** (page 32).

- Tackle an obstacle course or kick a field goal on the 45-yard indoor gridiron at the **College Football Hall of Fame** (page 34).

- Gasp at the playful beluga whales at the **Georgia Aquarium,** the largest indoor aquarium in the world (page 35).

- Visit the western lowland gorillas in their naturalistic habitat at **Zoo Atlanta,** the largest collection in the country (page 43).

- Explore the two-acre Children's Garden at the **Atlanta Botanical Garden,** which incorporates learning experiences into a playground-like atmosphere (page 45).

- Wow your toddler (age 2-8) with a romp through the colorful **Imagine It! The Children's Museum of Atlanta** (page 114).

- Hear a storyteller relate the adventures of rascally Br'er Rabbit at the **Wren's Nest House Museum** (page 114).

- Rub elbows with an actual Muppet at the **Center for Puppetry Arts**—or build your own (page 117).

- Experience an IMAX film or snap clever selfies with the dinosaur skeletons at **Fernbank Museum of Natural History** (page 51).

- Brave the enormous Goliath roller coaster at **Six Flags Over Georgia** (page 144).

a giant silverback gorilla named for former Atlanta mayor William B. Hartsfield. Though Willie B. passed away in 2000, his descendants now play among the other western lowland gorillas in the zoo's striking African rain forest area. More recently, the mascot mantle has been passed to the resident giant pandas, Lun Lun and Yang Yang, a prolific pair that has given birth to five cubs since 2006. The panda habitat is by far the zoo's most polished and up-to-date exhibition. Other highlights include the African lions, komodo dragons, a "living tree house" aviary and parakeet habitat, and an Australian-themed Outback Station, with a petting zoo and extensive playground. With the Cyclorama's exit from Grant Park, Zoo Atlanta has announced plans to transform the former Civil War Museum into a state-of-the-art events facility. It's also eyeing a major expansion of the African elephant habitat, which will more than triple in size by 2019.

MAP 1: 800 Cherokee Ave. SE, 404/624-9453, www.zooatlanta.org; Nov.-Mar. daily 9:30am-5:30pm, Apr.-Oct. Mon.-Fri. 9:30am-5:30pm and Sat.-Sun. 9:30am-6:30pm (last admission an hour before closing); $23 adult, $18 child, $19 senior

★ ATLANTA BOTANICAL GARDEN

With persistent growth in recent decades, the Atlanta Botanical Garden has blossomed into one of Midtown's greatest treasures, a serene oasis hidden in plain sight. It was once easy to jog around its fences inside Piedmont Park and never notice the expansive 30-acre garden. But ingenious renovations over the past few years have moved the main entrance to the park side of the garden and introduced several crowd-pleasing new features.

Any visit to the garden should start with the **Fuqua Conservatory,** a dazzling orchid center that hosts a superb collection of rare specimens from around the world. The moist, jungle-like atmosphere of the conservatory can feel more like a trip to a zoo than a garden. A 600-foot elevated canopy walk hovers over the **Southern Seasons Garden,** offering a rare up-close peek at the treetops of the **Storza Woods.** Below, a network of paths cuts through the hardwood forest, connecting the azalea walk with an 80-foot reflecting pool.

Harried travelers seeking a quiet afternoon can catch a moment of meditation in the peaceful **Japanese Garden.** The award-winning **Children's Garden** keeps young visitors splashing around in its always-busy **Sunflower Fountain,** while a summer concert series, seasonal art exhibitions, and crowded evening cocktail parties (May-Sept. Thurs. 6pm-10pm) have helped boost the garden's profile. More 155,000 visitors turn out to see **Garden Lights,** a holiday light show running November through January.

Tours are offered free with regular admission every Tuesday and Thursday at 1:30pm. Definitely a must-see, and not just for plant lovers.

MAP 2: 1345 Piedmont Ave. NE, 404/876-5859, www.atlantabotanicalgarden.org; Apr.-Oct. Tues.-Sun. 9am-7pm (Thurs. until 10pm May-Oct.), Nov.-Mar. Tues.-Sun. 9am-5pm; $19 adult, $13 child

★ FOX THEATRE

The "Fabulous Fox" defies easy characterization. It's an enormous, opulent 1920s movie house, a richly ornamented Moorish palace with a fetish for Egyptian accents, and an adored local monument whose history paved the way for Atlanta's modern preservation movement.

The Fox was built as the Yaarab Temple Shrine Mosque; the venue's original owners realized their lavish vision by securing financial aid from movie magnate William Fox, who agreed to lease its main auditorium as a movie hall. The 4,000-seat theater, replete with onion domes, minarets, and an interior sky full of sparkling stars, opened a few weeks after 1929's stock-market meltdown, leading to a decade of economic hardship and eventual bankruptcy. The Fox bounced back in the 1940s and became one of the city's premier cinemas and concert halls, wowing movie-goers with its 3,622-pipe Möller organ—the second-largest theater organ in the world. The early 1970s found the theater in decline, leading to a proposal by Southern Bell to demolish the property. A grassroots "Save the Fox"

Phantoms of the Fox

Anyone who's ever seen a show at the Fox Theatre will tell you that the cavernous old hallways just about drip with history. You can almost hear the murmurs of movie-goers from yesteryear as you climb the richly carpeted stairs to the upper balconies or descend into one of the echoing lounges below the lobby. After seven decades of continuous use as an entertainment venue, the theater has accumulated a couple of ghost stories.

One famous legend reports sightings of a Confederate soldier staring out of specific second-floor windows. It's a curious choice of a specter, considering that the venue wasn't built until 1929. Another tale that seems more rooted in actual history involves the basement, supposedly haunted by a Depression-era coal handler who slept on a cot next to the furnace. Apparently he never got the message that the place had switched to central heat.

At least one story of an unusual figure dwelling on the fringes of the Fox Theatre is *not* an urban myth. For more than 30 years, former technical director Joe Patten has lived on-site in the Fox's "secret" private residence, a well-appointed 3,600-square-foot apartment opposite the Egyptian Ballroom. Patten was granted the privilege of living at the Fox rent-free for the duration of his life, thanks to his vast efforts to save the building from demolition. Sometimes jokingly referred to as "the Phantom of the Fox," Patten enjoys unprecedented access to all areas of the theater, from the onion-shaped domes to the bowels of backstage.

Fox Theatre Tours (www.foxtheatre.org/tours) don't cover as much ground as its famous phantoms (living and otherwise), but they do offer tantalizing glimpses into several areas most visitors never see. The 60-minute walks hit highlights such as the Egyptian Ballroom, Spanish Room, and Grand Salon. Fox Theatre tours take place Monday, Thursday, and Saturday hourly 10am-1pm (canceled for special events); $18 adults, $15 seniors, children free.

campaign successfully halted the wrecking ball and landed the building a National Historic Landmark designation in 1976.

Today the Fox boasts one of the city's most varied cultural calendars, with touring Broadway shows, pop concerts, annual performances of Atlanta Ballet's *Nutcracker*, and a well-attended summer film series featuring a pre-show sing-along with the refurbished Mighty Mo organ. **MAP 2:** 660 Peachtree St. NE, 404/881-2100, www.foxtheatre.org; tours Mon., Thurs., and Sat. hourly 10am-1pm; $18 adults, $15 seniors, children free

★ HIGH MUSEUM OF ART

The majestic High Museum of Art rules over Midtown like a queen on the throne of Peachtree Street. Its extensive collection of antique works and contemporary masters makes it one of the busiest museums in the nation. Though its history dates back to 1905, in 1983 architect Richard Meier designed a grand minimalist masterpiece as its new home, a building later named one of the best works of American architecture of the 1980s.

In the mid-2000s, Italian superstar architect Renzo Piano added three new buildings to Meier's creation. The $124 million expansion complements

Clockwise from top left: Fernbank Museum of Natural History; Atlanta Botanical Garden; the High Museum of Art.

the gleaming white Meier building while also relocating the museum's center of gravity to a central campus that unites the High with the affiliated Woodruff Arts Center. The **Wieland Pavilion** houses the modern and contemporary collections, while the Meier building (now the **Stent Family Wing**) holds the permanent and folk art collections, including one of the most notable exhibitions of self-taught artists in the country. Make a point of seeing the grand rotunda of the Meier building.

Recent years have found the High hosting a prominent roster of touring shows. The **Anne Cox Chambers Wing** exhibits special collections. The upscale tapas bistro **Table 1280** provides stylish (if small) bites before shows at the High or the Alliance Theatre; make reservations. For snacks, pop by the **High Café** in the Stent Family Wing.

With street parking in short supply, your best bet is to pay at one of the Woodruff Arts Center's parking decks.

MAP 2: 1280 Peachtree St. NE, 404/733-4400, www.high.org; Tues.-Sat. 10am-5pm (Thurs. until 8pm), Sun. noon-5pm; $18 adult, $11 child, $15 senior; MARTA: Arts Center

MARGARET MITCHELL HOUSE AND MUSEUM

A famous snippet of Atlanta folklore notes that Margaret Mitchell showed little love for the tiny one-bedroom apartment she and husband John Marsh shared from 1925 to 1932: She reportedly called the place "the dump." While convalescing from an ankle injury, Mitchell passed her days in the shotgun-style flat by writing the bulk of *Gone With the Wind*—a novel that would eventually win both a Pulitzer Prize and a National Book Award and sell more copies worldwide than any other book except the Bible.

It would take another 50 years for the former Crescent Apartments to become a certified local landmark. Early efforts at its preservation met hot resistance. Arsonists struck the dilapidated Tudor Revival building in 1994 and 1996, though neither fire significantly damaged Mitchell's unit. The Margaret Mitchell House and Museum finally opened in 1996, thanks to a grant from the Daimler-Benz corporation, and has since become part of the Atlanta History Center.

The docent-led tour discusses Mitchell's early life and features a collection of her letters and personal effects on display in apartment No. 1, furnished similarly to when Mitchell lived there. Elsewhere on the property, visitors can check out exhibitions that explore the author's life and the philanthropy that dominated her later years. The highlight of the museum might be The Making of a Film Legend: Gone With the Wind, an exhibition that traces the transformation of *Gone With the Wind* to the silver screen. The Midtown MARTA station is one block away.

MAP 2: 990 Peachtree St. NE, 404/249-7015, www.gwtw.org; Mon.-Sat. 10am-5:30pm, Sun. noon-5:30pm; $13 adult, $8.50 child, $10 senior; MARTA: Midtown

★ PIEDMONT PARK

The 189-acre Piedmont Park remains a irresistible green playground for nature-craving Atlantans. The grassy slopes of **Oak Hill** tend to be packed with sunbathers and picnic blankets. The park also offers tennis courts, ball fields, a swimming pool, a dog park, and volleyball courts.

Above: Piedmont Park. **Below:** Atlanta History Center.

Originally a private fairground and racetrack, the land now known as Piedmont Park underwent major transformation to host the Cotton States and International Exposition of 1895, which drew 800,000 visitors from around the world. In 1904, the city of Atlanta purchased the park. Visitors today can spot remnants of the exposition, including the peaceful **Lake Clara Meer** and a few stone balustrades that once supported steps to the main building. Extensive projects since the late 1990s have updated and rejuvenated the park, adding new jogging paths, lookout points, restrooms, a parking deck, and the perennially busy dog park.

To access Piedmont Park's **Active Oval,** which includes jogging paths, playfields, and picnic tables, enter at 14th Street and Piedmont Avenue. Nearby, the unique and colorful **Noguchi Playscape,** designed by world-famous sculptor Isamu Noguchi in 1976, is a favorite destination for families. The southern edge of the park, including Oak Hill and the **Meadow,** opens along 10th Street from Myrtle Street to Monroe Drive.

Many of the city's most beloved and well-attended annual events traditionally take place in Piedmont Park, including the Dogwood Festival in April, the Atlanta Pride Festival in October, and the ending of the Peachtree Road Race in July.

MAP 2: 10th St. and Piedmont Ave., www.piedmontpark.org; daily 6am-11pm; free

Buckhead

Map 3

★ ATLANTA HISTORY CENTER

There's much more to the Atlanta History Center than the far-reaching collection of local relics. Its verdant 33-acre campus includes a research library, a restored antebellum farmhouse, and a Jazz Age mansion.

Start with the **Atlanta History Museum,** which has made a dramatic expansion. Improvements include a facelift of the front entrance, overhaul of the signature Metropolitan Frontiers exhibition, plus a new café and gift shop. In 2017, it will house the **Atlanta Cyclorama**.

The display of Civil War artifacts boasts 1,400 objects ranging from uniforms to firearms. A remarkable permanent exhibition is devoted to the 1996 Olympic Games. It offers a timeline of how the Olympic effort came about, a deep look at the city's hosting challenge, and a fun collection of memorabilia.

Save time to check out **Swan House,** the former residence of the aristocratic Inman family. Completed in 1928, the lavish estate was used as a film set for *The Hunger Games: Catching Fire*. Tours offer a taste of how upper-crust Atlantans lived during the 1930s and '40s. **Tullie Smith Farm** turns back the clock to 1845 via a humble yeoman-style farmhouse. Costumed interpreters lead tours of the farm and act out daily chores typical of 19th-century rural Georgia, including blacksmithing, candle-making, quilting, and weaving.

Because both Swan House and Tullie Smith Farm are open only during tours given at certain times, a visit to the Atlanta History Center might easily require three or four hours. The museum's basement café makes for a good refueling station.

MAP 3: 130 W. Paces Ferry Rd. NW, 404/814-4000, www.atlantahistorycenter.com; Mon.-Sat. 10am-5:30pm, Sun. noon-5:30pm; $16.50 adult, $11 child, $13 senior

GEORGIA GOVERNOR'S MANSION

The Georgia Governor's Mansion is not the most luxurious estate along glitzy West Paces Ferry Road, nor is it the most ostentatious. But the Greek Revival-style mansion has been the official residence of Georgia's first family since 1968. Located on 18 acres of forest in one of the city's most prestigious zip codes, the 24,000-square-foot mansion was designed by noted Georgia architect Thomas Bradbury and features 30 luxurious rooms spread out over three floors. The home's first occupant was Governor Lester Maddox, an outspoken segregationist. Later occupants have included Jimmy Carter, Zell Miller, and Nathan Deal.

The free, partly guided tour of the mansion includes a wealth of information about the home's museum-quality furnishings and antiques. Docents are stationed in each room to answer questions. Look for the signed first edition of Margaret Mitchell's *Gone With the Wind* on display in the library. The tour takes less than an hour.

MAP 3: 391 W. Paces Ferry Rd. NW, 404/261-1776, www.mansion.georgia.gov; Tues.-Thurs. 10am-11:30am; free

Virginia-Highland   Map 4

FERNBANK MUSEUM OF NATURAL HISTORY

Kids turn out in droves to stare wide-eyed at the giant *Argentinosaurus* skeleton that rules over the Great Hall of Fernbank Museum of Natural History, one of the many eye-popping oddities that have made the site a local favorite. The elegant 160,000-square-foot institution sits on the edge of an urban forest in a corner of the stately Druid Hills neighborhood. Permanent exhibits include A Walk Through Time in Georgia, a series of dioramas that detail the region's geological record, and Giants of the Mesozoic, which uses fossil casts to explore prehistoric life.

For budding fashionistas in the family, Reflections of Culture features a dazzling display of traditional and contemporary clothing, jewelry, and body art. Younger visitors will probably prefer NatureQuest, a hands-on forest expedition that feels more like a playground. Not everything here is kids' stuff. Adults can soak up the IMAX theater in a cocktail-party atmosphere on Friday nights with Martinis & IMAX.

MAP 4: 767 Clifton Rd. NE, 404/929-6300, www.fernbankmuseum.org; Mon.-Sat. 10am-5pm, Sun. noon-5pm; $18 adult, $16 child, $17 senior

Atlanta BeltLine Tours

the *Spinning Yarns* installation on the Atlanta BeltLine

It's been called Atlanta's biggest reinvention scheme since Reconstruction and the most ambitious smart-growth project in the country. After years of buzz, the Atlanta BeltLine is living up to the hype by improving the quality of life in key intown neighborhoods.

What is the BeltLine? Simply put, it's the redevelopment of a railroad corridor that circles central Atlanta, a project on the same scale as Boston's Big Dig. In 1999, a Georgia Tech graduate student proposed implementing light rail along the most abandoned tracks. The 22-mile loop touches 45 neighborhoods, giving it unprecedented potential to unify parts of town divided by interstates and other obstacles.

The idea soon flourished into a much more complex project. The plan includes 1,300 acres of new green space, 33 miles of trails and bike paths, new business districts, and affordable housing developments.

Although the most dramatic aspects of the BeltLine, including the proposed transit line, are still years away, its first phases have quickly become incredibly popular neighborhood hangouts. The award-winning **Atlanta BeltLine Eastside Trail**, a 2.5-mile pedestrian and bike path, connects Piedmont Park with Inman Park. Its **Art on the Atlanta BeltLine Lantern Parade** is a must-see spectacle of the fall. Nearby, **Historic Fourth Ward Park** features a well-designed and spacious skate park.

For a survey of the BeltLine's progress, claim a spot on one of the free tours offered by the **Atlanta BeltLine Partnership** (404/446-4400, http://beltline.org). Both the **BeltLine Bus Tour** (Fri. and Sat. 9:30am) and **Bicycle Tour** (Sat.10am, Sun. 2pm) follow the full path of the railway circle, delivering a fascinating slideshow of Atlanta life, warts and all. The **Arboretum Walking Tour** (Oct.-May Fri.-Sun. 10am, June-Sept. Fri.-Sun. 9am), led by Trees Atlanta docents, takes visitors on a pleasant stroll along the Eastside Trail.

Little Five Points and East Atlanta

Map 5

JIMMY CARTER PRESIDENTIAL LIBRARY AND MUSEUM

You can easily drive through the woods of Freedom Park and never notice the Jimmy Carter Presidential Library and Museum. Closer inspection reveals a cluster of circular buildings that encompasses not only a museum and research library but also the Carter Center, a not-for-profit organization devoted to advancing human rights. The 69,750-square-foot library hosts a sizable exhibition exploring the life of America's 39th president, from his childhood in rural Plains, Georgia, to his meteoric rise into national politics.

The museum includes relics from his campaigns and an amusing replica of the Oval Office presented as it was during the Carter presidency. First Lady Rosalynn Carter's inaugural gown is on display, along with gifts the Carters received from various heads of state. A comprehensive exhibit covers the Carters' humanitarian efforts since leaving the White House. The archives contain almost 27 million pages of Carter's White House materials, including documents, letters, and 500,000 photographs.

Beyond its function as a presidential museum, the Carter Center also serves as a key cultural center for Atlanta, with a busy schedule of lectures, literary events, and storytelling performances. Most events are free and open to the public.

MAP 5: 441 Freedom Pkwy., 404/865-7131, www.jimmycarterlibrary.gov; Mon.-Sat. 9am-4:45pm, Sun. noon-4:45pm; $8 adult, $6 senior, children free

Restaurants

Atlantans love to eat. Newcomers are some-times surprised to discover such an ani-mated—and ever-changing—restaurant scene, an embarrassment of riches for foodies and budget gourmands. The city maintains its fair share of ce-lebrity chefs and star-driven restaurants as well as see-and-be-seen epicurean carnivals. Some of the more interesting spots in town tend to be quieter, less showy establishments, though it's hard for a high-quality dining room to go undiscovered for long.

Southern cooking has experienced a renaissance of sorts in the new millennium, a trend that's hard to miss on many local menus. Don't be surprised if a place described as "Southern" features dishes that are any-thing but traditional. The city has also long enjoyed a tasty sample platter of international fare.

For years, Buckhead held sway as the center of Atlanta's culinary uni-verse, home to at least a dozen of the finest upscale restaurants in town. Though the well-heeled 'hood still features plenty of amazing options, there's been a noticeable movement southward for some of the most excit-ing startups. Inman Park and the Old Fourth Ward share what's probably the most compelling square mile in the city's competitive restaurant scene, with West Midtown and Decatur nearly tied for the distinction.

Unlike some other cities, Atlanta isn't necessarily a place where each neighborhood is identified with one type of food. Areas with lively res-taurants tend to have an assortment of options. For example, Virginia-Highland offers reliable pub grub, affordable mainstream Asian, and busy

Previous: Cockentrice; Front Page News.

HIGHLIGHTS

★ **Best Coffeehouse:** Trendy **Octane Coffee** has been named one of the coolest coffee spots in the country (page 62).

★ **Most Buzzed-About Restaurant:** With a list of awards and accolades to make any chef-owner blush, **Bacchanalia** remains one of the Southeast's critical darlings (page 62).

★ **Best Local Landmark:** Atlanta's been chowing down on the greasy chili dogs at **The Varsity** since 1928 (page 65).

★ **Best Pizza:** Experience West Midtown's growing "Little Italia" at **Antico Pizza Napoletana**, low on elbow room but high on flavor. (page 65).

★ **Best Classic Southern Dining: Mary Mac's Tea Room** is a portrait of local gentility and a fine choice for comfort food (page 68).

★ **Best Tacos:** If you can endure the long lines, savor the creative spin on Mexican street fare at **Taqueria del Sol** (page 71).

★ **Best Charcuterie:** Carnivores can't get enough of **The Cockentrice** in Krog Street Market, which brings bleeding-edge experimentation to meat cookery (page 79).

★ **Best Special-Occasion Restaurant: Rathbun's** pulls off the neat trick of creating civilized, sensual dining in an unexpected industrial setting (page 79).

★ **Best Breakfast: Thumbs Up Diner** does breakfast classics right and gets props for its healthy options (page 80).

★ **Most Romantic Patio: Barcelona Atlanta Wine Bar** has a seductive Spanish atmosphere and a wine list that's easy to love (page 82).

brunch spots. Next door in Midtown there's sophisticated pizza, healthy fusion, and down-home Southern.

As a city with more than 8,000 restaurants, Atlanta has a dining scene that could fill several volumes of guidebooks. The landscape changes fast. Today's has-been tofu house can quickly morph into tomorrow's white-hot tapas joint. The restaurants listed in this chapter represent a blend of the city's most-loved landmarks, buzzed-about staples, and auspicious new arrivals. Don't be afraid to set out on your own quest to discover the next big tastemakers.

Downtown

Map 1

Downtown has long catered to the convention market, whose middle-of-the-road preferences are reflected on many menus, but it has also sprouted a new batch of high-concept dining. The area has no lack of chain establishments, especially around **Peachtree Center,** though it's best known for a few of the more longstanding hotel restaurants. For more creative dining options, leave the hotel district and venture to **Edgewood Avenue, Cabbagetown,** or **Grant Park.**

BARBECUE
DADDY D'Z ❺

Daddy D'z has the personality of a laid-back juke joint where the waiters know your name, but the clientele ranges from Cabbagetown bohemians and Grant Park old-timers to Downtown execs rushing through their lunch breaks. Renowned especially for its sumptuous spare ribs, the menu swims in authentic Southern barbecue served in big daddy-sized portions. The chicken dishes and pulled pork are particular hits. Blues bands perform Friday and Saturday nights.

MAP 1: 264 Memorial Dr SE., 404/222-0206, www.daddydz.com; Mon.-Thurs. 11am-10:30pm, Fri.-Sat. 11am-midnight, Sun. noon-9:30pm

RIA'S BLUEBIRD ❺

What was once a dingy drive-through liquor store across from Oakland Cemetery remains one of the neighborhood's most reliable brunch spots even after the passing of its beloved namesake. Ria Pell, former chef for Floataway Café and Dish, opened Ria's Bluebird in 2001. The cozy, light-drenched diner quickly drew a following for its clever updates on classic Southern dishes and breakfast standards. The wait time on weekends can be mind-boggling.

MAP 1: 421 Memorial Dr. SE, 404/521-3737, www.riasbluebird.com; daily 8am-3pm

CONTEMPORARY AND NEW AMERICAN
THE SOUND TABLE ❺❺

The spirit of New York's East Village is alive and thumping at the Sound Table, a hipster bistro and lounge that hosts a rotating cast of touring DJs. The menu consists mostly of small plates loosely inspired by

Cheap Eats: Six Delicious Deals

- The heavier pasta dishes at **Noni's Bar and Deli** can set you back $13-14, but the $8-9 deli sandwiches are more budget friendly and just as filling (page 59).

- There's more to **Octane Coffee** than the espresso drinks. Chef Julia Schneider creates a delectable and affordable variety of breakfast bowls, soups, salads, and sandwiches—all under $7 (page 62).

- It's tempting to build a customized sandwich at **Yeah! Burger**, but doing so runs the risk of breaking the bank. Keep your meal under $10 by trying one of the tantalizing organic salads or hot dogs instead (page 64).

- Unless you're springing for the $20 "slab" of ribs, most of the sandwiches at **Fat Matt's Rib Shack** are well under $10 and finger-licking good (page 70).

- There's nothing on the menu over $10 at **Doc Chey's Noodle House.** Try the $9 Korean tacos, a spicy concoction of beef, kimchi, and powerful barbecue sauce (page 74).

- A longtime favorite for cash-strapped college students and blue-collar lunches, **Eats** has been slinging hearty, affordable pasta and jerk chicken since 1993 (page 76).

European fare (oxtail tacos, Belgian-style *frites*); the tapas can easily be big enough for a meal or a heavy snack before the late-night drinking begins. Another perk: The kitchen is open later than most any other restaurant around.

MAP 1: 483 Edgewood Ave. SE, 404/835-2534, www.thesoundtable.com; Tues.-Sat. 7pm-2:30am, Sun. 7pm-midnight

SUN DIAL RESTAURANT, BAR & VIEW $$$

Perched 73 stories above the city, the longstanding Sun Dial Restaurant has been a perennial tourist destination for decades. The trilevel complex features a revolving restaurant, cocktail lounge, and observation deck, all with gasp-inducing 360-degree views of Atlanta. The contemporary American fare, such as crab chowder and chicken pot pie, falls on the pricey side; go for drinks or a light lunch. Evening meals require business casual attire, including jackets for men.

MAP 1: Westin Peachtree Plaza Hotel, 210 Peachtree St., 404/589-7506, www.sundialrestaurant.com; Mon.-Fri. 11:30am-2:30pm and 6pm-10pm, Sat. 11:30am-2:30pm and 5:30pm-11pm, Sun. 11:30am-2:30pm; view open daily 10am until closing; $5 adult, $3 child for viewing only

TED'S MONTANA GRILL $$

Ted Turner's experiment in selling bison burgers has locations from Massachusetts to (duh) Montana, but the corporate headquarters is here. The quaint and classic atmosphere suits the traditional menu fine. You can choose between beef and bison for most of the entrées, which include tasty burgers and timeless blue-plate specials like meatloaf and slow-roasted pork. The bison pot roast is a particular delight. There are far less appealing places to end up Downtown.

MAP 1: 133 Luckie St. NW, 404/521-9796, www.tedsmontanagrill.com; Sun.-Thurs. 11am-10pm, Fri.-Sat. 11am-11pm

THRIVE ❺❺

So maybe it's trying a little too hard to be cool, but Thrive still gets points for effort. The restaurant brings a flashy, West Coast attitude into a once-sleepy Downtown office building. The impeccably modern dining room was designed with a fashionista crowd in mind. The Asian-American fusion menu defies easy explanation, ranging from upscale burgers and chicken dishes to a full sushi bar.

MAP 1: 101 Marietta St. NW, 404/389-1000, www.thriveatl.com; Mon.-Fri. 11:30am-10pm, Sat. 5:30pm-10pm; bar Thurs.-Sat. 11pm-2am

ITALIAN
NONI'S BAR AND DELI ❺❺

Edgewood Avenue used to be a street that nobody wanted to walk down after dark. These days, practically everybody's walking, skipping, running to check out the trendy strip of nightspots and restaurants. Noni's classifies as both. The dinner menu delivers classic Italian staples like lasagna Bolognese or chicken and eggplant parmesan. Later on (usually after the kitchen closes at 11pm), the dining room transforms into a dance floor, with a revolving DJ several nights a week.

MAP 1: 357 Edgewood Ave. SE, 404/343-1808, www.nonisdeli.com; Mon.-Sat. 11:30am-3am, Sun. 11:30am-midnight

MEXICAN
NO MAS! CANTINA ❺❺

This authentic Mexican cantina mixed with a furniture gallery and home accessories store has emerged as an unconventional success story. A warehouse has been dramatically revamped as a jovial two-story hacienda serving creative Mexican fare. If you fall in love with the margarita glasses or a hand-blown glass light fixture, pop next door to **No Mas! Hacienda** (404/215-9769, Tues.-Thurs. 11am-7pm, Fri.-Sat. 11am-9pm), where all the cantina's furniture is on sale, along with handcrafted pottery and other accessories imported from Mexico.

MAP 1: 180 Walker St. SW, 404/574-5678, www.nomascantina.com; Mon.-Thurs. 11am-11pm, Fri.-Sat. 10am-11pm

PIZZA
GRANT CENTRAL PIZZA AND PASTA ❺

The quintessential neighborhood pizza joint, Grant Central Pizza offers a peek into the casual dining habits of intown residents. The New York-style pizza has a dedicated local fan base, though the restaurant also serves great calzones, salads, and pasta dishes. Depending on the night, the place can sometimes have a more bar-like atmosphere, with drinkers almost outnumbering eaters. The building itself is also noteworthy, a charming former grocery store converted into an urban gathering spot.

MAP 1: 451 Cherokee Ave. SE, 404/523-8900, www.gcpatlanta.com; Mon.-Thurs. 11am-10pm, Fri.-Sat. 11am-11pm, Sun. noon-10pm

SLICE DOWNTOWN $

Fans of New York-style pizza who want to skip the long lines at other pizzerias can curb their craving at Slice Downtown. The low-key pub atmosphere also offers a welcome break from competing restaurants. This Fairlie-Poplar favorite is a cheap and easy destination for calzones, lasagna, and a decent beer selection. Slice hosts poker nights each Monday and can be busy during sporting events. Best of all, it's open late.

MAP 1: 85 Poplar St. NW, 404/917-1820, www.sliceatlanta.com; Mon.-Thurs. 11:30am-midnight, Fri. 11:30am-2am, Sat. 4pm-2am

SEAFOOD
SIX FEET UNDER $$

So (morbidly) named because of its proximity to Oakland Cemetery, Six Feet Under serves an exhaustive selection of seafood in a rowdy tavern environment. The menu doesn't shy away from deep-fried decadence; the catfish and shrimp baskets are some of the best you'll find in town. The restaurant is in the Jane, an eye-popping mixed-use redevelopment. Six Feet Under's west-side location (685 11th St., 404/810-0040, Mon.-Thurs. 11am-1am, Fri.-Sat. 11am-2am, Sun. 11am-midnight) features a rooftop deck with an outstanding view of the skyline.

MAP 1: 437 Memorial Dr. SE, 404/523-6664, www.sixfeetunder.net; Mon.-Thurs. 11am-1am, Fri.-Sat. 11am-2am, Sun. 11am-midnight

SOUL FOOD
PASCHAL'S $$

Paschal's was founded in 1947 and became a gathering spot for the likes of Martin Luther King Jr., Andrew Young, Hosea Williams, and John Lewis, who jokingly called the restaurant the "unofficial headquarters" of the civil rights movement. These days it feels more like a sociable hotel breakfast buffet. Known for fried chicken, authentic Southern sides, and busy weekend brunches, Paschal's draws tourists curious about its civil rights history and eager to sample soul food.

MAP 1: 180-B Northside Dr. SW, 404/525-2023, www.paschalsrestaurant.com; Mon.-Thurs. 11am-9pm, Fri.-Sat. 11am-11pm, Sun. 11am-9pm

SWEET GEORGIA'S JUKE JOINT $$

Don't let the lily pads and swamp creatures fool you. This delectable, down-home juke joint brings big-city class and attitude to its backwoods-inspired decor. Located in a former Macy's building, Sweet Georgia's is a fun place to sip creative moonshine cocktails while sampling crawfish tails and fried green tomatoes. It's open late for live soul and R&B.

MAP 1: 200 Peachtree St. NE, 404/230-5853, www.sweetgeorgiasjukejoint.com; Mon.-Thurs. 11am-midnight, Fri. 11am-2am., Sat. 4pm-2am., Sun. 4pm-midnight

VEGETARIAN

SOUL VEGETARIAN $

Although the "soul" can be a stretch—since when does "soul food" include pizza?—this West End vegan café gets major kudos for its creativity. It boasts a menu prepared with no preservatives, cholesterol, or excess sodium, a real challenge when featured items include mac-and-cheese or veggie country-fried steak (better than it sounds). Regulars swear by the Wheatloaf and the Garvey Burger, delicious vegan dishes that might just make you swear off meat altogether.

MAP 1: 879 Ralph David Abernathy Blvd. SW, 404/752-5194; Mon.-Thurs. 11am-10pm, Fri.-Sat. 11am-11pm, Sun. 9am-1:30pm and 5pm-10pm

Midtown

Map 2

Midtown's enduring restaurant row on **Crescent Avenue** boasts plenty of recommended bistros and lounges, but that's only part of the story in this rapidly evolving neighborhood. **West Midtown,** especially around the intersection of 14th Street and Howell Mill Road, is home to a selection of trendy restaurants and better-than-average cheap eats. **Juniper Street** between Ponce de Leon Avenue and 10th Street has also seen some interesting activity on the food front. Look for an eager—and ever-changing—cast of newcomers in the street-level spaces of the condo and office towers along **Peachtree Street,** starting around 5th Street and continuing north to 14th Street.

ASIAN

NAN THAI FINE DINING $$$

For years, Charlie and Nan Niyomkul's Tamarind was celebrated as one of the city's finest Thai restaurants, inspiring the kind of customer loyalty most chefs only dream of. The two continued their winning streak with Nan, an elegant big sister to Tamarind that upped the ante on Thai in Atlanta. Entrées tend to be appropriately exotic without straying too far from familiar seafood-and-short-rib territory. Plus, the service is frightfully attentive.

MAP 2: 1350 Spring St. NW, 404/870-9933, www.nanfinedining.com; Mon.-Thurs. 11:30am-10pm, Fri. 11:30am-11pm, Sat. 5pm-11pm, Sun. 5pm-10pm

TAKOREA $$

It's deceptive to group Takorea in with other Asian restaurants; the concept practically deserves its own category. Chef Tomas Lee mixes Korean ingredients with Mexican street food to create a fusion experience that defies easy description. The Korean Takos (rib-eye, grilled chicken, shrimp, and more) make a spicy kimchi delight. Like the food, the decor is colorful, warm, and witty, with shades of a classic cantina filtered through global goggles.

MAP 2: 818 Juniper St. NE, 404/532-1944, www.mytakorea.com; Mon.-Thurs. 11:30am-10pm, Fri.-Sat. 11:30am-11pm, Sun. noon-10pm

BRUNCH

EINSTEIN'S ⑤⑤

When you hear the words "brunch" and "patio" in Midtown, "Einstein's" often follows. This local institution has one of the most attractive outdoor dining spaces in town, but there's more to Einstein's than the Sunday-morning mimosa scene. The restaurant's interior keeps chilly nights warm and cozy with a lodge-like atmosphere and an active bar. The menu of comfort food, pasta, and sandwiches is hardly the draw: It's all about being seen on the patio.

MAP 2: 1077 Juniper St. NE, 404/876-7925, www.einsteinsatlanta.com; Mon.-Thurs. 11am-11pm, Fri. 11am-1am, Sat. 9am-1am, Sun. 9am-11pm

WEST EGG CAFÉ ⑤

Golden Egg is more like it. Weekend mornings almost always find this white-hot brunch spot swarming with diehard fans willing to wait more than an hour. The food itself is likable: traditional breakfast fare like buttermilk pancakes mixed in with fried green tomato wraps and turkey sausage patties. Perhaps the hype has more to do with the space itself, a West Midtown warehouse reborn as a sophisticated and classic-feeling American diner.

MAP 2: 1100 Howell Mill Rd., 404/872-3973, www.westeggcafe.com; Mon.-Fri. 7am-10pm, Sat.-Sun. 8am-10pm

COFFEEHOUSES

★ OCTANE COFFEE ⑤

In a city overrun with corporate coffeehouses, Octane brews a strong case for keeping your caffeine habit local. The hip and artsy espresso bar was a pioneer in its corner of rapidly changing West Midtown. It quickly drew a devoted crowd of laptop-bearing college students lured by the free wireless Internet and superior drink menu. The trendier-than-thou baristas are known for their attitude, but the erratic service is tempered by tasty sandwiches and great single-origin coffees. A Grant Park location shares its space with the **Little Tart Bake Shop** (437 Memorial Dr., Ste. A5, 404/348-4797, www.littletartatl.com, Mon. 7am-6pm, Tues.-Fri. 7am-11pm, Sat. 8am-11pm, Sun. 8am-10pm). The newest outpost is in Buckhead's **Tech Village** (3423 Piedmont Rd., Mon.-Fri. 7am-7pm, Sat.-Sun. 9am-4pm).

MAP 2: 1009-B Marietta St. NW, 404/815-9886, www.octanecoffee.com; Mon.-Thurs. 7am-11pm, Fri. 7am-midnight, Sat. 8am-11pm, Sun. 8am-11pm

CONTEMPORARY AND NEW AMERICAN

★ BACCHANALIA ⑤⑤⑤

Atlanta's most raved-about restaurant actually *deserves* all the fanfare. Since 1993, chef-owners Anne Quatrano and Clifford Harrison have frequently updated their contemporary American concept, carving a niche as the city's quintessential gathering spot for foodies. The seasonal prix-fixe menu offers only organic ingredients. Specials change daily, but a few old favorites like the crab fritters always get rave reviews. Hint: Skip the wait for reservations by ordering à la carte at the bar.

MAP 2: 1198 Howell Mill Rd. NW, 404/365-0410, www.starprovisions.com/bacchanalia; Mon.-Sat. 6pm-midnight

Clockwise from top left: Mary Mac's Tea Room; Octane Coffee; Bacchanalia.

HENRY'S MIDTOWN TAVERN ⑤

"Come, sit, stay," says the motto of Henry's, a nod to the restaurant's pet-friendly policies and busy patio. Named for owner Maureen Kalmanson's dog, the casual tavern deserves an award for turning a drab Thai shack into an instantly popular hangout with one of the best decks around for people-watching. The menu features pub grub and upscale comfort food (hot dogs, pulled pork, meatloaf)—a significant step above other neighborhood hangouts.

MAP 2: 132 10th St. NE, 404/537-4477, www.henrysatl.com; Sun.-Thurs. 11am-11pm, Fri.-Sat. 11am-1am

THE LAWRENCE ⑤⑤⑤

St. Lawrence, the patron saint of cooks and chefs, rules over this lively and forward-thinking lounge. The superb cocktail program and wine list keep the bar busy during happy hour, but drinkers shouldn't overlook chef Mark Nanna's evolving menu of creative Southern and international favorites. The decor is refined and relaxed. To experience the Lawrence's charms without breaking your bank account, check out the terrific Sunday brunch.

MAP 2: 905 Juniper St. NE, 404/961-7177, www.thelawrenceatlanta.com; Sun.-Mon. 11am-2pm and 5:30pm-10pm, Tues.-Thurs. 11am-2pm and 5:30pm-10:30pm, Fri.-Sat. 11am-2pm and 5:30pm-11:30pm

MILLER UNION ⑤⑤⑤

You could drive past Miller Union's anonymous storefront location and never know how close you'd come to one of the city's most buzzed-about restaurants. Since opening in late 2009, this farm-to-table powerhouse has remained a critical darling among even the most jaded of foodies. The focus is on freshly harvested veggies and meats, prepared with a certain rustic earnestness. The menu changes constantly, but expect dishes such as braised pork cheek or Florida red grouper.

MAP 2: 999 Brady Ave. NW, 678/733-8550, www.millerunion.com; lunch Tues.-Sat. 11:30am-2:30pm, dinner Mon.-Thurs. 5pm-10pm and Fri.-Sat. 5pm-11pm

THE OPTIMIST ⑤⑤⑤

This trendy seafood bistro and oyster bar with a wood-burning oven comes from the same foodie masterminds behind JCT Kitchen. Its lobster rolls have been hailed as some of the best in town. Reservations are highly recommended: Even with a 180-seat dining room (plus a cool mini-golf playground out front and charming patio), The Optimist is rarely empty.

MAP 2: 914 Howell Mill Rd. NW, 404/477-6260, www.theoptimistrestaurant.com; Mon.-Thurs. 11:30am-2:30pm and 5-10pm., Fri. 11:30am-10pm, Sat. 5pm-11pm., Sun 5pm-10pm

YEAH! BURGER ⑤

Don't dismiss Yeah! Burger as just another entry in the crowded boutique burger market. Owner Shaun Doty ensures that his sandwiches are crafted with as many organic ingredients impossible, using locally raised meats free

of antibiotics, growth hormones, and synthetic pesticides and herbicides.
The burgers (including turkey and chicken variations) truly are some of
the most scrumptious in town. The restaurant's playful energy is front and
center with cartoony murals and clever signage. The Virginia-Highland location (1017 N. Highland Ave., 404/437-7845, Mon.-Thurs. 11:30am-10pm,
Fri. 11:30am-11pm, Sat. 11am-11pm, Sun. 11:30am-10pm) is also popular.

MAP 2: 1168 Howell Mill Rd. NW, Ste. E, 404/496-4393, www.yeahburger.com;
Mon.-Thurs. 11:30am-10pm, Fri. 11:30am-11pm, Sat. 11am-11pm, Sun. 11:30am-10pm

CONTINENTAL
APRÈS DIEM ❶❶

Is Après Diem a cozy coffee bar that serves gourmet sandwiches, a casually chic lounge with a robust liqueur list, or a late-night wine bar with an
irresistible dessert display? Try all of the above. Though there's a steady
brunch crowd, Après Diem ("after the day") is most often mentioned as
an after-dinner destination and great place for romance. The menu offers
a mixed bag of international influences from *baba ghanouj* to truffle pâté.

MAP 2: 931 Monroe Dr. NE, 404/872-3333, www.apresdiem.com; Mon.-Thurs.
11:30am-midnight, Fri. 11:30am-2am, Sat. 11am-2am, Sun. 11am-midnight

DINERS
★ THE VARSITY ❶

Atlanta without the Varsity would be like summer without sunshine. The
bona fide homegrown institution boasts its own catchphrases ("What'll ya
have?"), costumes (free red paper hats), and wacky names (ask about the
Naked Dog Walking). What started in 1928 as a carhop for Georgia Tech
students has grown into a sprawling lunch counter serving comfort food
to a melting pot of locals, with a deep-fried menu sure to inspire pangs of
guilt for today's health-conscious diners.

MAP 2: 61 North Ave., 404/881-1706, www.thevarsity.com; Sun.-Thurs. 10am-11:30pm,
Fri.-Sat. 10am-12:30am

ITALIAN
★ ANTICO PIZZA NAPOLETANA ❶❶

Giovanni Di Palma's growing empire in West Midtown includes an artisan
grocery store, chicken shack, and seasonal bar, but it all began with Antico's
brick-oven pizza. Be prepared for long lines and zero elbow room at his
crowded, no-frills pizzeria. Luckily, the hot and greasy Neapolitan pies
are (almost) worth the wait. The connected **Caffé Gio** (Mon.-Sat. 11:30am-
10pm) serves truly sublime gelati and sorbets. Antico's kitchen closes when
the daily batch of dough runs out.

MAP 2: 1093 Hemphill Ave. NW, 404/724-2387, www.littleitalia.com; Mon.-Sat.
11:30am-close

PASTA DA PULCINELLA ❶❶

Crescent Avenue has long been a destination for busy restaurants, but for
a quieter, more gracious experience, wander one street over to the nearly

What'll Ya Have, What'll Ya Have?

The Varsity

After almost 90 years of business and with eight locations across the state, **The Varsity** has grown into something far bigger than just another hamburger joint: It's an Atlanta tradition. The restaurant boasts that it whips up two miles of hot dogs, a ton of onions, 2,500 pounds of potatoes, 5,000 fried pies, and 300 gallons of chili each day. A visit to the "world's largest drive-in" can be intimidating for a first-timer. The counter workers—though friendly—bark "What'll ya have?" in a booming baritone. The scene reeks of chaos to the uninitiated. It's helpful to know the lingo before you order. Here are some of the more colorful menu terms:

- Naked Dog: plain hot dog

- Yellow Dog: naked dog with mustard

- Red Dog: naked dog with ketchup

- Naked Dog Walking: plain hot dog to go

- Heavy Weight: hot dog with extra chili

- Glorified Steak: hamburger with mayo, lettuce, and tomato

- Mary Brown Steak: hamburger with no bun

- Bag of Rags: potato chips

- Ring One: onion rings

- Squirt One: the Varsity's signature orange beverage

hidden Pasta Da Pulcinella. Elegant without being pretentious, the quaint, converted bungalow serves some of the most satisfying pasta dishes in town, including the dazzling Granny Smith apple ravioli—all at prices that won't break the bank. A candlelit meal on the breezy front porch makes for an unforgettable night.

MAP 2: 1123 Peachtree Walk NE, 404/876-1114, www.pastadapulcinella.com; Mon. 5:30pm-10pm, Tues.-Thurs. 11:30am-10pm, Fri. 11:30am-11pm, Sat. 5:30pm-11pm, Sun. 5:30pm-9pm

VARUNI NAPOLI ❸❸
It's hard to find forgotten commercial spaces in Midtown ripe for a bold reinvention, which makes Giancarlo Pirrone's gamble with Varuni Napoli all the more special. The Naples native took a 4,000-square-foot warehouse in an almost-invisible strip mall and somehow created an enchanting pizzeria complete with a roomy courtyard. Serving authentic Neapolitan pies, Italian wines, and *cuoppo* (paper cones of fried goodies), Varuni Napoli can teach the neighborhood a timely lesson in ingenuity.

MAP 2: 1540 Monroe Dr. NE, 404/709-2690, http://varuni.us; Tues.-Thurs. 5:30pm-10pm, Fri. 5:30pm-11pm, Sat. noon-midnight, Sun. noon-10pm

MEDITERRANEAN
ECCO ❸❸❸
The years have been kind to Ecco since it was named one of America's best new restaurants in 2006 by *Esquire*. Even if the hype has subsided, it's still an in-demand Midtown institution. Ecco sprouted from a family of much-loved local eateries (including La Tavola Trattoria and South City Kitchen). It's labeled "Mediterranean," though a broader "European" label better fits the menu, which changes seasonally. Ecco delivers sophistication.

MAP 2: 40 7th St. NE, 404/347-9555, www.ecco-atlanta.com; Sun.-Thurs. 5:30pm-10pm, Fri.-Sat. 5:30pm-11pm

SOUTHERN
EMPIRE STATE SOUTH ❸❸❸
Empire State South takes the notion of "word of mouth" to a different level. If it weren't for the impeccable reputation, you might never know it existed. The restaurant sits in a blind courtyard on the backside of an office building, yet it's always packed with in-the-know devotees. Empire State South mixes backwoods comfort food (catfish, pork belly, farm eggs) with big-city elegance. Reservations at dinner can be a challenge, but lunch is just as delicious.

MAP 2: 999 Peachtree St. NE #140, 404/541-1105, www.empirestatesouth.com; Mon.-Fri. 7am-11pm, Sat. 5:30pm-11pm, Sun. 10:30am-11pm

GLADYS KNIGHT & RON WINANS CHICKEN AND WAFFLES
Yes, you can catch the Midtown Train for Southern fried jumbo chicken wings and a waffle, but there's more to this soul food outpost than its breakfast menu. Atlanta native Gladys Knight established her first cozy café back in 1997, eventually bringing the late gospel legend Winans into the mix. The

crowded Peachtree Street location has since expanded into a major brunch spot that's especially popular among out-of-towners.

MAP 2: 529 Peachtree St. NE, 404/874-9393, www.gladysandron.net; Tues.-Thurs. 11am-11pm, Fri.-Sat.11am-4am, Sun.11am-8pm

JCT KITCHEN & BAR 🟢🟢

JCT Kitchen & Bar has defied the odds and transformed what was once a cursed corner of the Westside Urban Market into a thriving business. Promoted as "Southern farmstead cooking," the menu tweaks many down-home favorites, arriving at combinations like crispy duck leg confit served with sheep's milk ricotta dumplings or wood-grilled pork tenderloin paired with blue-cheese potatoes. The fried chicken is some of the best in town, the servers some of the most gracious.

MAP 2: 1198 Howell Mill Rd. NW, Ste. 18, 404/355-2252, www.jctkitchen.com; Mon.-Thurs. 11am-2:30pm and 5pm-10pm, Fri.-Sat. 11am-2:30pm and 5pm-11pm, Sun. 5pm-9pm

★ MARY MAC'S TEA ROOM 🟢🟢

Finding quality food from the Old South can be a tall order even in the capital of the New South. Mary Mac's Tea Room, though, has been offering the same genteel goodness since 1945, earning the nickname "Atlanta's Dining Room." The restaurant remains a packed brunch destination for both the retired Sunday School set and college students humoring their parents. The menu, heavy on fried items, also includes a few healthier choices and vegetarian-friendly options.

MAP 2: 224 Ponce de Leon Ave. NE, 404/876-1800, www.marymacs.com; daily 11am-9pm

SOUTH CITY KITCHEN 🟢🟢

South City Kitchen is not the flashiest restaurant on Crescent Avenue, but it's certainly one of the most satisfying. Located in a renovated bungalow with a lovely front patio, it whispers an understated Southern gentility. That same attitude shines through in the contemporary Southern fare—with an urbane twist—heavy on Lowcountry favorites like she-crab soup, shrimp and grits, and buttermilk-fried chicken. The main dining room seems almost always packed, so ask for a table outside. South City also has a location in Vinings (1675 Cumberland Pkwy., 770/435-0700, Mon.-Thurs. 5pm-10pm, Fri.-Sat. 5pm-10:30pm, Sun. 10am-3pm and 5pm-9:30pm).

MAP 2: 1144 Crescent Ave. NE, 404/873-7358, www.southcitykitchen.com; Mon.-Thurs. 11am-10pm, Fri.-Sat. 11am-10:30pm, Sun. 11am-3pm and 5pm-10pm

SPANISH
COOKS & SOLDIERS 🟢🟢🟢

The Castellucci restaurant empire brings mouthwatering Basque tapas to West Midtown. The curious name Cooks & Soldiers gives a nod to the annual Tamborrada festival of San Sebastian in Spain. The menu is largely composed of *pinchos* ("thorns" or "spikes"), small snacks found in Spanish bars, such as braised pork fritters, *chistorra* sausage, and soft scrambled

eggs. For heartier options, try the larger (and shareable) wood-fire grill
entrées, heavy on pork and seafood.

MAP 2: 691 14th St. NW, 404/996-2623, www.cooksandsoldiers.com; Sun.-Wed.

5pm-10pm, Thurs. 5pm-11pm, Fri.-Sat. 5pm-midnight

STEAK HOUSES
STK $$$

The lights, the DJ booth, the sequins: It would be easy to mistake flashy STK for a velvet-rope nightclub. The difference is that this multistory export from Manhattan's Meatpacking District also delivers high-end steaks and seafood. Though the spotlight shines brightest on attitude and atmosphere, STK is worth the fuss with a menu that's pricey but gratifying. The energy level and in-your-face waitstaff make a visit less of a meal and more of an event.

MAP 2: 1075 Peachtree St. NE, 404/793-0144, www.stkhouse.com; Sun.-Thurs.

5pm-10:30pm, Fri.-Sat. 5pm-11:30pm

TAPAS
TABLE 1280 $$

No restaurant in town can rival the architectural chops of Table 1280, which was unveiled as part of the vast expansion of the High Museum by the internationally acclaimed Renzo Piano. The restaurant features full-service American brasserie-inspired fare, or the tapas lounge offers up small plates of upscale, seasonal ingredients. Table 1280 is wedged in the courtyard between the High Museum and the Woodruff Arts Center, making it a convenient choice after browsing the art.

MAP 2: 1280 Peachtree St. NE, 404/897-1280, www.table1280.com; Tues.-Wed.

11:30am-6pm, Thurs. 11:30am-8pm, Fri. 11:30am-9:30pm, Sat. 11:30am-8pm, Sun.
11am-3:30pm

Buckhead

Map 3

Buckhead's reputation for doing glitzy, over-the-top dining isn't going away anytime soon. The upscale neighborhood still has plenty of classic favorites to choose from, largely high-end Italian and French places that will keep a certain luxury-loving segment of the population coming back for years to come. The heart of the restaurant scene has traditionally been near the intersection of **East Paces Ferry and Peachtree Roads,** though there are also some notable options near Lenox Square Mall. For cheaper, less stuffy fare, venture southeast to **Cheshire Bridge Road.**

ASIAN
RU SAN'S BUCKHEAD AT TOWER PLACE $$

If you like your sushi served in a sedate, meditative environment, then Ru San's is absolutely not the place for you. If you're looking for a sake-fueled college party where blasting music shakes your table and the chefs yell at each other from behind the bar, then you just might join the legions of locals who swear by Ru San's. The sushi is serviceable without being stellar; the multi-page menu might be daunting for beginners. Ru San's Midtown location (1529 Piedmont Rd., 404/875-7042, daily 11:30am-midnight) is usually just as raucous.

MAP 3: 3365 Piedmont Rd. NE, 404/239-9557, www.rusans.com; daily 11:30am-midnight

BARBECUE
FAT MATT'S RIB SHACK $

Be prepared to stand in line at this bare-bones barbecue joint, known not only for its mouthwatering ribs but also for the nightly blues bands. The menu keeps it simple—ribs, chopped pork, or chicken—but be sure to sample the rum-baked beans and other Southern sides. Getting a table after the music cranks up can take a minor miracle, and forget about carrying on a conversation. With ribs this tasty, who needs to talk?

MAP 3: 1811 Piedmont Ave. NE, 404/607-1622, www.fatmattsribshack.com; Mon.-Thurs. 11:30am-11:30pm, Fri.-Sat. 11:30am-12:30am, Sun. 1pm-11:30pm

BRAZILIAN
FOGO DE CHÃO CHURRASCARIA $$$

Fogo de Chão brings something distinctive to Atlanta: an authentic all-you-can-eat Brazilian *churrasco*. Guests first encounter slabs of beef roasting in the front window, then receive a card used to signal when they're ready for a parade of meats to be brought to the table: Green means *"Sim por favor"* ("Yes, please"), while red signals *"Não obrigado"* ("No thanks"). Vegetarians are directed toward the salad bar—but really should steer clear altogether.

MAP 3: 3101 Piedmont Rd. NE, 404/266-9988, www.fogodechao.com; Mon.-Thurs. 11:30am-2pm and 5pm-10pm, Fri. 11:30am-2pm and 5pm-10:30pm, Sat. 4:30pm-10:30pm, Sun. 4:30pm-9:30pm

BRUNCH
OK CAFE $$

Opened in 1987, OK Cafe claims to serve more customers than any other full-service restaurant in Georgia. Judging from the crowds outside on weekend mornings, you might think it was the only brunch spot in Buckhead. The family-friendly diner menu is heavy on hot sandwiches, omelets, and comfort food, which suits the retro-inspired roadhouse atmosphere just fine. The café also has a great takeaway station and is open later than most restaurants in this area.

MAP 3: 1284 W. Paces Ferry Rd. NW, 404/233-2888, www.okcafe.com; Sun.-Thurs. 7am-10pm, Fri.-Sat. 7am-11pm

CONTEMPORARY AND NEW AMERICAN
ARIA $$$

This Buckhead gem has been pushing the envelope on New American fare since 2000, hyping what head chef (and owner) Gerry Klaskala calls his own unusual take on the "slow food" movement. The "slow" here seems to refer mainly to process, with meats that are braised, roasted, and simmered to perfection, along with a pleasantly unpredictable menu of seafood entrées.

The dining room is intimate, minimally decorated, and barely lit—perfect for a romantic evening.

MAP 3: 490 E. Paces Ferry Rd. NE, 404/233-7673, www.aria-atl.com; Mon.-Sat. 6pm-10pm

RESTAURANT EUGENE ❸❸❸

Owner Linton Hopkins earned the top prize on the Food Network's *Iron Chef*—but you'd never know it from a visit to Restaurant Eugene, an exercise in restraint and quiet charm. Hopkins strikes the right balance between mannerly Southern influences and elegant, upscale classics. He goes to astounding lengths to include local ingredients in his dishes, a goal sometimes reflected in the eye-popping prices. Serious gourmands should reserve the private Chef's Table for 6-8 guests.

MAP 3: 2277 Peachtree Rd. NW, 404/355-0321, www.restauranteugene.com; Mon.-Thurs. 5:30pm-10pm, Fri.-Sat. 5:30pm-11pm, Sun. 5:30pm-9pm

SOUPER JENNY ❸❸

When she's not busy heating up some of the most mouthwatering soups in Atlanta, Jenny Levison is a popular actress on local stages. Souper Jenny is one of the neighborhood's most in-demand lunch spots, with a line that curves out the door. The café usually serves six hot soups daily, including vegetarian and vegan options, plus sandwiches and salads. Thursday is grilled-cheese night, with later hours. The last hour of each day is take-out only.

MAP 3: 56 E. Andrews Dr. NW, 404/239-9023, www.souperjennyatl.com; Mon.-Wed. 11am-5pm, Thurs. 11am-10pm, Fri.-Sat. 11am-5pm

MEXICAN
★ TAQUERIA DEL SOL ❸

Technically speaking, the West Midtown location (1200-B Howell Mill Rd., 404/352-5811, lunch Mon.-Fri. 11am-2pm and Sat. noon-3pm, dinner Tues.-Thurs. 5:30pm-9pm and Fri.-Sat. 5:30pm-10pm) was the original Taqueria del Sol—but the experiment in creative, cross-cultural tacos began here on Cheshire Bridge in the former Sundown Café. The owners stumbled upon a winning concept with their spin-off cantina, serving authentic Mexican street tacos and creative specials in a crisp, urban setting, and eventually ditched the Sundown name in favor of the more popular brand. Be prepared for lines, although the wait time can be tempered with one of TDS's signature margaritas. There's a third location in Decatur (359 W. Ponce de Leon Ave., 404/377-7668, lunch Mon.-Fri. 11am-2pm and Sat. noon-3pm, dinner Tues.-Thurs. 5:30pm-9pm and Fri.-Sat. 5:30pm-10pm).

MAP 3: 2165 Cheshire Bridge Rd. NE, 404/321-1118, www.taqueriadelsol.com; lunch Mon.-Fri. 11am-2pm, dinner Mon.-Thurs. 5:30pm-9pm and Fri.-Sat. 5:30pm-10pm

SEAFOOD
CHOPS LOBSTER BAR ❸❸❸

Chops was once known as one of Atlanta's most exclusive steak houses. These days the clientele has drifted down-market some, with more curious suburbanites filling the art deco dining room, but the menu remains a study in exorbitance. Downstairs, the more cozy Lobster Bar features seafood as well as steaks from the Chops menu (which also offers all items from the Lobster Bar menu). Business attire is suggested, but the dress code is not strictly enforced.

MAP 3: 70 W. Paces Ferry Rd. NW, 404/262-2675, www.buckheadrestaurants.com; Mon.-Thurs. 11:30am-2:30pm and 5:30pm-10pm, Fri. 11:30am-2:30pm and 5:30pm-11pm, Sat. 5:30pm-11pm, Sun. 5:30pm-10pm

OCEAN PRIME $$$

Even though it's part of a national chain, Buckhead's Ocean Prime has all the trappings of an upscale neighborhood hangout: bartenders who remember your name and usual order, waiters who'll stop and gossip, and a crew of sassy, well-dressed regulars holding court at the front bar. The chef-driven menu feels extensive and accessible. The signature cocktails do not disappoint, even the fun and frivolous Berries and Bubbles—Belvedere Citrus vodka served over dry ice.

MAP 3: 3102 Piedmont Rd. NE, 404/846-0505, www.oceanprimeatlanta.com; Mon.-Thurs. 5pm-10pm, Fri.-Sat. 5pm-11pm, Sun. 5pm-9pm

SOUTHERN
THE COLONNADE $$

The polar opposite of pretentious, the Colonnade feels like it fell into a time warp during the Carter administration and hasn't changed since. It serves some of the most authentic—and unapologetic—Southern food in town, from greasy fried chicken to collard greens and frog legs. Have a drink at the bar, if you dare: The cocktails are some of the stiffest around, even on seedy Cheshire Bridge Road. Cash only.

MAP 3: 1879 Cheshire Bridge Rd. NE, 404/874-5642, www.colonnadeatl.com; Mon.-Thurs. 5pm-9pm, Fri. 5pm-10pm, Sat. noon-10pm, Sun. 11:30am-9pm

ROASTERS $

Roasters has made a name for itself by serving dependable comfort food to a diverse clientele, ranging from families from the surrounding neighborhood and shoppers en route from Lenox Square Mall to imports from Midtown and Brookhaven who swear that the rotisserie chicken is worth the drive. It's also a tremendous value, with a meat-and-three with fresh veggies—plus rolls and cornbread—costing far less than food at most of the trendy restaurants in the area.

MAP 3: 2770 Lenox Rd. NE, 404/237-1122, www.roastersfresh.com; Mon.-Thurs. 11am-10pm, Fri.-Sat. 11am-10:30pm, Sun. 11am-10pm

WATERSHED ON PEACHTREE $$$

Those who remember the glory days of the original Watershed in Decatur may be pleasantly surprised to find its latest incarnation in south Buckhead. The updated space features an elegant dining room while still focusing on locally sourced dishes steeped in Southern flavors. The much-raved-about Southern fried chicken is as delicious as ever, however it's only served on Wednesdays.

MAP 3: 1820 Peachtree Rd. NW, 404/809-3561, www.watershedrestaurant.com;
Tues.-Thurs. 11:30am-3pm and 5pm-10pm, Fri.-Sat. 11:30am-3pm and 5pm-11pm, Sun.
11:30am-3pm

73

SOUTHWESTERN
GEORGIA GRILLE ❸❸❸

The name comes from Georgia O'Keeffe, not the state, which explains a lot
about the Southwestern-inspired menu. Georgia Grille has been a word-
of-mouth favorite since 1990—a miracle considering the tiny restaurant's
nearly invisible location in a strip mall. Inside, eclectic Southwestern artifacts adorn the walls (including a very O'Keeffe cow's skull). The food
is both creative and familiar, with twists on traditional Tex-Mex dishes,
such as lobster enchiladas, cowboy shrimp, and some potent margaritas.

MAP 3: 2290 Peachtree Rd. NW, 404/352-3517, www.georgiagrille.com; Tues.-Thurs.
6pm-10pm, Fri.-Sat. 6pm-11pm, Sun. 5:30pm-10pm

STEAK HOUSES
BONE'S ❸❸❸

Bone's has racked up many accolades, including being named as one of
the best steak houses in America by *USA Today* and the *New York Times*.
The elite Buckhead dining room was a gathering spot for local power brokers and retains the posture of an exclusive gentlemen's club. The service
is impeccable, and the steaks still deserve their reputation. The menu includes prime cuts of beef, Maine lobster, and seafood options, along with
Southern favorites.

MAP 3: 3130 Piedmont Rd. NE, 404/237-2663, www.bonesrestaurant.com; Mon.-Fri.
11:30am-2:30pm and 5:30pm-10pm, Sat.-Sun. 5pm-10pm

VEGETARIAN
CAFE SUNFLOWER ❸❸

The influences vary wildly at Cafe Sunflower, from Asian spring rolls and
edamame to soy chili burritos, but the one constant is a complete devo-
tion to vegetarian dishes. Located in a busy Buckhead strip mall, the inconspicuous diner has a relaxed, sunny ambience and a cheery staff. The
black bean quesadilla is to die for, though customers craving meat might
settle for one of the many faux chicken options. There's also a Sandy Springs
location (5975 Roswell Rd., 404/265-1675, Mon.-Thurs. 11:30am-2:30pm
and 5pm-9pm, Fri. 11:30am-2:30pm and 5pm-9:30pm, Sat. noon-2:30pm
and 5pm-9:30pm).

MAP 3: 2140 Peachtree Rd. NW, 404/352-8859, www.cafesunflower.com; Mon.-Thurs.
11:30am-2:30pm and 5pm-9:30pm, Fri. 11:30am-2:30pm and 5pm-10pm, Sat.
noon-2:30pm and 5pm-10pm

R. THOMAS DELUXE GRILL ❸❸

Richard Thomas's funky, San Francisco-inspired restaurant has prided
itself on promoting healthy and sustainable diet choices since its opening
in 1985. The menu is heavy on vegetarian and vegan-friendly dishes (like
the walnut sunflower loaf or the veggie sloppy joe), though it also includes

RESTAURANTS
BUCKHEAD

free-range chicken and beef options. The restaurant itself is an eclectic roadside attraction, with multicolored windmills and tropical parrots on display. It's one of the few restaurants in town open all night.

MAP 3: 1812 Peachtree St. NW, 404/872-2942, www.rthomasdeluxegrill.net; daily 24 hours

Virginia-Highland

Map 4

You could spend weeks sampling the food along **North Highland Avenue**, starting around East Rock Springs Road and working your way south, and never try the same place. The itinerary would hit some of Atlanta's most-loved restaurants. This busy street alone has dozens of delectable favorites representing a huge range of cuisines, from sushi to Southern, and many are budget-friendly places. For even cheaper favorites, check out **Ponce de Leon Avenue** between Monroe Drive and North Highland Avenue, a favorite stomping ground of college students and thrifty locals.

ASIAN
DOC CHEY'S NOODLE HOUSE ❸
The concept has been copied plenty in Atlanta, but never topped: cheap, tasty, and Americanized noodle dishes served fast. Doc Chey's has been a Morningside landmark for more than a decade and has since expanded into Athens and the Carolinas. The bargain prices and enormous portions draw crowds of young people, as well as neighborhood yuppies. Its large outdoor patio overlooks nothing special but manages to be romantic and convivial during the warmer months.

MAP 4: 1424 N. Highland Ave. NE, 404/888-0777, www.doccheys.com; daily 11:30am-10pm

HARRY & SONS ❸❸
The inconspicuous entrance of Harry & Sons hardly hints at the commotion inside, let alone the busy back patio—one of the cutest in the neighborhood. The menu sticks to Thai and Chinese favorites like curry chicken or Thai noodle dishes but includes a full selection of sushi options—some of the best in the area. The exposed-brick dining room is tastefully adorned with contemporary artwork. Really, you should ask for the patio.

MAP 4: 820 N. Highland Ave. NE, 404/873-2009, www.harryandsonsrestaurant. com; Mon.-Thurs. 11:30am-2:30pm and 5:30pm-10:30pm, Fri. 11:30am-2:30pm and 5:30pm-11:30pm, Sat. noon-11:30pm, Sun. noon-10:30pm

BRUNCH
MURPHY'S ❸❸
Somehow Atlanta never got the hint that having just a handful of quality brunch options causes major headaches on weekends. Which is only good news for Murphy's, one of the most in-demand brunch spots in Virginia-Highland. The wait time for a table on a Sunday morning can be ludicrous, especially after 11am, but luckily the killer Bloody Marys can help

Above: Harry & Sons. **Below:** Yeah! Burger.

you cope. The restaurant has the tasteful ambience of a French bistro, but without the attitude.

MAP 4: 997 Virginia Ave. NE, 404/872-0904, www.murphys-atlanta-restaurant.com; Mon.-Thurs. 11am-10pm, Fri. 11am-midnight, Sat. 8am-11pm, Sun. 8am-10pm

DESSERT
PAOLO'S GELATO ITALIANO $

Paolo's is one of the few dessert counters in town offering authentic Italian gelato, with a rotating selection of more than 50 flavors. Proprietor Paolo, whose smiling face figures prominently in all the marketing goods, brings gelato-making expertise from his homeland of Italy and is often on hand to educate customers in the closet-sized shop. It sits on one of the busiest corners of Virginia-Highland and does a brisk after-dinner business. It's cash only.

MAP 4: 1025 Virginia Ave. NE, 404/607-0055, www.paolosgelato.com; Tues.-Thurs. 2pm-10pm, Fri. 2pm-10:30pm, Sat. noon-11pm, Sun. noon-10pm

ITALIAN
EATS $

After two decades of slinging cheap pasta to an eclectic crowd, Eats deserves a spot as a genuine ATL institution, up there with the Varsity. The bare-bones spaghetti shack has a rough-around-the-edges charm. Diners choose either the pasta counter, offering simple noodle dishes with a choice of sauces and toppings, or the chicken counter, famous for its spicy jerk chicken and Southern sides like collard greens and baked sweet potatoes.

MAP 4: 600 Ponce de Leon Ave. NE, 404/888-9149, www.eatsonponce.net; daily 11am-10pm

FLOATAWAY CAFÉ $$$

Floataway Café is the dreamy sibling of the celebrated Bacchanalia, but the small and wistful bistro has a style all its own. Located in a renovated warehouse on a scary-looking industrial side street north of Morningside, Floataway might get more attention if it were in a more visible spot. Still, a trip there feels like finding a hidden treasure. The menu changes daily and features seasonal cuisine created with country French, Mediterranean, and Italian influences.

MAP 4: 1123 Zonolite Rd. NE, Ste. 15, 404/892-1414, www.starprovisions.com; Tues.-Sat. 6pm-10pm

LA TAVOLA TRATTORIA $$

La Tavola ("the table" in Italian), a charming and chatty café on a busy intersection, is about as close as Virginia-Highland comes to Little Italy. The small restaurant somehow feels larger as it fills up; there's a warm jubilance that suits the menu of pasta and seafood favorites (baked manicotti, veal scaloppini) just fine. The food itself might not set off fireworks, but La Tavola does boast an impressive wine list and gracious staff.

MAP 4: 992 Virginia Ave. NE, 404/873-5430, www.latavolatrattoria.com; Mon.-Thurs. 5:30pm-10pm, Fri.-Sat. 5:30pm-11pm, Sun. 11am-3pm and 5:30pm-10pm

LA FONDA LATINA $

Mexican, Cuban, and Latin American dishes all collide at La Fonda, a
bargain staple that has a tendency to polarize patrons—people either
love it or hate it. Detractors say the "Latin" label is too generous, that it's
really just a Mexican joint with a broad menu. Loyalists swear that La
Fonda offers consistently fresh and tasty quesadillas, Cuban sandwiches,
and paella. The Ponce de Leon location has a breezy second-story patio
that's perfect for summer nights; there are also locations in Candler Park
(1639 McLendon Ave., 404/378-5200, Mon.-Thurs. 11am-11pm, Fri.-Sat.
11am-midnight, Sun. noon-11pm) and Buckhead (2813 Peachtree Rd.,
404/816-8311, Mon.-Thurs. 11am-11pm, Fri.-Sat. 11am-midnight, Sun.
noon-11pm).

MAP 4: 923 Ponce de Leon Ave. NE, 404/607-0665, www.fellinisatlanta.com/lafonda.
html; Mon.-Thurs. 11am-11pm, Fri.-Sat. 11am-midnight, Sun. noon-11pm

SOUTHERN

ATKINS PARK $$

This Virginia-Highland survivor often gets mentioned for its bar credentials, mainly because of its designation as Atlanta's oldest continuously
licensed tavern, open since 1922. The drinking crowd that fills the place
later on is only half the story. Atkins Park also serves great comfort food
several notches above the usual pub fare. The Southern fried chicken is a
guilty pleasure served just the way your grandmother made it, with mac-
and-cheese and green beans.

MAP 4: 794 N. Highland Ave. NE, 404/876-7249, www.atkinspark.com; Mon.-Sat.
11am-3am, Sun. 11am-midnight

Little Five Points
and East Atlanta   Map 5

Bohemian Little Five Points is better known as a destination for thrift stores
or dive bars than fine dining—but the quality of some of the cheap eats
here really can't be beat (nor can the people-watching). Nearby **Old Fourth
Ward** and **Inman Park** have benefited from an ongoing building boom,
with outstanding new restaurants sprouting regularly. East Atlanta, like
Little Five, doesn't exactly swim in culinary greatness, but even the grungy
set gotta eat sometime.

ASIAN

GU'S DUMPLINGS $$

This in-demand Krog Street Market counter carries on the tradition of Gu's
Bistro, a Buford Highway favorite that closed in 2014. The menu features
Gu's highly acclaimed Zhong-style dumplings and noodle dishes. It's billed
as "the first authentic Szechuan restaurant" to open in the area. Items such

as the Chongqing Spicy Chicken or Spicy Crispy Beef bring on the heat, and even some of the "cold" noodle dishes can be anything but.

MAP 5: 99 Krog St. NE, 404/527-6007, www.gusdumplings.com; Tues.-Thurs. 5:30pm-11pm, Fri.-Sat. 5:30pm-midnight, Sun. 5:30pm-11pm

BRUNCH
THE FLYING BISCUIT CAFE ❸❸

The original Flying Biscuit remains a colorful Candler Park icon, with sunflowers painted on the walls and an endearing girly-girl personality. The food can be less creative than the setting but does include some stand-outs, such as a delicious turkey meatloaf and pudge (mashed potatoes with sun-dried tomatoes, basil, and olive oil), plus, of course, the signature biscuits. Skip the brunch crowds by going for dinner or a late lunch. Breakfast is served all day. There are less zany locations in Midtown (1001 Piedmont Ave., 404/874-8887, daily 7am-10pm) and Buckhead (3280 Peachtree Rd., 404/477-0013, daily 6:30am-4pm).

MAP 5: 1655 McLendon Ave. NE, 404/687-8888, www.flyingbiscuit.com; daily 7am-9:30pm

HIGHLAND BAKERY ❸❸

Highland Bakery scores points for its exquisite whole-grain breads and the extensive brunch menu. The setting is a converted redbrick warehouse that just oozes character and warmth; the staff is attentive and polite, if often a little harried. The bakery grinds its flour on-site daily using a unique Austrian stone mill. Though busiest during breakfast hours, the bakery also offers a choice selection of sandwiches and salads for lunch.

MAP 5: 655 Highland Ave. NE, 404/586-0772, www.highlandbakery.com; Mon.-Fri. 7am-4pm, Sat.-Sun. 8am-4pm

RADIAL CAFÉ ❸❸

Radial Café is the kind of place where you can sip some organic fair-trade coffee and listen in as the millennials at the next table dish about the art show they saw the night before. Radial opened in 1999, but it's still relatively easier to get a table here than at other nearby brunch destinations. The food tends to be eclectic remakes of breakfast classics (such as biscuits and vegetarian gravy, or organic buckwheat pancakes).

MAP 5: 1530 DeKalb Ave. NE, 404/659-6594, www.radial.us; Sun.-Wed. 7:30am-4pm, Thurs.-Fri. 7:30am-10pm, Sat. 8:30am-10pm

COFFEEHOUSES
JAVAVINO ❸

There are plenty of quality coffeehouses near Poncey-Highland, but JavaVino gets extra credit for its unique concept, adding wine to the mix. The intimate espresso house serves a wide range of coffees and wines from around the world. The house coffee is truly a family affair: Co-owner Heddy Kühl's coffee-growing relatives in Nicaragua hand-pick the beans, and the roast is made in-house at JavaVino. JavaVino also serves desserts, cheese plates, and a few sandwiches.

MAP 5: 579 N. Highland Ave. NE, 404/577-8673, www.javavino.com; Mon. 6:30am-11am, Tues.-Thurs. 6:30am-10pm, Fri. 6:30am-midnight, Sat. 8am-midnight, Sun. 8am-8pm

CONTEMPORARY AND NEW AMERICAN
CARROLL STREET CAFÉ $$

Carroll Street Café beams with bohemian personality, a reflection of its location in gentrifying Cabbagetown. The featured paintings are by local artists, and a folksy ambience overflows into both the staff and the food. Healthy salads, serviceable sandwiches, and pasta dishes fill the menu, though things get more complicated at dinner when steaks and seafood show up. Visit during lunch on a sunny day, and snag one of the few tables on the sidewalk.

MAP 5: 208 Carroll St. SE, 404/577-2700, www.carrollstcafe.com; Sun.-Sat. 8am-midnight

★ THE COCKENTRICE $$$

The unwieldy menus at the Cockentrice can seem overwhelming, a dense catalog of meat-market terminology that may make even the most sophisticated carnivores pause. Luckily, chef Kevin Ouzts's sublime experiments in charcuterie and meat cookery are far more easily digested than their descriptions. The much-anticipated restaurant mixes classic Southern cooking techniques with cutting-edge tastes. Freshly butchered meats and locally sourced ingredients are delivered daily. Portion sizes can be unpredictable and vary greatly from entrée to entrée.

MAP 5: 99 Krog St. NE, 470/428-2733, http://thecockentrice.com; Tues.-Thurs. 5:30pm-11pm, Fri.-Sat. 5:30pm-midnight, Sun. 5:30pm-11pm

GUNSHOW $$$

Brace yourself for theatrics at this much-hyped Glenwood Park bistro designed to eliminate the separation between guests and the kitchen. Owner Kevin Gillespie, a *Top Chef* fan favorite and former co-owner of Woodfire Grill, leads a team of chefs who bring their latest creations around to each table dim-sum style. The eclectic menu changes weekly, with inspirations varying from classic Southern dishes to fanciful updates of international favorites. Reservations are essential and can be made online.

MAP 5: 924 Garrett St., Suite C, 404/380-1886, www.gunshowatl.com; Tues.-Sat. 6pm-9pm

★ RATHBUN'S $$$

Kevin Rathbun reigns as one of Atlanta's go-to celebrity chefs, with a slew of television appearances and a winning turn on the Food Network's *Iron Chef.* The trendy Old Fourth Ward restaurant that bears his name is a study in contrasts: an ultramodern space carved out of an industrial urban complex, and an upscale dining experience that's also curiously relaxed. The playful menu goes from roasted pork belly tacos to Maine lobster without missing a beat. The chef's empire includes nearby **Kevin Rathbun Steak** (154 Krog St., 404/524-5600, Mon.-Thurs. 5:30pm-10pm, Fri.-Sat. 5:30pm-11pm) and tapas lounge **Krog Bar** (112 Krog St., 404/524-1618, www.krogbar.com, Mon.-Sat. 4:30pm-midnight).

MAP 5: 112 Krog St.NE, 404/524-8280, www.rathbunsrestaurant.com; Mon.-Thurs. 5:30pm-10pm, Fri.-Sat. 5:30pm-11pm

SERPAS TRUE FOOD $$

Chef Scott Serpas delivers irresistible Cajun comfort food blended with Asian and Southwestern influences. Expect spicy and unpredictable twists on old favorites like seafood gumbo and sausage jambalaya. The lofty space itself feels at once modern and classic; the noise level can be a nuisance when the place gets packed. *GQ* named Serpas True Food as one of the 10 best new restaurants in the country in 2009, cementing its reputation.

MAP 5: 659 Auburn Ave. NE #501, 404/688-0040, www.serpasrestaurant.com; Tues.-Thurs. 5:30pm-10pm, Fri.-Sat. 5:30pm-11pm, Sun. 11am-3pm and 5:30pm-9pm

TWO URBAN LICKS $$$

With sky-high ceilings, hushed lighting, and an exposed kitchen that fills the center of the dining room, Two Urban Licks doesn't skimp on atmosphere or extravagance; its unique 26-foot wine wall holds 42 stainless-steel barrels of wine, while elsewhere a towering rotisserie cooks up an army's worth of poultry. The menu features New American fare that's inventive without being too intimidating, including its famous ribs and a couple of inspired seafood dishes.

MAP 5: 820 Ralph McGill Blvd. NE, 404/522-4622, www.twourbanlicks.com; Mon.-Thurs. 5:30pm-midnight, Fri.-Sat. 5:30pm-1am, Sun. 11am-3pm and 5:30pm-10pm

THE VORTEX BAR AND GRILL $$

The Vortex is a snarling 18-and-up burger joint whose clientele tends to be more mixed (and middle class) than the aggressive artwork might suggest. The star of the kitchen is the half-pound hamburger dressed up in a wide variety of incarnations, including the bizarre Elvis Burger (king-sized with peanut butter and bacon). The menu warns, "Don't come in here and start acting like a damned fool," which says everything you need to know about the service.

MAP 5: 438 Moreland Ave. NE, 404/688-1828, www.thevortexbarandgrill.com; Sun.-Thurs. 11am-midnight, Fri.-Sat. 11am-2am

DINERS
★ THUMBS UP DINER $

"Relax, it's just eggs," says the motto of Thumbs Up Diner, though the mood on busy Sunday mornings can be anything but relaxed. Folks flock to Thumbs Up for the dependable and hearty breakfast menu, which really is one of the most consistently satisfying in town. Favorites include the Skillet Heap (seasoned spuds with cheddar-jack) and the Belgian waffle (topped with 100 percent pure Vermont maple syrup). Thumbs Up also offers burgers and sandwiches. Its other locations are just as busy, including

West Midtown (826 Marietta St., 404/745-4233, Mon.-Fri. 7am-3pm, Sat.-Sun. 8am-4pm) and Decatur (174 W. Ponce de Leon Ave., 404/687-0999, Mon.-Sun. 9am-3pm). Thumbs Up accepts cash only.

MAP 5: 573 Edgewood Ave. SE, 404/223-0690, www.thumbsupdiner.com; Mon.-Fri. 7am-3pm, Sat.-Sun. 8am-4pm

ICE CREAM
JAKE'S ICE CREAM ⑤

Just when the Atlanta BeltLine Eastside Trail seems like it may never end, rest assured there's a double scoop of hand-crafted happiness awaiting you at the finish line. Jake's Ice Cream has been a constantly evolving local staple since 1999, famous for its fun flavor names (Chocolate Slap Yo Mama remains a perennial favorite) and yummy dairy-free and vegan options. Don't be intimidated by the long line: Jake's is well worth the wait.

MAP 5: 660 Irwin St. NE, 678/705-7945 www.jakesicecream.com; Tues.-Thurs. 8am-10pm, Fri. 8am-11pm, Sat. 9am-11pm, Sun. 9am-10pm

ITALIAN
AMMAZZA ⑤⑤

Ammazza's (in)famous Inferno pizza—swimming in spicy sopressata, basil, house mozzarella, and fiery calabria peppers—brings new meaning to "the burning of Atlanta." For those less courageous, this 5,000-square-foot Edgewood Avenue hot spot offers a wide variety of better-than-average Neapolitan wood-fired pizzas served family-style (think: rustic dining room, stiff drinks). The Italian street food sides, especially the sausage-and-pepperoni Carnosa, shouldn't be missed; the salads are also a treat.

MAP 5: 591-A Edgewood Ave. SE, 404/228-1036, www.ammazza.com; Sun.-Thurs. 5pm-midnight, Fri.-Sat. 5pm-2am

FRITTI ⑤⑤

A craze for fussy thin-crust pizza swept through Atlanta a few years back, and perhaps no place does it better than Fritti. The fashionable younger sister of longstanding Italian restaurant **Sotto Sotto** (404/523-6678, www.urestaurants.com, Mon.-Thurs. 5:30pm-11pm, Fri.-Sat. 5:30pm-midnight, Sun. 5:30pm-10pm) next door, this stylish Inman Park destination offers two dozen varieties of Neapolitan pizzas—pies that have actually been certified by the Verace Pizza Napoletana Association in Naples, Italy—cooked in handmade wood-burning ovens. The festive patio is always full of young professionals sipping Chardonnay and folks heading to the Atlanta BeltLine nearby.

MAP 5: 309 N. Highland Ave. NE, 404/880-9559, www.frittirestaurant.com; Mon.-Thurs. 11:30am-11pm, Fri.-Sat. 11:30am-midnight, Sun. 12:30pm-10pm

MEXICAN
PURE TAQUERIA ⑤⑤

Don't tell the urbanites who frequent this stylish Inman Park cantina, but the concept originated way out in the northern suburb of Alpharetta. The attractive North Highland location marks the local chain's first venture into town, and it's been an unqualified success so far. Affordable Mexican standards like chipotle chicken tacos and ceviche come paired with a decent beer menu and serviceable margaritas. The patio is pure fun.

MAP 5: 300 N. Highland Ave. NE, 404/522-7873, www.puretaqueria.com; Mon.-Wed. 11am-10pm, Thurs.-Sat. 11am-11pm, Sun. 11am-10pm

SOUTHERN
FRONT PAGE NEWS 🄢🄢

While some folks swear by the original Midtown location (1104 Crescent Ave., 404/897-3500, Sun.-Wed. 11am-11pm, Thurs. 11am-1am, Fri.-Sat. 11am-2am), the larger Little Five Points incarnation of Front Page News has a couple of distinct advantages. Located in a gorgeous 100-year-old warehouse, the restaurant features an irresistible patio and a cavernous dining room (which can get noisy on busy nights). The restaurant taps into a playful French Quarter energy, with a menu influenced, but not overwhelmed, by Creole favorites. Sunday's Live Jazz Brunch is immensely popular.

MAP 5: 351 Moreland Ave. NE, 404/475-7777, www.frontpageatlanta.com; Mon.-Wed. 11am-11pm, Thurs. 11am-midnight, Fri.-Sat. 11am-1am, Sun. 10am-11pm

PARISH BRASSERIE AND NEIGHBORHOOD CAFÉ 🄢🄢🄢

The building frenzy that broke out on the border of Inman Park and the Old Fourth Ward a few years back included the restoration of a historic 1890s pipe factory into Parish, an instant neighborhood staple. Equal parts market and eclectic restaurant, Parish offers broad-based Southern comfort food. The downstairs market features a communal table for fast bites from the deli, as well as a handsome assortment of housewares, flowers, homemade ice creams, and other unexpected delights.

MAP 5: 240 N. Highland Ave. NE, 404/681-4434, www.parishatl.com; Tues.-Thurs. 8am-10pm, Fri.-Sat. 8am-11pm, Sun. 8am-9pm

SOUTHWESTERN
AGAVE 🄢🄢

Agave is the plant that produces tequila, and this cantina prides itself on offering 100 varieties of the coveted Mexican liquor. It opened in 2000 and was fast to attract a following. The dining room is both upscale and boisterous. The creative Southwestern fare varies from traditional New Mexican dishes (like posole or Hatch green-chile stew) to more Americanized options (short ribs or tenderloin medallions). Agave also features an extensive wine list and a dedicated parking lot.

MAP 5: 242 Boulevard SE, 404/588-0006, www.agaverestaurant.com; Sun.-Thurs. 5pm-10pm, Fri.-Sat. 5pm-11pm

SPANISH
★ BARCELONA ATLANTA WINE BAR 🄢🄢

Catalonia came to the Old Fourth Ward in 2011 with the arrival of Barcelona Atlanta Wine Bar, an overnight sensation thanks largely to its expansive patio and sultry ambience. The concept originated in Connecticut, of all places, with a close-knit clan of tapas lounges that selected Atlanta

Clockwise from top left: The Vortex Bar and Grill; Atkins Park; Front Page News.

for its first Southern outpost. The reasonably priced entrées reference traditional Spanish dishes without being completely foreign; the tapas also tend to be bigger than you might expect.

MAP 5: 240 N. Highland Ave. NE, 404/589-1010, www.barcelonawinebar.com; Mon.-Thurs. 11:30am-12:30am, Fri. 11:30am-1:30am, Sat. 11:30am-2am, Sun. 11:30am-midnight

Decatur   Map 6

While the sparkle has faded in some of metro Atlanta's scattered commercial outposts in recent years, the absolute opposite has been true of Decatur's **downtown square.** The concentration of restaurants and shops only seems to grow more bustling, with a charming blend of brew houses, ethnic fare, and casually elegant eateries. Nearby **Oakhurst** has its own burgeoning restaurant scene, where a smattering of comfortable neighborhood joints double as pubs for locals.

BRUNCH
SWEET MELISSA'S $

The weekend brunch rush in Atlanta can be extremely hectic, with wait times reaching the red zone and irate customers howling for tables. Sweet Melissa's gets just as full as some of the other places in town, but the relaxed vibe in this quaint Decatur café helps to mitigate the aggravation. The food won't ever win awards; expect reliable and familiar omelets, wraps, and club sandwiches. It's been around since 1989.

MAP 6: 127 E. Court Sq., Decatur, 404/370-1111, www.sweetmelissas.com; Mon.-Fri. 8am-2:30pm, Sat.-Sun. 8am-3pm

COFFEEHOUSES
JAVA MONKEY $

Leave it to hipper-than-thou Decatur to show ambivalence toward a place like Java Monkey, a charming coffee shop (and sandwich counter) that most any other small town would be thrilled to call its own. Locals hang out here to make a statement about choosing independent businesses over corporate chains—but then they gripe about the service or the spotty wireless Internet. Java Monkey shines for its tasty sandwiches and wine selection. It also hosts open-mic nights.

MAP 6: 425 Church St., Decatur, 404/378-5002, www.javamonkeydecatur.com; Mon.-Thurs. 7am-11pm, Fri.. 7am-midnight, Sat. 7:30am-midnight, Sun. 7:30am-11pm

CONTEMPORARY AND NEW AMERICAN
CAKES & ALE $$$

Chef Billy Allin's Cakes & Ale is a comfortable, elegant bistro and bakery that has quickly become one of the square's standby spots. With a focus on products sourced from sustainable farms and fisheries, the menu feels at once curatorial and also as if it's not trying to please everyone. The first

Sunday of each month features a special family-style prix fixe meal that usually books weeks in advance.

MAP 6: 155 Sycamore St., Decatur, 404/377-7994, www.cakesandalerestaurant.com; Tues.-Thurs. 6pm-10pm, Fri.-Sat. 5:30pm-10:30pm

FARM BURGER $\$$

Grass-fed beef burgers topped with arugula and basil goat cheese; sautéed chicken livers swimming in kale and sherry vinaigrette; fried mac-and-cheese finished with pickled Vidalia onions. Is it any wonder that Farm Burger is always packed to the point of bursting? The meat comes from cows raised free from antibiotics, hormones, or grain. The difference is in the taste. The prices here are a lot more reasonable than at some of the other high-concept burger shacks.

MAP 6: 410B W. Ponce de Leon Ave., Decatur, 404/378-5077, www.farmburger.net; Sun.-Thurs. 11:30am-10pm, Fri.-Sat. 11:30am-11pm

SUN IN MY BELLY $\$$

Modeled after a relaxed European café, Sun in My Belly is probably best enjoyed for a lingering Sunday brunch. The first Sunday of each month features live jazz performances. The restaurant might be most famous for its bacon, a decadent but delicious side that comes glazed in honey. The menu also includes a persuasive selection of sandwiches (try the balsamic grilled veggies with goat cheese) and seasonal entrées ranging from traditional meatloaf to adobe-spiced pork tenderloin.

MAP 6: 2161 College Ave. NE, Atlanta, 404/370-1088, www.suninmybelly.com; Mon. 8am-4pm, Tues.-Sat. 8am-4pm and 6pm-10pm, Sun. 9am-4pm

UNIVERSAL JOINT $\$$

Universal Joint—named for the auto part—converted a dilapidated gas station into a busy Oakhurst watering hole. The large patio is packed almost year-round, weather permitting. Though it's known to many of its patrons as a bar first, the Joint also serves tasty burgers, sandwiches, and quesadillas that are in a class well above the usual pub fare. The spicy egg rolls—stuffed with chicken, cream cheese, grapes, and jalapeños—are a guilty pleasure.

MAP 6: 906 Oakview Rd., Decatur, 404/373-6260, www.ujointbar.com; Mon. 11:30am-1am, Tues.-Thurs. 11:30am-2am, Fri.-Sat. 11:30am-3am, Sun. 11:30am-2pm

GASTROPUBS

BRICK STORE PUB $\$$

Perhaps no place in Atlanta has better Brunswick stew, but the Brick Store Pub is more famous for its selection of Belgian beers, including eight rotating Belgian drafts and more than 120 Belgian bottled beers—plus the 17 drafts and 75 bottled beers on its regular menu. It has the feeling of an English tavern from the turn of the 20th century, though it actually opened in 1997. Don't expect prompt or impressive service.

MAP 6: 125 E. Court Sq., Decatur, 404/687-0990, www.brickstorepub.com; Mon. 11am-1am, Tues.-Sat. 11am-2am, Sun. noon-1am

Waffle House and Dwarf House

When the world's first Waffle House opened in Atlanta on Labor Day 1955, neither Joe Rogers nor Tom Forkner had any sense that their diner would eventually become a Southern icon. Most often found along interstates and famous for being open 24 hours a day, seven days a week, Waffle House now operates more than 1,600 locations in 25 states. In 2008 the company reopened its original Avondale Estates café as the **Waffle House Museum** (2719 E. College Ave., 877/992-3353, www.wafflehouse.com/waffle-house-museum). The 13-stool diner has been stocked with antique equipment, classic Waffle House uniforms, displays of memorabilia, and place settings with plastic food.

The jukebox offers a selection of original Waffle House songs. The museum is free but open by appointment only, Tuesday and Thursday 10am-2pm.

Another national chain that emerged from Atlanta has taken a different route with its original location. Though it's known today as Chick-fil-A, Truett Cathy's chicken-sandwich empire started as the Dwarf Grill in 1946 in Hapeville, a stone's throw from what is now Hartsfield-Jackson Atlanta International Airport. Now called the **Dwarf House** (461 Central Ave., 404/762-1746, www.cfarestaurant.com/hapevilledwarfhouse), the busy restaurant serves the usual Chick-fil-A menu—but with table service.

LEON'S FULL SERVICE ❺❺

The retro aesthetic has become a cliché in Atlanta restaurants, with every second newcomer twisting itself into knots to do nostalgia better than the neighbors. But at Leon's, the hints of yesteryear's roadhouses are only window dressing for a gastropub experience that's fresh and modern. The menu is admittedly scattered: turkey schnitzel, skirt steak gyros, pan-roasted trout. Leon's has one of the best patios in Decatur and some of the most inventive cocktails in town.

MAP 6: 131 E. Ponce de Leon Ave., Decatur, 404/687-0500, www.leonsfullservice.com; Mon. 5pm-1am, Tues.-Thurs. 11:30am-1am, Fri.-Sat. 11:30am-2am, Sun. 11:30am-1am

MEXICAN
MATADOR MEXICAN CANTINA ❺

Matador may look like your typical Americanized Mexican cantina, but beyond the usual round-up of combo plates and fajitas, the extensive menu also features some surprises. Several dishes were inspired by traditions of the Michoacán region of central Mexico. The unique tacos are a particular treat. This lively Oakhurst hole-in-the-wall also touts an extensive tequila list and is known for hosting a noisy crowd for Team Trivia on Wednesdays.

MAP 6: 350 Mead Rd., Decatur, 404/377-0808, www.matadorcantina.com; Mon.-Thurs. 7am-10pm, Fri.-Sat. 7am-11pm, Sun. 7am-10pm

SPANISH
THE IBERIAN PIG ❺❺❺

In case you aren't up to snuff on geography, the Iberian Peninsula includes Spain, Portugal, Andorra, and Gibraltar. The name of this unassuming

Decatur gem serves it well due to the diversity of flavors and textures. In comparison to typical Spanish tapas bars, the menu at the Iberian Pig includes old faves like Serrano ham and bacon-wrapped dates as well as some new twists like wild boar meatballs and veal ravioli.

MAP 6: 121 Sycamore St., Decatur, 404/371-8800, www.iberianpigatl.com; Mon.-Thurs. 5pm-11pm, Fri.-Sat. 5-midnight, Sun. 4pm-9pm

Greater Atlanta   Map 7

Atlanta's outer suburbs may not have the same density of trendy dining rooms as neighborhoods like Buckhead or Midtown, but that's not to say that everything outside of the Perimeter is a culinary wasteland. The most interesting—and non-corporate—spots tend to pop up around historic small-town centers, such as in quaint **Roswell** or in the crossroads at **Vinings.** Finding fine dining in Greater Atlanta requires research and a lot more driving, but there are definitely some hidden treasures waiting to be discovered.

BARBECUE
THE SWALLOW AT THE HOLLOW 🟢🟢

A canoe filled with iced beer greets guests at the Swallow at the Hollow, a down-home barbecue joint that doubles as a music venue. The longstanding Roswell restaurant has live country music Friday and Saturday nights. The menu includes heaps of Southern favorites and even some vegetarian-friendly dishes. Be prepared for communal seating; on a busy night you might end up rubbing elbows with strangers at one of the larger tables.

MAP 7: 1072 Green St., Roswell, 678/352-1975, www.theswallowatthehollow.com; Wed.-Thurs. 11am-9pm, Fri.-Sat. 11am-10pm, Sun. 11am-9pm

CONTEMPORARY AND NEW AMERICAN
CANOE 🟢🟢🟢

Landlocked Atlanta holds a real grudge against cities with waterfronts, which makes Canoe all the more outstanding. It's nestled on a quiet bank of the Chattahoochee River near Vinings, about 10 minutes outside of Buckhead. Many tables feature prominent views of the water, but the main dining room is urbane and comfortable even without a window or patio seat. Canoe's menu features original and creative seafood along with upscale New American fare. It's definitely worth the trip.

MAP 7: 4199 Paces Ferry Rd. SE, 770/432-2663, www.canoeatl.com; Mon.-Thurs. 11:30am-2:30pm and 5:30pm-10pm, Fri. 11:30am-2:30pm and 5:30pm-11pm, Sat. 5:30pm-11pm, Sun. 10:30am-2:30pm and 5:30pm-9:30pm

HORSERADISH GRILL 🟢🟢🟢

Horseradish Grill sits a stone's throw from scenic Chastain Park. The converted barn has the feel of a pleasant—if somewhat somber—garden café. The menu swears by the mantra, "What grows together, goes together," and is heavy on heirloom varieties of local produce, some of which are grown behind the restaurant. Though the menu is thick with Southern influences (fried chicken, North Georgia trout), the overall scope is more middle-of-the-road American and full of wood-grilled specialties.

MAP 7: 4320 Powers Ferry Rd., Atlanta, 404/255-7277, www.horseradishgrill.com; Mon.-Thurs. 11:30am-2:30pm and 5:30pm-9pm, Fri. 11:30am-2:30pm and 5pm-10pm, Sat. 11am-2:30pm and 5pm-10pm, Sun. 11am-2:30pm and 5pm-9pm

MEXICAN
NUEVO LAREDO CANTINA $$

Located on a distant industrial edge of town, the eternally crowded cantina is a spot locals would rather no one else find—because the line's long enough already. Serving authentic, homey Mexican fare since 1992, the place is known for its fresh salsas, sauces, and delicious chicken mole. For extra credit, order the Cadillac Margarita Grande, which might help you make sense of the oddball decor downstairs.

MAP 7: 1495 Chattahoochee Ave., Atlanta, 404/352-9009, www.nuevolaredocantina. com; Mon.-Thurs. 11am-10pm, Fri.-Sat. 11am-11pm, Sun. noon-9:30pm

SOUTHERN
OLD VININGS INN $$

The first thing you notice when approaching the Vinings Inn is the building itself, a gently renovated monument of a house that has previously held a post office, an antiques store, and apartments. The setting inside is white tablecloths and measured gentility. The menu, billed as Southern, includes many regional standards like fried green tomatoes and sweet corn grits, but it could just as easily be categorized as New American. **Attic Bar,** a part of Vinings Inn, is above the restaurant and books music acts Tuesday-Saturday and can get quite boisterous—for Vinings.

MAP 7: 3011 Paces Mill Rd. SE, Atlanta, 770/438-2282, www.oldviningsinn.com; Mon.-Thurs. 5pm-9pm, Fri. 5pm-10pm, Sat. 11:30am-10pm, Sun. 11:30am-3pm

ONE FLEW SOUTH $$$

Located in a prime corner spot in Terminal E, this jet-setting bistro serves "Southernational," a mixture of high-end local favorites (often with a twist) along with a variety of sushi creations. The restaurant can fill up depending on delays around the airport. Reservations are not accepted, but takeout options are available.

MAP 7: Hartsfield-Jackson Atlanta International Airport, Terminal E, Atlanta, 404/816-3464, www.oneflewsouthatl.com; daily 11am-10pm

SOUTHBOUND $$

Nobody goes to Chamblee for the food—unless the destination happens to be Southbound. Housed in a century-old factory and former Masonic Lodge, the shotgun-style dining room is a delicious throwback peppered with contemporary sophistication. The "supper" options draw heavily on farm-to-table options and regional standards (fried North Carolina catfish,

Above: The Iberian Pig. Below: Nuevo Laredo Cantina.

wood-grilled rib eye) mixed with diverse small plates (beef tartare, wood-grilled octopus).

MAP 7: 5394 Peachtree Rd., Chamblee, 678/580-5579, www.baconsnobs.com; Tues.-Thurs. 11am-10pm, Fri.-Sat. 11am-11pm

STEAK HOUSES
MCKENDRICK'S STEAK HOUSE $$$

McKendrick's Steak House has been feeding the northern suburbs since 1995. Located in the bustling business district around Perimeter Mall, it's a bit less stuffy than most of the business-class steak houses found farther south in Buckhead. The place still has a sophistication worthy of the power brokers who dine there. The cuts of beef are appropriately high-end, the waitstaff knowledgeable and attentive.

MAP 7: 4505 Ashford Dunwoody Rd., Atlanta, 770/512-8888, www.mckendricks.com; Mon.-Thurs. 11:30am-2:30pm and 5:30pm-10pm, Fri. 11:30am-2:30pm and 5:30pm-11pm, Sat. 5:30pm-11pm, Sun. 5:30pm-10pm

Nightlife

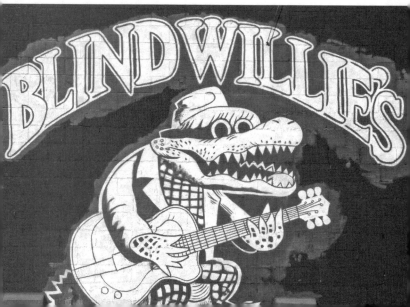

Look for ★ to find recommended nightlife.

Highlights

★ **Best Hipster Hangout:** A charismatic congregation keeps the spirit(s) flowing at **Sister Louisa's Church of the Living Room & Ping Pong Emporium,** famous for its table tennis and kitschy velvet-Jesus decor (page 94).

★ **Best Patio:** Perhaps no place in town has a larger outdoor space than **Park Tavern,** tucked into a scenic corner of Piedmont Park (page 96).

★ **Best Gay Bar:** Open since 1987, **Blake's on the Park** remains one of the city's busiest stand-and-model bars for gay guys of all ages (page 96).

★ **Best Speakeasy:** Famous for its "secret" entrance via a telephone booth, **Prohibition** pays homage to cabarets and cigar bars of yesteryear (page 100).

★ **Best Dive Bar:** Definitely not for the squeamish, **Clermont Lounge** is a dingy 1960s-era strip club now famous as a hipster hangout and destination for visiting celebrities (page 103).

★ **Best Neighborhood Bar: Manuel's Tavern** has been a go-to spot in Poncey-Highland for generations, a great place to vent about local politics (page 106).

★ **Best Brewpub: Wrecking Bar Brewpub** serves sophisticated craft beers and a mile-long whiskey list in the basement of a historic Victorian mansion (page 106).

★ **Best Acoustic Music Venue:** An intimate retreat with a long-standing and well-deserved reputation for excellence, **Eddie's Attic** is a Decatur landmark (page 109).

Hip-hop superstars Jermaine Dupri and Ludacris solidified Atlanta's party town credentials in a hit 2002 single: "Welcome to Atlanta, where the playas play," the duo proclaimed, the "new Motown" where "parties don't stop till 8 in the morning." This reputation as the spiciest club scene in the South dated back decades, thanks to 24-hour discotheques perpetually thumping and a rowdy, multi-block nightlife quarter in Buckhead infamous for its excesses.

But in the years since "Welcome to Atlanta" was released, seismic changes have shaken the places that go bump in the night. New liquor laws and a few outspoken neighborhood associations have led to the departure of many legendary venues.

The reign of the megaclubs may have ended, but the ATL's resilient sot set refuses to go gentle into that good night. Local nightlife has evolved into a different sort of party animal. Eager new speakeasies, underground lounges, gastropubs, game rooms, and art bars keep bubbling up. Many restaurants take advantage of legal loopholes by doubling as gin joints. It's not uncommon for a dining room to downshift into a martini lounge after the kitchen closes. Atlantans have a particular love for brewpubs, a trend that keeps building steam.

Night owls of the new generation tend to be less dedicated to particular venues and inclined to follow erratic crowds. This week's white-hot champagne bar might be deserted a month from now—then back at full throttle six weeks later. Promoters have perfected the art of one-off events, with semi-regular electronic dance music (EDM) and hip-hop parties popping

---

Previous: Manuel's Tavern; Blind Willie's.

up in unexpected corners of town. Atlanta has long been a city for ballers and bottle-service bars, a legacy that lives on in innumerable velvet-roped meat markets.

The city can also brag about its music venues, ranging from fanatical emo dive bars to sophisticated jazz joints and folkie hangouts. The many blues clubs here enjoy a particularly devoted clientele. Locals gather at beloved neighborhood taverns and scream at TVs in sports bars. While many American cities have seen gay and lesbian nightlife decline, Atlanta has bucked the trend with an energetic strip of new and updated venues.

Any given weekend finds DJ gigs, concerts, beer busts, open-mic nights, and after-hours parties raging somewhere in the city. Check the listings in *Creative Loafing*, *Rolling Out*, or *The GA Voice* to get a handle on what Atlanta's ever-changing nightlife has on tap. Here is a smattering of the most unsinkable and effervescent hot spots.

Downtown
Map 1

BARS
JOYSTICK GAMEBAR
Joystick Gamebar brings a sweet taste of nostalgia to the many flavors of Edgewood Avenue's diverse nightlife strip. Lose yourself in the pixelated bliss of yesteryear via the collection of vintage arcade games and pinball machines. The games on hand change from month to month, but old-school favorites like Donkey Kong and Ms. Pac-Man are always a given. Gobbling ghosts can become extra challenging after you sample the cocktail menu, which also updates regularly.

MAP 1: 427 Edgewood Ave. SE, 404/525-3002, http://joystickgamebar.com; Mon.-Fri. 5pm-2:30am, Sat. noon-2:30am, Sun. 5pm-midnight; no cover

SIDEBAR ATLANTA
Despite its many busy hotels and restaurants, Downtown has yet to figure out a winning formula for nightlife. The lack of options in the central business district led a couple of neighborhood residents to launch Sidebar, a sports bar that enjoys a devoted following among Georgia State University students and nearby loft dwellers. The place is famous for its Cuban sandwiches and giveaways for sporting event tickets.

MAP 1: 79 Poplar St. NW, 404/588-1850, www.sidebaratlanta.com; Mon.-Thurs. 11am-1am, Fri. 11am-2am, Sat. 5pm-2am, Sun. noon-midnight; no cover

★ SISTER LOUISA'S CHURCH OF THE LIVING ROOM & PING PONG EMPORIUM
Heaven help us all, but Grant Henry knows how to throw one helluva party. His alter-ego Sister Louisa plays grande dame at this groovy and gritty Old Fourth Ward dive bar, which covers every possible centimeter of its exposed-brick walls with wacky (and often wildly sacrilegious) pop art.

The titular Ping Pong Emporium is no joke; look for intense tournaments upstairs, sometimes with celebrity guests. No doubt the joint would be dubbed a den of Satan anyplace else in the Bible Belt, but here it's been a divine addition to a once-desolate neighborhood.

MAP 1: 466 Edgewood Ave. SE, 404/522-8275, www.sisterlouisaschurch.com; Mon.-Sat. 5pm-3am, Sun. 5pm-midnight; no cover

TRADER VIC'S
This colorful and nostalgic Polynesian-themed tiki bar and restaurant has been a Downtown favorite since 1976. Located in the basement of the Hilton Atlanta, the truly unique dining room feels like a kitschy-fun excursion to the South Pacific, with a dark-bamboo interior and an earnest appreciation for Tahitian accents. The mai tai is known as one of the best in town.

MAP 1: 255 Courtland St. NE, 404/221-6339, www.tradervicsatl.com; Mon.-Sat. 5pm-midnight; no cover

BREWPUBS
MAX LAGER'S AMERICAN GRILL AND BREWERY
Downtown is overrun with brand-name restaurants and bars inside swanky hotels, but Max Lager's is an entertaining exception. The roomy, 10,000-square-foot brew house has the character of a renovated industrial plant, with a loft-like urban bar and dining room. On tap you'll find German- and Vienna-inspired ales and lagers, including the popular Max Gold pilsner. Most menu items are wood-fired, leading to a distinctive dining experience rarely discovered this far south on Peachtree Street.

MAP 1: 320 Peachtree St. NE, 404/525-4400, www.maxlagers.com; Mon.-Sat. 11:30am-10:30pm, Sun. 4pm-10:30pm, bar open daily until 11pm or later; no cover

Midtown
Map 2

BARS
LOCA LUNA
When Loca Luna moved to its cavernous new digs at Amsterdam Walk, regulars worried that the tapas bar might lose its convivial (read: smashed) atmosphere. While the focus did shift, slightly, to the dinner menu of postage-stamp-sized Latin American and Brazilian dishes, the venue still delivers ear-splitting merengue and salsa music from live bands and a dance floor filled with hapless gringos swilling mojitos.

MAP 2: 550 Amsterdam Ave. NE, 404/875-4494, www.loca-luna.com; Tues.-Thurs. 5-10pm, Fri.-Sat. 5pm-2:30am, Sun. 5pm-10pm; no cover

ORMSBY'S
Time has a way of quickening at Ormsby's, an enormous gastropub and game room. Blame it on the lack of sunlight: The two-story tavern lies beneath the White Provision building, a 1910 meat-packing plant refurbished as a posh urban market. Hours underground tend to fly by—especially

when you're caught up in a heated game of pool, bocce, shuffleboard, or darts. The age range spans from millennials to soccer moms.

MAP 2: 1170 Howell Mill Rd. NW, 404/968-2033, http://ormsbysatlanta.com; Mon.-Fri. 11am-3am, Sat. noon-3am, Sun. noon-midnight; no cover

BREWPUBS
★ PARK TAVERN

Bars with large, crowded patios are about as common as traffic jams in Atlanta, but few can match the view at Park Tavern, overlooking the vast playing fields of Piedmont Park's Meadow. The tavern brews a handful of colorful, locally named drafts (Piedmont Pilsner, Eastside Trail Pale Ale). Even in the chilly months, the tavern draws a crowd with the addition of its indoor ice rink. Discount drafts are offered on rainy days: "When it rains, we pour!"

MAP 2: 500 10th St. NE, 404/249-0001, www.parktavern.com; Mon.-Fri. 4:30pm-midnight, Sat.-Sun. 11:30am-midnight; no cover

DANCE CLUBS
OPERA

This venue holds a storied history. The opulent auditorium first arrived in 1921 as an extension of the Atlanta Woman's Club. It became the Peachtree Playhouse in the 1970s, followed by infamous nightclub Petrus. Techno wonderland eleven50 reinvigorated the forgotten dance floor in 2000 and dominated Atlanta nightlife for the next decade. Now, as Opera, the space returns to its fussy, opulent roots and brings in a rotating lineup of well-known house DJs.

MAP 2: 1150 Crescent Ave. NE, 404/874-3006, www.operaatlanta.com; Wed.-Sat. 10pm-3am; $10-50

GAY AND LESBIAN
AMSTERDAM CAFÉ

The name doesn't really fit. Rather than evoking a smoky Dutch coffee shop, this Amsterdam feels more like a classic black-box boozer, complete with pool tables and televisions at every turn. The sports bar draws a crowd of regular blue-jean guys looking for a less pretentious atmosphere than at some of the glitzier Midtown haunts. Look for the entrance in the remote back corner of Amsterdam Walk, far away from the shopping center's more visible businesses.

MAP 2: 502 Amsterdam Ave. NE, 404/892-2227, www.amsterdamatlanta.com; Mon.-Thurs. 11:30am-2am, Fri.-Sat. 11:30am-3am, Sun. 11:30am-midnight; no cover

★ BLAKE'S ON THE PARK

Blake's on the Park has defied the odds and emerged as one of the most resilient gay bars in the country. Midtown's quintessential stand-and-model scene somehow hasn't slipped in popularity despite gentrification in the surrounding gayborhood. The potent, affordable well drinks bring in a diverse mix of gay guys and straight women who co-opt the downstairs drag

Midtown's Own Boystown

The 2012 closing of Outwrite Bookstore and Coffeehouse caused a major stir for some longtime residents of Midtown. Alarmists declared the passage another nail in the coffin for Atlanta's rapidly gentrifying gayborhood.

But those doomsday predictions have proven wildly inaccurate. A bumper crop of bars and restaurants have transformed 10th Street into a mini version of Montreal's Gay Village or Chicago's Boystown, with more foot traffic than ever before.

On weekends, the Midtown gay bar crawl begins at either **Henry's Midtown Tavern** (132 10th St., 404/537-4477, http://henrysatl.com) or **Joe's on Juniper** (1049 Juniper St., 404/875-6634, http://joesonjuniper.com), both popular among day drinkers thanks to their enormous decks. A block east, **Ten Atlanta** (990 Piedmont Ave., 404/347-3360, http://tenatlanta.com) serves comfort food by day, then transitions into a congested bar and dance club at night; **10th & Piedmont** (991 Piedmont Ave., 404/602-5510, www.communitashospitality.com/10th-and-piedmont) and the connected gastropub, **G's Midtown** (219 10th St., 404/872-8012, www.gilbertscafe.com) go for more of a lounge vibe, with one-off parties and karaoke.

Any tipsy tour of Midtown invariably ends at **Blake's on the Park** (227 10th St., 404/892-5786, www.blakesontheparkatlanta.com), which benefited from a much-needed interior facelift in 2015. The grande dame of the gayborhood delivers drinks as stiff as kerosene and drag shows running until Judgment Day.

"stage" as a dance floor after midnight. A 2015 renovation modernized the interior. Check out the breezy upstairs patio.

MAP 2: 227 10th St. NE, 404/892-5786, www.blakesontheparkatlanta.com; Mon.-Thurs. 3pm-3am, Fri.-Sat. 1pm-3am, Sun. 1pm-midnight; no cover

G'S MIDTOWN

Perhaps brothers Sean and Gilbert Yeremyan never saw it coming, but their polite little Gilbert's Mediterranean Café somehow mutated into a urbane cocktail lounge, G's Midtown. Dinner and brunch still draw devotees. The real party happens on nights when G's benefits from the foot traffic between other 10th Street hot spots. A back hallway connects G's to its sister bistro, **10th & Piedmont** (991 Piedmont Ave., 404/602-5510, www.communitashospitality.com/10th-and-piedmont, Sun.-Mon. 11am-midnight, Tues.-Sat. 11am-2am), which hosts occasional lesbian parties, tea dances, and other one-off events.

MAP 2: 219 10th St. NE, 404/872-8012, www.gilbertscafe.com; Sun.-Thurs. 5pm-11pm, Fri.-Sat. 5pm-midnight., bar until 2:30am Tues.-Sat., brunch Sat.-Sun. 10am-4pm; no cover

TEN ATLANTA

Ten Atlanta will never win awards for its cleverness. The interior decor is almost unchanged from the space's previous occupant, a burger café. New features include the DJ booth, open patio arrangement, and the masses of men that swarm the narrow dance floor most weekend nights. Since opening in early 2013, Ten has brought in a reliable clientele of clean-cut bro-mosexuals and randy guys ranging in age from "Emory undergrad" to "fourth face-lift."

MAP 2: 990 Piedmont Ave. NE, 404/347-3360, http://tenatlanta.com; Mon.-Fri. 5pm-3am, Sat. 11am-3am, Sun. 11am-midnight; no cover

JAZZ CLUBS
CHURCHILL GROUNDS

Churchill Grounds draws a busy pre-show crowd headed to the Fox Theatre next door. The real magic happens later in the night when the intimate nightclub hosts a packed schedule of jazz acts for discerning fans of the genre. The cover charge on weekends can feel like a stretch, with an additional $10 drink minimum. Pop by on a weeknight to beat the crowd and get a better taste of Churchill Grounds' potent charms.

MAP 2: 660 Peachtree St. NE, 404/876-3030, www.churchillgrounds.com; Tues.-Fri. 5pm-2am, Sat. noon-2am, Sun. 5pm-midnight; $10-15

LIVE MUSIC
APACHE CAFÉ

Urban music enclave Apache Café features a vivacious calendar of entertainment, from open-mic hip-hop nights to R&B and even comedy showcases. Equal parts lounge, restaurant, and art gallery, the café's exposed-brick interior gives it an off-the-radar Greenwich Village feel—an impression bolstered by its location on a dingy, dead-end street near the interstate. Beware: The area nearby can be borderline unsafe at night, so be sure to park in a secure lot.

MAP 2: 64 3rd St. NW, 404/876-5436, www.apachecafe.info; Mon.-Wed. 8pm-12:30am, Fri.-Sat. 8pm-3am; up to $15

NORTHSIDE TAVERN

The exterior of Northside Tavern looks like a roadside honky-tonk transplanted from the dusty backwoods of south Georgia. But inside is one of the city's oldest and most respected blues clubs, with a history dating to 1972. The live blues calendar features a standing lineup of local musicians with loyal followings on weeknights, along with touring acts on weekends. The music generally starts at 10pm each night but begins earlier on Sundays and for special acts.

MAP 2: 1058 Howell Mill Rd. NW, 404/874-8745, www.northsidetavern.com; daily noon-2:30am; $10

RED LIGHT CAFÉ

Bluegrass, folk, jazz, Americana—and belly dancing? The boxy Red Light Café, tucked in a quiet strip mall on the far side of Piedmont Park, gets points for versatility, even if the venue's acoustics and traffic flow can be cumbersome. Billed as "Atlanta's Living Room," Red Light hosts up-and-coming singer-songwriters, various local and touring bands, plus crowded open-mic nights. The name may imply naughtiness, but the café's sparse interior errs on the demure side.

MAP 2: 553 Amsterdam Ave. NE, 404/874-7828, www.redlightcafe.com; Mon.-Wed. and Fri.-Sun. 7:30pm-2am, Thurs. 6pm-2am; $3-15

LOUNGES

HALO LOUNGE

It can be tricky to sniff out Halo Lounge, in the basement of the historic Biltmore Hotel (refurbished as an office building). The doorway is on 6th Street and looks like a service entrance. Inside, the multilevel space connects via cool, industrial surfaces. Crowded nights can make it hard to appreciate the color changes in the illuminated downstairs bar, but the ultramodern interior is visual catnip. Hours can be somewhat sporadic; have a backup plan.

MAP 2: 817 W. Peachtree St. NW, 404/962-7333; Mon.-Sat. 10pm-3am; up to $10

LOBBY AT TWELVE

The creators of Lobby at Twelve lose points for uninspired naming (it's in the lobby of the Twelve Atlantic Station Hotel) but deserve props for launching a winning cocktail bar in Atlantic Station. The atmosphere is a jolt of urban fashionista, though not so fussy as to keep common folk from camping out in the cozy lounge. Bring your A game—but skip the always-backlogged valet parking and look for spaces on the street.

MAP 2: 361 17th St. NW, 404/961-7370, www.lobbyattwelve.com; Mon. 6:30am-10pm, Tues.-Fri. 6:30am-11pm, Sat. 11am-11pm, Sun. 11am-10pm; no cover

Buckhead

Map 3

BARS

FADÓ IRISH PUB

When a place brags about pouring the best Guinness in town, the proof is in the pint. Fadó lives up to the claim and makes its respect for authentic Irish pub culture undeniable. Much of the three-level tavern was imported from Dublin in 2007. Weekends find boisterous gatherings of fans of European sports. The unruly St. Patrick's Day festivities seem to last a month. In 2015, Fadó opened a second Midtown location (933 Peachtree St., 404/260-7910, www.fadoirishpub.com/atlanta-midtown, Mon.-Fri. 11am-2am, Sat. early-2am, Sun. early-midnight).

MAP 3: 273 Buckhead Ave. NE, 404/841-0066, www.fadoirishpub.com/atlanta; Mon.-Thurs. 11am-2am, Sat. early-3am, Sun. early-midnight; no cover

HAVANA CLUB

The skirts are short, the dance floors are sweaty, the air is thick with cigar smoke. What else would you expect from a (loosely) Cuban-themed discotheque in the heart of Buckhead? This colossal club evolved from a much smaller cigar bar. The calendar includes guest appearances from celebrity

DJs and different music styles in three main rooms (a mix of Top 40, EDM, and Latin). Dress code is business casual for guys, slightly more permissive for women.

MAP 3: 3112 Piedmont Rd. NE, 404/869-8484, www.havanaclubatl.com; Thurs.-Sat. 8pm-3am; $10 and up

THE IVY BUCKHEAD

The glory days of boozy Buckhead live on at the Ivy, which apparently never got the memo that the neighborhood is averse to nightlife. Weekends at this converted two-story mansion tend to be packed with a hard-drinking early-twenties crowd; it's a place where recently graduated fraternity and sorority types come to do shots and flirt while keeping track of sports scores. Its four owners met while living in Athens, Georgia, known for its wild watering holes.

MAP 3: 3717 Roswell Rd., 404/941-3081, www.theivybuckhead.com; Mon.-Fri. 4pm-3am, Sat. noon-3am, Sun. noon-midnight; up to $10

★ PROHIBITION

Half the fun of a visit to Prohibition comes from the James Bond routine required to find the door. Guests enter a red British telephone box, dial a "secret" number, then push a hidden door to discover a well-appointed 1920s speakeasy and cigar bar. With its dress code (blazers and skirts, no jeans or tennis shoes) and $13 cocktails, this throwback to classic jazz cabarets aims for a more sophisticated set than some of its neighbors.

MAP 3: 56 E. Andrews Dr. NW, 404/869-1132, http://prohibitionatl.com; Mon.-Sat. 5pm-3am, Sun. 5pm-midnight; no cover

THE TAVERN AT PHIPPS

There's something peculiar about a restaurant in a shopping mall that attracts a singles scene. But this is Buckhead. For years the Tavern at Phipps has done a brisk lunch business for power brokers and mall moms. After happy hour, the New Orleans-inspired restaurant gets more of a meat-market feel, with lots of flirty glances exchanged across the bar. Its patio is often listed as one of the best in Buckhead.

MAP 3: Phipps Plaza, 3500 Peachtree Rd., 404/814-9640, www.thetavernatphipps.com; Sun.-Mon. 11am-midnight, Tues.-Sat. 11am-1am; no cover

DANCE CLUBS

GOLD ROOM

The Gold Room fills the dance floor every weekend with butt-shaking electronic beats and a polished clientele that's dressed to impress (thanks, in part, to the stricter-than-usual dress code). The futuristic interior decor feels inspired by chic European megaclubs; it's about as close as Buckhead gets to the Balearic Beat. Love it or hate it, the Gold Room deserves a gold star for mixing the classy with the trashy.

MAP 3: 2416 Piedmont Rd. NE, 404/898-1707, www.goldroomnightclub.com; Thurs.-Sat. 10pm-3am; $5-25

The Rebirth of Buckhead Nightlife

The rise, fall, and return of Atlanta's most notorious nightlife district might be a parable about urban planning gone astray—or amusing proof that some watering holes refuse to run dry.

Throughout the 1990s, the dense concentration of bars in Buckhead Village made Peachtree Street look more like Bourbon Street. The rowdy club scene came under national scrutiny in 2000 when a linebacker for the Baltimore Ravens was charged in the late-night stabbings of two men outside the upscale Cobalt Lounge. Though charges against Ray Lewis were eventually dropped, the murders added credence to outraged neighborhood groups who had long complained about bars bringing crime and noise to Buckhead.

The Atlanta City Council responded by shutting down 24-hour nightclubs and rolling back last call to 2:30am. The change drew criticism from the nightlife industry once it was revealed that Underground Atlanta, a city-owned property, would be allowed to serve alcohol until 4am. Attempts to lure crowds downtown quickly faltered.

Meanwhile, neighborhood activists started covert efforts to convince Buckhead Village property owners to stop renting to bars. The campaign was successful, and several once-hot clubs shuttered. Real estate developer Ben Carter began a quiet crusade to buy buildings in the heart of the village's nightlife strip. In 2007, Carter unveiled an $850 million redevelopment plan for the area, which led to the bulldozing of four blocks of prime real estate to make way for an upscale shopping quarter.

Carter's project soon collapsed due to the Great Recession; the stalled construction site festered as a giant mud hole for years. The mixed-use complex now known as **Buckhead Atlanta** (www.buckhead-atl.com) finally opened the first of its luxury stores and restaurants in 2014.

But the razing of Buckhead Village didn't exactly ring the death knell for local nightlife. Favorites like **Tongue & Groove, Fadó Irish Pub,** and the **Havana Club** relocated and flourished in other pockets of the neighborhood. The wild spirit of the old village roared back to life a few blocks away. The **East Andrews Drive bar district** (www.andrewsdistrict.com) and adjacent **Irby Avenue** host a cluster of busy spots, ranging from cigar bars to dance clubs. Slightly north, the tipsy masses fill **the Ivy Buckhead** on weekends. The lesson here is clear: Atlanta bar-goers may be a lot of things, but quitters they are not.

NIGHTLIFE
BUCKHEAD

TONGUE & GROOVE

Once a main stop on the Buckhead Village bar crawl, Tongue & Groove relocated to Lindbergh in 2007. The dance club has continued to evolve and renovate its new digs over the years, adding futuristic lights, plush VIP areas, and stylish bar updates. Guest DJs play house and remixes of Top 40 pop songs. You might get lucky and spot a celebrity (drop-ins have ranged from Justin Bieber to Mick Jagger).

MAP 3: 565 Main St. NE, 404/261-2325, www.tandgonline.com; Mon. and Wed.-Sat. 9pm-2:30am; $10-20

Above: Limerick Junction Irish Pub. **Below:** Krog Bar.

GAY AND LESBIAN
JUNGLE ATLANTA

Jungle carries on the tradition of big-room beat factories of yesteryear. This warehouse space is the city's largest predominantly gay dance club. The crowd (sometimes 18-and-up) can range from glitter-soaked Gaga groupies to seen-it-all circuit veterans, with a smattering of women. Most Saturdays feature locally known house DJs with occasional celebrity appearances. The quarterly body-paint parties are a big draw, but not the sort of event you want to stumble into accidentally.

MAP 3: 2115 Faulkner Rd. NE, 404/844-8800, www.jungleclubatlanta.com; Wed. 10:30pm-3am, Fri.-Sat. 10pm-3am; $10-20

Virginia-Highland
Map 4

BARS
★ CLERMONT LOUNGE

"Dive" doesn't begin to describe this legendary Atlanta strip club, which has earned its status as an honest-to-goodness late-night landmark. Open since 1965 in the basement of the former Clermont Motor Hotel, the bar is much adored by a certain ironic, hipster clientele who brave the $10 cover on Saturday nights and fill the place to capacity, barely paying attention to the middle-aged ladies wiggling for tips on stage.

MAP 4: 789 Ponce de Leon Ave. NE, 404/874-4783, www.clermontlounge.net; Mon.-Sat. 1pm-3am; Mon.-Thurs. no cover, Fri. $3, Sat. $10

DARK HORSE TAVERN

A Virginia-Highland mainstay since 1990, this roomy multilevel man-cave seems enormous on an off night (which is rare) and impossibly tiny once the regulars start squeezing in. The crowd piles up three or four deep at the main U-shaped bar for a vibe that feels like a college meat market populated by young professionals from the neighborhood. Downstairs, the tavern's live-music room **10 High** features live-band karaoke, metal nights, and party bands.

MAP 4: 816 N. Highland Ave. NE, 404/873-3607, www.darkhorseatlanta.com; Mon.-Sat. 4pm-3am, Sun. 4pm-midnight; no cover

EL BAR

You could easily walk past El Bar and never realize you're within spitting distance of a raucous late-night bender. The tiny venue is improbably located on the backside of a Mexican restaurant. There's barely room inside to swing a bat at a piñata. The bar attracts an in-the-know crowd of boisterous hipsters and a rotation of up-and-coming DJs spinning everything from indie rock to old-school hip-hop. Probably not the best destination for big groups or the claustrophobic.

MAP 4: 939 Ponce de Leon Ave. NE, 678/613-3807; Wed.-Sat. 10pm-3am; no cover

HIGHLAND TAP

Although the Highland Tap bills itself as Virginia-Highland's only steak house, the subterranean pub keeps getting listed as one of the city's best martini bars. Opened in 1989, it does a reliable and subdued dinner business in the early evening; the mob of upwardly mobile drinkers arrives after midnight for a scene that's loud and flirty. Order one of the martinis (including a bizarre Sweet Teeni concoction, made with sweet tea) or the better-than-average burger.

MAP 4: 1026 N. Highland Ave. NE, 404/875-3673, www.nnnwcorp.com/highlandtap.html; Mon. 4pm-1am, Tues.-Thurs. 11am-1am, Fri.-Sat. 11am-2:30am, Sun. 12:30pm-midnight; no cover

LIMERICK JUNCTION IRISH PUB

Everything you'd want from an intimate Irish pub—the Guinness, the Gaelic folk songs, the shepherd's pie—you'll find at Limerick Junction, but the tiny taproom also defies easy stereotypes. The free wireless Internet gives it more of a laptop-friendly Starbucks vibe during happy hour, and the live music lends more to a casual neighborhood pub environment. A mature and often mixed crowd makes the cozy space feel full almost any night of the week.

MAP 4: 822 N. Highland Ave. NE, 404/874-7147, www.limerickjunction.com; Mon.-Wed. 5pm-1am, Thurs.-Sat. 5pm-2am, Sun. 5pm-midnight; no cover

THE LOCAL

The Local is about as no-frills as a nightspot can come: wood-paneled walls, sticky floors, and scruffy waiters. Yet the place has a devoted—borderline maniacal—following that just keeps coming back for more, no doubt hooked on the *Cheers*-like neighborhood vibe and familiarity of the crowd. Known equally for its cheap drinks and famous tater tots, the Local also boasts one of the best barbecue sandwiches in town.

MAP 4: 758 Ponce de Leon Ave. NE, 404/873-5002; Mon.-Sat. 5pm-3am, Sun. 5pm-midnight; no cover

RIGHTEOUS ROOM

Next door to the nostalgic Plaza Theatre, the intimate Righteous Room is an easy, no-frills place to grab a beer—as long as you're not part of a big group. The narrow bar fills up with regulars. Early on you'll find fewer drinkers and more nibblers (the Fatty Grilled Cheese is a particular delight). Later, this shotgun shack gets loud and full. The bar also features art shows by local painters and photographers.

MAP 4: 1051 Ponce de Leon Ave. NE, 404/874-0939, www.stayrighteous.com; Mon.-Thurs. 11:30am-2am, Fri.-Sat. 11:30am-3am, Sun. noon-midnight; no cover

DANCE CLUBS
MJQ CONCOURSE & THE DRUNKEN UNICORN

Located beneath a nondescript Poncey-Highland parking lot, this subversive discotheque lures in a racially diverse, hard-partying, and widely mixed crowd for its EDM, hip-hop, and reggae nights. It's also known to

Orpheus Brewing Company

- **Sweetwater Brewing Company** (195 Ottley Dr., 404/691-2537, www.sweetwaterbrew.com, Wed.-Fri. 5:30pm, Sat. 2:30pm, free) boasts a 49,000-barrel production of "aggressive, West Coast-style" beers. The award-winning brewery manufactures Sweetwater Blue, Sweetwater IPA, and an innovative line of seasonal microbrews.

- Open since 1993, **Red Brick Brewing** (2323 Defoor Hills Rd., 404/355-5558, www.redbrickbrewing.com, Wed.-Fri. 7pm, Sat. 4pm, $10) bills itself as the oldest operational craft brewery in Georgia. The company produces Red Brick Ale and Laughing Skull Amber Ale.

- Sample the famous Atalanta Tart Plum Saison at **Orpheus Brewing Company** (1440 Dutch Valley Pl., www.orpheusbrewing.com, Thurs.-Fri. 6pm-8pm, Sat. 2pm-4pm, $12). The artisanal brew house got lucky in the real estate department; it sits next to a much-anticipated Atlanta BeltLine trail expansion.

- Even the kids can enjoy tours of **Red Hare Brewery** (1998 Delk Industrial Blvd., Marietta, 678/401-0600, www.redharebrewing.com, Thurs.-Fri. 5:30pm-7:30pm, Sat. 2pm-4pm, $10), which serves samples of sweet, old-fashioned root beer to young guests and a half dozen original craft beers to adults.

- For a truly authentic taste of the South, try swigging a beer called Cooter Brown out of a Mason Jar at **Jekyll Brewing** (2855 Marconi Dr., Alpharetta, 844/453-5955, www.jekyllbrewing.com, Tues.-Fri. 5pm-9pm, Sat. 1pm-9pm, $12). The Alpharetta upstart was voted RateBeer's Best New Brewery in the South in 2013.

- **Wild Heaven Craft Beers** (135B Maple St., Decatur, 404/997-8589, www.wildheavencraftbeers.com, Fri. 5:30pm-8pm, Sat. 2pm-5pm, Sun. 2pm-4pm, $12) gets points for its cheeky sample glasses, including an Emergency Drinking Beer pint and its signature Wild Heaven "goblet."

- Farther afield, **Terrapin Brewery** (265 Newton Bridge Rd., Athens, 706/549-3377, www.terrapinbeer.com, Wed.-Thurs. 5:30pm-7:30pm, Fri.-Sat. 4:30pm-7:30pm, Sun. 1:30pm-3:30pm, $10) is worth the trip to Athens to experience its hopped-up Recreation Ale or brave the chocolate and peanut butter Liquid Bliss porter.

host bizarre theme parties (ninjas vs. cowboys, anyone?) and features a live-music space, **The Drunken Unicorn.** The only predictable thing about MJQ is its utter unpredictability. If you can't find the front door, you probably shouldn't be looking for it in the first place.

MAP 4: 736 Ponce de Leon Ave. NE, 404/870-0575, www.thedrunkenunicorn.net; Wed. 11pm-3am, Fri.-Sat. 11pm-3am; $5-20

LIVE MUSIC
BLIND WILLIE'S

Blind Willie's has the atmosphere of a sticky blues joint lifted off some Bourbon Street back alley. Cofounders Eric King and Roger Gregory asked local blues musicians to pitch in with the carpentry and painting when it opened in 1986, so you could say that the place has the blues in its bones. Expect an always-full house to hear touring and regional acts six nights a week. Blind Willie's serves a light menu.

MAP 4: 828 N. Highland Ave. NE, 404/873-2583, www.blindwilliesblues.com; Mon.-Sat. 7pm-late; Mon.-Thurs. $3-8, Fri. and Sat. $12

Little Five Points and East Atlanta
Map 5

BARS
THE ARGOSY

Named for a merchant ship, this gigantic East Atlanta pub swims in dark-wood everything. Equally massive is the beer menu—32 seasonal brews on tap that change weekly, plus several pages of bottles from microbrews. The energetic atmosphere and tasty gastropub fare quickly established the Argosy as a go-to neighborhood hangout, the ideal spot for killing a pint or six while observing hipster mating rituals.

MAP 5: 470 Flat Shoals Ave. SE, 404/577-0407, http://argosy-east.com; Mon.-Fri. 5pm-2:30am, Sat. noon-2:30am, Sun. 12:30pm-midnight; no cover

★ MANUEL'S TAVERN

If you're looking for a passionate debate about the state of Georgia politics, pull up a stool at Manuel's Tavern. It has long been a crossroads for politicos and journalists, with lots of movers and shakers in the mix. The joint dates back to 1956 and still has the feel of a genuine greasy spoon. Some employees have worked there for more than 30 years. Manuel's has a clientele that transcends race, class, and generation.

MAP 5: 602 N. Highland Ave. NE, 404/525-3447, www.manuelstavern.com; Mon. 11am-midnight, Tues.-Fri. 11am-1am, Sat. 9:30am-1am, Sun. 9.30am-midnight; no cover

BREWPUBS
★ WRECKING BAR BREWPUB

Owners Bob and Kristine Sandage unveiled this much-anticipated Little Five Points taproom in the basement of a renovated Victorian mansion in 2011. Wrecking Bar's unique pub grub and whiskey list are worth the drive, but the craft beers are the real draw. The cavernous space fills to capacity even on random weeknights, the thick granite walls echoing like a medieval fortress. If Beowulf were craving a stout microbrew, this would be his cave of choice.

MAP 5: 292 Moreland Ave. NE, 404/221-2600, http://wreckingbarbrewpub.com; Mon.-Thurs. 4pm-11pm, Fri.-Sat. noon-midnight, Sun. 11am-10pm; no cover

GAY AND LESBIAN
MARY'S

Compared to Midtown's meat-market bars, the hipster, alternative ambience of Mary's can feel like a completely different planet. Its wacky karaoke nights, offbeat theme parties, and smarter-than-you DJs bring in East Atlanta eccentrics and misfit scene queens. The closet-sized kitsch wonderland can fill to the point of aggravation. Escape the madness by venturing to the upstairs balcony, a prime spot for cruising the crowd. Various publications have dubbed it the best gay bar in Atlanta.

MAP 5: 1287 Glenwood Ave. SE, 404/624-4411, www.marysatlanta.com; Mon.-Sat. 5pm-3am; up to $2

MY SISTER'S ROOM

Atlanta has a spotty track record for keeping lesbian establishments afloat, but My Sister's Room has proven to be the exception to the rule. This nimble nightlife survivor has a long, colorful history dating back to 1996. Weekend nights find the intimate space packed with butch gals and lipstick ladies bouncing to Top 40 house and EDM. There are also karaoke nights, comedy sets, and drag king shows.

MAP 5: 1271 Glenwood Ave. SE, 678/705-4585, www.mysistersroom.com; Tues. varies, Wed. 8pm-2am, Thurs. 9pm-3am, Fri. 9pm-4am, Sat. 8pm-3am, Sun. 7pm-midnight; free-$10

LIVE MUSIC
THE EARL

This East Atlanta staple is nothing if not reliable: reliably grungy, reliably loud, and reliably crowded. One of the city's best-known spots for the local indie rock scene, the Earl brings in a hard-partying coolerthan-cool crowd that likes to slam back PBRs and scream to be heard, even if a band happens to be playing on stage. A roomy lounge up front serves a menu better than bar food, from jerk chicken to a portobello mushroom burger.

MAP 5: 488 Flat Shoals Ave. SE, 404/522-3950, www.badearl.com; Mon.-Sat. 11:30am-2:30am, Sun. 11:30am-midnight; up to $20

529

It's a tiny venue even by East Atlanta standards, as smoky as an East Berlin brothel and with a vibe that's distinctly insiders-only. However, 529 is one of the best places in town to catch off-the-radar indie acts, thanks to its weekly calendar, always chock-full of eclectic performances. Many shows are cheap—or even free. Though the space can be ridiculously loud during some live sets, you can always escape to the large patio.

MAP 5: 529 Flat Shoals Ave. SE, 404/228-6769, www.529atlanta.com; Mon.-Sat. 7pm-3am; $5-10

THE MASQUERADE

Depending on the night, a trip to the Masquerade can be either heaven or hell—literally. The live-music space, dubbed Heaven, features indie rock, goth, and punk acts in a hall that can accommodate 1,000 fans. Downstairs, the dance club Hell is reserved for DJs spinning everything from electro to old-school hip-hop, along with performances by smaller acts. In between, there's Purgatory, a pub with pool tables. Some events at the Masquerade are 18 and up.

MAP 5: 695 North Ave. NE, 404/577-8178, www.masqueradeatlanta.com; 7pm-2am; $8-30

STAR COMMUNITY BAR

Depending on the night, it can be a funky Little Five Points roost for rockabilly or divey dance floor ideal for screaming along to 1980s favorites. Star Community Bar also hosts a full lineup of singer-songwriters, tribute bands, comedy shows and open-mic nights. Its zealous regulars keep coming back for the cheap PBRs, while newcomers come through to glimpse the divinely tacky shrine to Elvis Presley, a Little Five Points landmark.

MAP 5: 437 Moreland Ave. NE, 404/681-9018, www.starbar.net; Mon.-Tues. 8pm-3am, Wed.-Sat. 5pm-3am; up to $5

LOUNGES
KROG BAR

Kevin Rathbun launched his eponymous restaurant and its tiny sibling, Krog Bar, in the Old Fourth Ward long before the buzz began about the neighborhood's renaissance. The dimly lit wine bar channels the ambience of a seductive Spanish bistro with a dizzying wine list and tapas menu. Krog Bar is best experienced late in the evening when a different sort of buzz sets in and passion ensues at a corner table. No wonder the neighbors call it "snog bar."

MAP 5: 112 Krog St. NE #27, 404/524-1618, http://krogbar.com; Mon.-Sat. 4:30pm-midnight; no cover

Decatur

Map 6

LIVE MUSIC
★ EDDIE'S ATTIC

Fans waxing poetic about Eddie's Attic describe the welcoming upstairs club in spiritual terms, with talk of musical "pilgrimages" to see this "shrine" to acoustic legends. The humble space itself defies such grandiose language, but you can't argue with its track record. John Mayer, Sugarland, the Indigo Girls, Shawn Mullins, and other acts can thank Eddie's for early exposure. The Music Room hosts up to 185 fans in a smoke-free environment, and it's often filled to capacity.

MAP 6: 515-B N. McDonough St., Decatur, 404/377-4976, www.eddiesattic.com; Mon.-Fri. 5pm-1am, Sat.-Sun. 6pm-1am; $5-25

Greater Atlanta

Map 7

BREWPUBS
5 SEASONS BREWING

A Sandy Springs staple since 2001, 5 Seasons Brewing serves authentic handcrafted beers in a laid-back, gracious environment. Located in an upscale strip mall, this sprawling brewpub usually features seven or eight creative drafts brewed in-house, along with a menu that's organic and locally grown when possible. Its suburban locale leads to a yuppie-ish crowd of parents and young professionals. There's a similar West Midtown location (1000 Marietta St., 404/875-3232) that has a more urban feel—and a killer patio.

MAP 7: 5600 Roswell Rd., Sandy Springs, 404/255-5911, www.5seasonsbrewing.com; Mon.-Thurs. 11am-10pm , Fri.-Sat. 11am-11pm, Sun. noon-10pm; no cover

Arts and Culture

When it comes to the arts, Atlanta sometimes shows symptoms of an inferiority complex. The city seems to be figuratively always looking over its shoulder, nervous that the most promising local talent and arts leaders are planning escapes to towns more hospitable to cultural careers, or eyeing with envy the creative vitality of places like New York or Austin. Such fears stem from many mitigating circumstances, including the reality that some of the city's most successful artists and authors *have* fled Atlanta in the last two decades, coupled with a very Southern insecurity of being dismissed as a cultural backwater.

The irony is that the city has a bounty of cultural attractions to be proud of, with a thriving theater scene, scores of galleries, exceptional concert halls, and a wealth of performance groups dedicated to everything from opera to improv. Visitors here will find museums filled with classic works and contemporary masterpieces, jaw-dropping natural history exhibitions, one-of-a-kind collections of artifacts, and cultivated displays of local color. The literary scene has gained momentum in recent years, as seen in the rising prestige of the Decatur Book Festival, the popularity of many offbeat reading events, and big-name author appearances. The city's many galleries serve an assortment of tastes, from the bleeding edge to ethnic and outsider art. The Woodruff Arts Center, which includes the Alliance Theatre, the Atlanta Symphony, and the High Museum of Art, remains a pervasive force in the city's cultural life. It's also the largest arts center in the Southeast.

Atlanta's love of the arts is celebrated most obviously through its countless festivals, including the much-hyped Atlanta Dogwood Festival in April,

---

Previous: Center for Puppetry Arts; Atlantic Station's Millennium Gate.

Highlights

★ **Best Place to Pamper Your Inner Child:** The **Center for Puppetry Arts** is a performance space for kids' shows and also features a museum of puppet history (page 117).

★ **Best Small Theater:** With a reputation for excellence, **Actor's Express** has been producing daring stagecraft for decades (page 119).

★ **Best Regional Theater:** The **Alliance Theatre** showcases recent Broadway hits, crowd-pleasing classics, and world premieres (page 121).

★ **Best Ancient Artwork:** The **Michael C. Carlos Museum of Emory University** features one of the most impressive collections of Egyptian funerary artifacts in the nation (page 125).

★ **Best Music Venue:** The intimate Little Five Points landmark **Variety Playhouse** lives up to its name, featuring a killer lineup of indie rock, folk, pop, and alternative acts (page 125).

★ **Best Comedy Troupe:** Even after 20 years of improv acrobatics and an unexpected venue change, **Dad's Garage Theatre** is as sophomoric and hilarious as ever (page 125).

★ **Best Trip Down Memory Lane:** You don't have to be an aviation buff to get swept away by the vintage aircraft and nostalgic airline memorabilia on display at the **Delta Flight Museum** (page 130).

the ongoing calendar of the National Black Arts Festival, and a revitalized Music Midtown Festival at the end of summer. The Atlanta Film Festival has been a regional hit since it began in 1976, while the citywide Atlanta Celebrates Photography has grown into a major draw each autumn.

Downtown

Map 1

CONCERT VENUES
PHILIPS ARENA
Is it a sports complex that moonlights as a concert venue or a rock arena that hosts NBA games? Opened in 1999 as a snazzy new home for the Atlanta Hawks, Philips Arena was ranked as the fourth busiest arena in the United States in 2014. Over the years, ticket sales have been stronger for concerts than sports events—a trend the Atlanta Hawks would love to reverse. Philips Arena is the place to go to experience blockbuster bands on tour.

MAP 1: 1 Philips Dr., 404/878-3000, www.philipsarena.com; MARTA: Dome/World Congress Center; ticket prices vary

TABERNACLE
This historic Downtown concert hall was an active Baptist church from 1910 until the 1980s. It was converted into a House of Blues club for the 1996 Olympics. These days it qualifies as one of the city's favorite midsize music venues, accommodating 2,600 fans. Few flourishes from the church era remain other than the sheer size of the sanctuary and the striking chandelier. Most interior walls are decorated with funky folk-art designs left over from the House of Blues days.

MAP 1: 152 Luckie St. NW, 404/659-9022, www.tabernacleatl.com; ticket prices vary

GALLERIES
CLARK ATLANTA UNIVERSITY ART GALLERIES
Located on the second floor of Trevor Arnett Hall on the Clark Atlanta University campus, these galleries boast an extensive and noteworthy collection of more than 600 works by African American artists. Items on display change seasonally. The galleries are most famous for housing Hale Woodruff's *Art of the Negro* murals. Other artists represented include Curtis Patterson, Radcliffe Bailey, and Freddie Styles.

MAP 1: 223 James P Brawley Dr., 404/880-6102, www.cau.edu; by appointment only; free

EYEDRUM ART AND MUSIC GALLERY
Eyedrum held sway as Atlanta's de facto destination for underground arts for years, until losing the lease on its Old Fourth Ward warehouse space in 2011. The nonprofit arts collective roared back to life in 2014. Now located across from the Martin Luther King Jr. Federal Building, Eyedrum brings avant-garde art installations, experimental music jams, life-drawing classes, film screenings, and much more to a pocket of Downtown that's definitely still in transition.

MAP 1: 88 Forsyth St. SW, www.eyedrum.org; cost varies

MARCIA WOOD GALLERY

In 2003, longtime Atlanta art guru Marcia Wood decamped from South Buckhead and relocated her popular contemporary gallery to Castleberry Hill, which helped to kick-start an obvious renaissance in a previously forgotten pocket of Downtown. Wood's relentlessly hip space remains one of the city's most respected galleries and a cornerstone of the monthly Castleberry Hill Art Stroll. Marcia Wood Gallery specializes in contemporary painting and sculpture, with a taste for provocateurs.

MAP 1: 263 Walker St. SW, 404/827-0030, www.marciawoodgallery.com; Tues.-Sat. noon-5pm

MUSEUMS

THE APEX MUSEUM

A Downtown fixture since 1978, the African American Panoramic Experience Museum aims to preserve the culture, traditions, and history of people of African descent. Worth noting is its collection of African art and a detailed replica of the Yates & Milton Drug Store, one of Atlanta's earliest black-owned businesses. The small space is crammed full of artifacts, photographs, and colorful exhibitions—but could use a more discerning curatorial eye to make the "experience" feel less jumbled.

MAP 1: 135 Auburn Ave. NE, 404/523-2739, www.apexmuseum.org; Tues.-Sat. 10am-5pm; $4 adult, $3 child and senior

IMAGINE IT! THE CHILDREN'S MUSEUM OF ATLANTA

The Downtown attraction welcomes visitors into a colorful fantasy land of interactive educational exhibits ideal for kids ages eight and under. The bright, family-friendly space is filled with clever diversions for the pre-K set. It's divided into a variety of "learning zones," designed to inspire creative thinking while also teaching concepts such as nutrition, environmental awareness, and the importance of teamwork. All children must be accompanied by an adult; no adults are admitted without kids.

MAP 1: 275 Centennial Olympic Park Dr. NW, 404/659-5437, www. childrensmuseumatlanta.org; Mon.-Tues. 10am-4pm, Thurs.-Fri. 10am-4pm, Sat.-Sun. 10am-5pm; $12.75, free under 2

SPELMAN COLLEGE MUSEUM OF FINE ART

This hidden gem on the Spelman College campus bills itself as the only museum in the nation emphasizing art by and about women of the African diaspora. Works on display range from ceramics and mixed-media folk art to bronze sculpture and paintings. Of note are the rare and important works by Hale Woodruff, including paintings that were previously presumed lost and a series of linocuts.

MAP 1: 350 Spelman Ln., 404/270-5607, museum.spelman.edu; hours vary, closed in summer; $3 suggested donation

WREN'S NEST HOUSE MUSEUM

Atlanta author Joel Chandler Harris became a household name in the late 1800s thanks to his clever retelling of African American folktales featuring

Clockwise from top left: Tabernacle; the Millennium Gate; The Goat Farm Arts Center.

the characters Br'er Rabbit and Uncle Remus. Harris's home has been a museum and memorial to the writer since 1913. The farmhouse stands preserved as the Harris family left it. Storytellers appear Saturdays at 1pm to bring new life to Harris's Uncle Remus tales; the Wren's Nest also hosts literary events.

MAP 1: 1050 Ralph David Abernathy Blvd. SW, 404/753-7735, www.wrensnest.org; Tues.-Sat. 10am-2:30pm; $9 adult, $6 child, $8 seniors and students

THEATER
AGATHA'S: A TASTE OF MYSTERY
Agatha's calls itself a "comedy murder mystery dinner theater," but it doesn't take a detective to gather that the emphasis is on cornball comedy. Heavy on audience participation, the "plot" of each original whodunit unfolds in various spots around the dining room. Guests are shamelessly drafted into the action. The show comes with a five-course meal buffet and a glass of wine. The experience can be killer fun for big groups but murder on a first date.

MAP 1: 161 Peachtree Center Ave. NE, 404/480-5244, www.agathas.com; Mon.-Thurs. 7:30pm-10pm, Fri. 8pm-10:30pm, Sat. 7:30pm-10pm, Sun. 6pm-8:30pm; Sun. and Tues.-Fri. $65, Sat. $70

THEATRICAL OUTFIT
Theatrical Outfit has somehow found success in the hit-or-miss in Downtown historic Fairlie-Poplar business district, not exactly a friendly landscape for any cultural group. This lively and professional theater company steadfastly produces compelling stagecraft. Its current home, the lovely 200-seat Balzer Theater at Herren's, was previously the site of one of Downtown's most legendary restaurants. Theatrical Outfit stages classic and modern works, with a taste for spiritual themes and stories tied to the South.

MAP 1: 84 Luckie St. NW, 678/528-1500, www.theatricaloutfit.org; $15-45

Midtown   Map 2

CINEMAS
MIDTOWN ART CINEMA
Way back in 2003, Landmark Theatres revamped a ragged eight-screen multiplex into one of the city's most interesting movie houses. Midtown Art Cinema screens an unusual blend of big studio releases, foreign films, and off-the-radar art-house flicks. It hosts Atlanta Film Festival and Out on Film, the gay and lesbian film festival. The lobby and concession area serves pastries, espresso drinks, and beer. The theater is overdue for another round of upgrades, especially to the auditoriums.

MAP 2: 931 Monroe Dr. NE, 678/495-1424, www.landmarktheatres.com; $8-11

GALLERIES

THE ATLANTA CONTEMPORARY ART CENTER

Founded in 1973 as a cooperative gallery by a faction of photographers, the Contemporary has evolved into a cornerstone of the local cutting-edge arts scene. The multidisciplinary nonprofit features an expansive exhibition space and a dozen artist studios in an eye-catching 35,000-square-foot warehouse complex. Beyond its series lectures, film screenings, and workshops, the annual end-of-summer Art Party is a spirited bacchanal set among interactive installations. Note that opening times only apply during active exhibition periods.

MAP 2: 535 Means St. NW, 404/688-1970, www.thecontemporary.org; Tues.-Wed. and Fri.-Sat. 11am-5pm, Thurs. 11am-8pm; $5 adult, $3 child and senior

THE GOAT FARM ARTS CENTER

The Goat Farm calls itself a "creative industrial complex," efficient shorthand that doesn't quite cover this category-defying arts incubator. The 12-acre West Midtown site, previously a cotton gin factory from the early 1900s, brings a rustic, hipster-meets-farmer ethos to a hodgepodge of gallery spaces, artist studios and residences, performance venues, and an organic farm with real, live goats. The dilapidated brick buildings provide a mesmerizing backdrop for experimental art shows and recitals.

MAP 2: 1200 Foster St. NW, no phone, www.facebook.com/TheGoatFarmArtsCenter; hours vary

KAI LIN ART

An air of youthful exuberance characterizes many of the shows at Kai Lin Art, a fun and fearless West Midtown art oasis. The gallery established its credentials with locations in Midtown and Buckhead before hitting its stride in the current, edgier west-side digs. Owner Yu-Kai Lin fills the gallery's frantic exhibition calendar (new shows every eight weeks) with unpredictable works by emerging artists and returning favorites. Expect whimsy and bold statements.

MAP 2: 999 Brady Ave. NW, 404/408-4248, www.kailinart.com; Wed.-Fri. noon-6pm, Sat. noon-5pm

MUSEUMS

★ CENTER FOR PUPPETRY ARTS

The largest American organization dedicated to puppetry theater doubles as performance space and museum. The permanent collection boasts a delightful menagerie of familiar foam faces, from well-known Muppets to prototypes for Disney's Broadway hit *The Lion King*. There's plenty to keep the ankle-biters busy, such as puppet-building workshops and family-friendly shows. Adults should check out the provocative Xperimental Puppetry Theater performances—definitely not for the squeamish. A 2015 expansion houses the museum's extensive Jim Henson Collection.

MAP 2: 1404 Spring St. NW, 404/873-3391, www.puppet.org; Tues.-Fri. 9am-3pm, Sat. 9am-5pm, Sun. noon-5pm; $8 adult, $6 child, $7 senior

Arts All Over

What's the center of gravity for Atlanta's art scene? Opinions are mixed, but one answer may be: There is no gravity. Art galleries are sprinkled like constellations in scattered neighborhoods. The movement of a star player into a previously sleepy (read: gentrifying) area can bring other upstarts into orbit—or predicate a supernova. The most obvious success story used to be Castleberry Hill, though recent years have brought big movement in West Midtown and renewed sparks in the **Miami Circle Art and Design District.**

Castleberry Hill was once a seedy intersection of urban decay and crime in the backwater of the Georgia Dome. It became a federally recognized historical district in 1985. A new, well-heeled generation of residents soon arrived, driving property values up and leading to a renovation boom. A handful of prominent art-gallery owners followed the migration, with pioneers like Marcia Wood Gallery leading the charge. In 2014, USA Today listed Castleberry Hill as one of the 10 best city arts districts in the nation. Sample the scene at the free **Castleberry Hill Art Stroll** (www.castleberryhillartstroll. com), held 7pm-10pm on the second Friday of each month, which typically hits more than a dozen galleries, restaurants, and shops. Street parking is available around the neighborhood or in the lot at the corner of Trinity and Spring Streets.

The fledgling **Westside Arts District** has had less luck supporting regular gallery walks, even as new businesses have flourished in West Midtown. The gallery scene continues to coalesce, loosely, around the **Westside Cultural Arts Center** (760 10th St., 678/218-3740, www. westsideartscenter.com), stretching north to 14th Street and south to the Atlanta Contemporary Art Center.

THE MILLENNIUM GATE

It's no Arc de Triomphe, but the Millennium Gate does add gravitas to an otherwise anonymous intersection in Atlantic Station. Designed in the style of classical Roman triumphal arches, the seven-story stucco-and-limestone structure houses a 12,000-square-foot history museum with galleries focusing on Georgia history. Meticulously appointed period rooms recreate the homes of famous Georgians from each of the past three centuries. It has become a popular spot for wedding photos.

MAP 2: 395 17th St. NW, 404/881-0900, www.thegateatlanta.com; Mon.-Fri. 10am-5pm; $12 adult, $10 senior

MUSEUM OF DESIGN ATLANTA

The Southeast's only museum devoted exclusively to design is still the "new" kid on the block in Midtown's nexus of cultural attractions. MODA moved into its current eye-catching, 6,500 square-foot gallery space in 2011. Though perhaps overshadowed by the indomitable High Museum nearby, MODA hosts chic and accessible exhibitions on everything from interior design and fashion to 3D printing. Guided tours are offered each Thursday at 6:30pm (free with the price of admission).

MAP 2: 1315 Peachtree St. NE, 404/979-6455, www.museumofdesign.org; Tues.-Wed. and Sun. noon-6pm, Thurs. noon-8pm, Sat. 10am-6pm; $10 adult, $5 student, $8 senior

119

RHODES HALL

Authentic reminders of local history are almost nonexistent in built-yesterday Atlanta, which makes stately Rhodes Hall all the more remarkable. The "Rhineland castle on Peachtree" was built in 1904 by furniture magnate Amos Rhodes and appointed with high-Victorian flourishes. Visitors today can marvel at the luminous stained-glass windows depicting the rise and fall of the Confederacy and learn about the evolution of Peachtree Street. The $7 ticket gives visitors a tour of all four floors.

MAP 2: 1516 Peachtree St. NE, 404/885-7800, www.georgiatrust.org; Tues. 11am-3pm, Sat. 10am-2pm, tours hourly; $7 four floors, $5 first floor only

WILLIAM BREMAN JEWISH HERITAGE MUSEUM

From the notorious Leo Frank murder trial to the bombing of the Atlanta synagogue in 1958, the local Jewish community has often found itself entangled in issues of justice and equality—even in "the city too busy to hate." This museum takes visitors on a rich and comprehensive tour of Atlanta's colorful Jewish history. The Breman hosts permanent exhibitions exploring the roots of the city's Jewish population and its reaction to the Holocaust.

MAP 2: 1440 Spring St. NW, 678/222-3700, www.thebreman.org; Sun.-Thurs. 10am-5pm, Fri. 10am-4pm; $12 adult, $4 child, $8 senior

PERFORMING ARTS
ATLANTA SYMPHONY ORCHESTRA

Atlantans have a love-hate relationship—mostly hate—with the acoustically challenged **Symphony Hall,** but their derision doesn't extend to its resident arts company, the Atlanta Symphony Orchestra. Under the musical direction of Robert Spano and Donald Runnicles since 2004, the Grammy-winning orchestra has bolstered its international credentials and cultivated a reputation for commissioning works by living composers. During warmer months, the orchestra performs at Verizon Wireless Amphitheatre in Alpharetta and Chastain Park in Buckhead.

MAP 2: 1280 Peachtree St. NE, 404/733-4900, www.atlantasymphony.org; ticket prices vary

THEATER
★ ACTOR'S EXPRESS

Since 1988, Actor's Express has put forth some of the most provocative, eyebrow-raising theater in town. Famous for its penchant for male nudity on stage and for championing challenging works by local playwrights, the Express knows how to brew up a season that's topical and tantalizing. The 200-seat black-box theater is located in the charming King Plow Arts Center, a 19th-century factory whose renovation helped presuppose West Midtown's current building boom.

MAP 2: 887 W. Marietta St. NW, Ste. J-107, 404/875-1606, www.actors-express.com; $25-35

Above: Rhodes Hall. **Below:** Museum of Design Atlanta.

Discount Tickets

Looking to catch a show in Atlanta? **AtlanTIX** is a smart option for finding same-day half-price tickets to theater, dance, and musical performances. Though the selection varies, the service lists a surplus of shows daily and almost never disappoints. AtlanTIX operates a ticket booth at **Underground Atlanta** (at the corner of Upper Alabama St. and Pryor St.) open Tuesday-Saturday 11am-6pm and Sunday noon-4pm. Go early for the best selection.

Many of the discount tickets available at the AtlanTIX booths can be purchased online at **Atlanta Performs** (www.atlantaperforms.com), a handy resource for finding happenings around town. The official site of the 400-member Atlanta Coalition of Performing Arts, Atlanta Performs serves up a comprehensive list of theatrical productions throughout the metro area, with an easy-to-use search engine.

★ ALLIANCE THEATRE

On the crowded stage of Atlanta theater, the Alliance plays the role of the admired prima donna who refuses to give up the spotlight. The theater has been a standard-bearer of stagecraft in the Southeast for more than four decades, launching three Tony Award winners to Broadway: *The Color Purple, Aida,* and *The Last Night of Ballyhoo.* The 770-seat main auditorium tends to show crowd-pleasers and classics, while more cutting-edge fare occupies the cozy Hertz Stage.

MAP 2: 1280 Peachtree St. NE, 404/733-4650, www.alliancetheatre.org; $40-85

NEW AMERICAN SHAKESPEARE TAVERN

The Atlanta Shakespeare Company holds an unusual pedigree: It's the first professional troupe in the nation to have performed Shakespeare's entire 39-play canon. The company's host theater has the look and feel of a classic British pub, which gives the crowd the chance to kick back a few Irish ales and munch on traditional English fare before each show. Performances are mounted purist style in classic Elizabethan costumes. Arrive early to get a good seat.

MAP 2: 499 Peachtree St. NE, 404/874-5299, www.shakespearetavern.com; Thurs.-Sat. 7:30pm, Sun. 6:30pm; $15-45

Buckhead

Map 3

GALLERIES
THE BILL LOWE GALLERY

Local arts legend Bill Lowe can't be still for long. In 2014, he celebrated his gallery's 25th anniversary with a dramatic move into the burgeoning Miami Circle Arts and Design District. The tasteful and understated new 10,000-square-foot space feels a tad less flashy and more furtive than previous iterations, yet no less refined. The gallery specializes in powerful,

Gay Atlanta

Atlanta has long been recognized as the gay capital of the Southeast, a tolerant oasis that draws queer residents and tourists from all over the country. The city's enormous annual **Atlanta Pride Festival** (www.atlantapride.org) began in 1971 and today brings in hundreds of thousands of revelers to the city, with a deluge of events happening around Piedmont Park each autumn. Atlanta also hosts one of the world's largest black gay pride festivals, **Atlanta Black Gay Pride** (www.inthelifeatl.com), each year over Labor Day weekend. **Out on Film** (www.outonfilm.org), the gay film festival, takes place each spring, while the **Atlanta Queer Literary Festival** (http://atlqueerlitfest.blogspot.com) presents sporadic programming throughout the year.

For decades, Atlanta's most visible gay neighborhood was Midtown—especially around the intersection of Piedmont Avenue and 10th Street—with its concentration of bars and gay-friendly shops and restaurants. While one of the city's much-loved gay landmarks, Outwrite Bookstore, has since closed, local favorites **Blake's on the Park** (www.blakesonthepark.com) and **G's Midtown** (219 10th St., 404/872-8012, www.gilbertscafe.com) remain as packed as ever. Recent years have found Midtown becoming more mixed and gay Atlantans less confined to any one part of town, with queer bars and businesses popping up from Decatur to Marietta.

Lesbians in Atlanta have an enviable resource in Little Five Points with **Charis Books and More** (www.charisbooksandmore.com), a fixture that's served the feminist community for three decades. Charis Circle, its programming arm, hosts a vibrant assortment of events and workshops. The city has had less luck keeping a girls-only nightlife scene afloat over the years. **My Sister's Room** (www.mysistersroom.com) in East Atlanta deserves major props for outlasting the odds.

For gay men, the bar and club scene in Atlanta offers several options on any given night of the week. **Mary's** (www.marysatlanta.com) in East Atlanta has been cited as one of the best gay bars in the country, drawing an eclectic clique of hipsters and bears. **Burkhart's Pub** (1492 Piedmont Ave., 404/872-4403, www.burkharts.com, Mon.-Fri. 4pm-3am, Sat. 2pm-3am, Sun. 2pm-midnight, no cover) is full of the blue-jeans-and-ball-cap crowd; it shares a parking lot with **Felix's on the Square** (1510 Piedmont Ave., 404/249-7899, Mon.-Fri. 2pm-2:30am, Sat. noon-2:30am, Sun. 12:30pm-midnight, no cover) and **Oscar's Atlanta** (1510 Piedmont Ave., 404/815-8841, www.oscarsatlanta.com, Mon.-Sat. 2pm-3am, no cover). **Bulldogs Bar** (893 Peachtree St., 404/872-3025, Mon.-Sat. 4pm-3am, no cover) remains a longtime favorite for African American men. The leather scene congregates at the **Atlanta Eagle** (306 Ponce de Leon Ave., 404/873-2453, www.atlantaeagle.com, Mon.-Fri. 7pm-3am, Sat. 5pm-3am, cover varies, up to $5), but it's become far more mixed as a younger crowd has cycled in.

The biggest and most popular gay dance club, **Jungle Atlanta** (www.jungleclubatlanta.com) is the go-to spot for touring DJs and theme nights. **The Heretic** (2069 Cheshire Bridge Rd., 404/325-3061, www.hereticatlanta.com, Mon.-Sat. 9am-3am, cover varies, up to $10), an Atlanta standard for more than two decades, still knows how to fill a dance floor on weekends.

Gay travelers should check out the **Atlanta Gay and Lesbian Travel Guide** (www.gay-atlanta.com), a portal operated by the Atlanta Convention and Visitors Bureau that features a wealth of listings for lodging, events, and community organizations. The city's main gay publications, *The GA Voice* (www.thegavoice.com) and *David Atlanta* (www.davidatlanta.com), are also handy resources.

content-driven works. The monthly opening parties tend to be well attended and less stuffy than at certain other galleries.

MAP 3: 764 Miami Cir. NE, 404/352-8114, www.lowegallery.com; Tues. 10am-5:30pm, Sat. 11am-5:30pm

TULA ART CENTER

At the end of a sleepy industrial street in south Buckhead, the TULA Art Center holds a remarkable enclave of creative activity. The 50,000-square-foot former manufacturing plant houses 17 working artist studios producing everything from mixed-media canvas works to couture and jewelry. The Museum of Contemporary Art of Georgia relocated to TULA in 2008, adding new cultural cred to an already respected arts district. It's best enjoyed during an evening art opening or on a weekday afternoon.

MAP 3: 75 Bennett St. NW, 404/351-3551, www.tulaartstudios.com; prices vary

MUSEUMS
MUSEUM OF CONTEMPORARY ART OF GEORGIA

The Museum of Contemporary Art of Georgia has calmly grown into a significant cultural player. Conceived in 1989, the museum tripled its exhibition space in 2007 by moving into TULA Art Center, off the beaten path on a funky south Buckhead cul-de-sac. Today, MOCA GA hosts up to five exhibitions in galleries on two levels. Its permanent collection boasts 750 works by more than 200 Georgia artists.

MAP 3: 75 Bennett St. NW, 404/367-8700, www.mocaga.org; Tues.-Sat. 10am-5pm; $8 adult, $5 students and seniors, free under 6

THEATER
BUCKHEAD THEATRE

The former Roxy Theatre underwent an extensive $6 million renovation in 2010 and reopened with swanky new decor and a return to its original name. The venue began as a movie palace in the 1930s. Over the next eight decades it hosted everything from racy stage shows to boxing matches, though it was best known as a place to binge drink while listening to really loud music. These days the calendar features perfectly polite guitar-based bands.

MAP 3: 3110 Roswell Rd. NE, 404/843-2825, www.thebuckheadtheatre.com; ticket prices vary

Virginia-Highland

Map 4

CINEMAS
IMAX THEATRE AT FERNBANK MUSEUM OF NATURAL HISTORY

Atlanta has two IMAX theaters, and only one shows Hollywood blockbusters. Fernbank Museum reserves its five-story screen for educational films. The programming choices haven't kept the crowds away from Fernbank's weekly Martinis & IMAX, a festive Friday night cocktail party that serves

Movies Under the Stars

As if summers in Atlanta weren't packed enough with neighborhood festivals, concerts, and events every night of the week, city dwellers have also come to love outdoor movie screenings.

Atlantic Station: Movies in Central Park (http://atlanticstation.com) tends to be the festival with the most titles, at least inside city limits. Screenings start in mid-May (usually) and run weekly through August. The free series shows musicals, cartoons, and recent blockbusters on a super-sized portable screen—no doubt a sore spot for the Regal Atlantic Station 18 a block away.

Candler Park Movie Night (http://friendsofcandlerpark.org) goes for a much more nostalgic feel with its lineup of family-friendly favorites. Locals put down blankets for pre-show picnics in front of the park's pool house. The free series of five or six classics begins in April and returns on sporadic Saturdays through September.

The new city of Brookhaven (as of 2012) has had success with its summer film series, **Movies on the Town** (http://townbrookhaven.net), launched in 2013. The Thursday-night screenings take place at Town Brookhaven, a mixed-use retail and residential complex, from May through July. The only downside: No outside food or drinks are allowed.

After 14 years at the Starlight Six, **Drive-Invasion** (www.drive-invasion.com) moved its retro-flavored movie and music festival to Turner Field in 2014. The Labor Day weekend celebration of drive-in culture shows vintage B-movie creature-features on a 40-foot screen, with tailgating encouraged.

The always entertaining **Coca-Cola Film Festival** at the Fox Theatre (www.foxtheatre.org) also happens under the stars—albeit fake ones. (The historic movie palace's enormous ceiling is painted to mimic a romantic night sky, complete with twinkling stars.) A beloved Atlanta summer tradition, the series features a pre-show sing-along with the Mighty Mo pipe organ and vintage cartoons. The movies shown on the Fox's gigantic screen vary from summer blockbusters to classics. The festival kicks off in June or July. Doors open at 6:45pm. It's perfect for folks who prefer their summer movies in the comfort of air-conditioning.

drinks and hors d'oeuvres in the Great Hall before screenings of movies such as *Humpback Whales and Mysteries of the Unseen World*. The theater sometimes sells out, so buy tickets ahead of time.

MAP 4: 767 Clifton Rd. NE, 404/929-6400, www.fernbankmuseum.org; $13 adult, $12 student and senior, $11 child

PLAZA THEATRE

It may not have the amenities of modern stadium-seating arenas, but the Plaza Theatre serves as a cherished flashback to the golden age of small neighborhood cinemas. Atlanta's oldest movie house announces its presence on Ponce de Leon Avenue via a nostalgic neon marquee. The theater's two screens show everything from indie flicks to Hollywood fare and cult classics. Costumed performers do the "Time Warp" at midnight screenings of *The Rocky Horror Picture Show* every Friday.

MAP 4: 1029 Ponce de Leon Ave. NE, 404/873-1939, www.plazaatlanta.com; $8-10.50

MUSEUMS

FERNBANK SCIENCE CENTER

Not to be confused with Fernbank Museum of Natural History, this educational facility encompasses a museum, planetarium, observatory, and nature complex. Most of the programming is geared toward field trips for student groups (the center is owned by the DeKalb County School System), but its free exhibitions and astronomy events can prove fascinating for science lovers of any age. The biggest attraction for adults is the planetarium, one of the largest in the country.

MAP 4: 156 Heaton Park Dr., 678/874-7102, www.fernbank.edu; Mon.-Wed. noon-5pm, Thurs.-Fri. noon-9pm, Sat. 10am-5pm (observatory Thurs.-Fri. 9pm-10:30pm); free (planetarium shows $7 adult, $5 student and senior)

★ MICHAEL C. CARLOS MUSEUM OF EMORY UNIVERSITY

Several high-profile acquisitions and an elegant interior renovation from architect Michael Graves have helped bolster the Michael C. Carlos Museum's reputation nationally. It features a vast and dazzling display of Egyptian mummies and breathtaking relics, including the oldest Egyptian mummy in North America. The exhibitions run the gamut from ancient Greek and Roman ceramics to modern art. Perhaps because of its somewhat remote location on the Emory campus, the Carlos can be blissfully free of crowds.

MAP 4: 571 S. Kilgo Circle, 404/727-4282, www.carlos.emory.edu; Tues.-Fri. 10am-4pm, Sat. 10am-5pm, Sun. noon-5pm; $8 adult, $6 child, student, and senior, free under 5

Little Five Points and East Atlanta

Map 5

CONCERT VENUE
★ VARIETY PLAYHOUSE

This bare-bones music club maintains an eclectic and unpredictable lineup of acts: indie rock one night, bluegrass the next. The sloped space, a former movie theater, provides clear sight lines to the stage. The standing-room-only pit up front fills up early. More relaxed fans can see and hear just as well in the upper balcony. The staff is low-key and always friendly, serving microbrews and cocktails at reasonable prices. It's great for a casual night out.

MAP 5: 1099 Euclid Ave. NE, 404/524-7354, www.variety-playhouse.com; prices vary

THEATER
★ DAD'S GARAGE THEATRE

A fly-by-night improv troupe has evolved into one of the South's preeminent comedy houses—minus the house. In 2013, Dad's Garage took up temporary residence at 7 Stages Theatre when its longtime Inman Park location was demolished. Despite the venue change, Dad's hasn't lost the subversive, sophomoric energy that put its improv marathons on the map.

Drinking and audience participation are encouraged. The company plans to occupy a former church in the Old Fourth Ward in 2016.

MAP 5: 1105 Euclid Ave. NE, 404/523-3141, www.dadsgarage.com; Thurs.-Sat. 10:30pm; $4-23

HORIZON THEATRE COMPANY

Since 1983, cofounders Lisa and Jeff Adler have kept Atlanta audiences hooked on Horizon Theatre. The reliably crowded Little Five Points stage, located in a funky former elementary school, often hosts the Atlanta premieres of off-Broadway shows and debuts by lesser-known contemporary playwrights. Productions in the intimate 180-seat theater have a do-it-yourself charm, though the talent seen here is anything but unprofessional. Horizon hosts the annual New South Young Playwrights Festival.

MAP 5: 1083 Austin Ave. NE, 404/584-7450, www.horizontheatre.com; $20-50

Greater Atlanta   Map 7

CINEMAS
CINÉBISTRO

CinéBistro screens first-run films in an upscale, accommodating setting. The 21-and-up venue goes for an exclusive yet casual vibe: high-back leather rocking chairs; draft beer from local breweries; a gourmet-inspired menu and full bar. Plan to arrive at least 30 minutes before showtime. An hour will give you time to enjoy the food and atmosphere before the feature begins.

MAP 7: 1004 Town Blvd. SE, 404/333-0740, www.cobbcinebistro.com; $9-12

STARLIGHT SIX DRIVE-IN

During the 1950s, Georgia could brag about having almost 130 drive-in movie theaters. Atlanta's venerable Starlight Six Drive-In is one of only four in business today. Open since 1949, this local institution remains relevant and busy by showing current studio releases—usually double features—at the bargain price of $9 per adult ($1 for kids under 9).

MAP 7: 2000 Moreland Ave. SE, Atlanta, 404/627-5786, www.starlightdrivein.com; $9 adult, $1 child

CONCERT VENUES
AARON'S AMPHITHEATRE AT LAKEWOOD

This open-air arena—which will now and forever be referred to as "Lakewood Amphitheatre" by stubborn locals—offers 4,000 covered seats, 3,000 "starlight" seats, and room on the sloped lawn for an additional 12,000 fans. (Spring for the reserved seats. The lawn often turns into a mudslide.) The summer concert schedule is full of high-profile rock and country acts. Parking and traffic around the area can be a real nightmare; plan to arrive—and exit—early.

MAP 7: 2002 Lakewood Ave., Atlanta, 404/443-5000, www.aaronsamphitheatre.net; ticket prices vary

Clockwise from top left: Dad's Garage Theatre; Variety Playhouse; Michael C. Carlos Museum of Emory University.

Hooray for Y'allywood: Top Film and TV Sites

Sorry, peaches: Georgia's favorite cash crop may now be popcorn.

The state's film industry has exploded in recent years. Hollywood crews have set up shop from Atlanta to Savannah, lured South by the climate, scenery, and, most of all, irresistible tax credits. Film and television productions pumped more than $5 billion into the local economy in 2014, according to officials.

Major studios have built sound stages around the metro area to shoot anything from summer blockbusters (*Ant-Man*, later *Hunger Games* entries) to sitcoms (*Drop Dead Diva*) and game shows (*Family Feud*). The rise of so-called "Y'allywood" (a tongue-in-cheek nickname that's gained traction in local media) and record-breaking ratings of locally filmed shows have spawned side industries: wigs, fashion, and forgettable pop music from Bravo's *The Real Housewives of Atlanta*; a competitive field of would-be undead extras for AMC's *The Walking Dead* or the CW's *The Vampire Diaries*.

A cottage industry of tourism has also spread like kudzu. Visitors determined to bump into the cast of VH1's *Love & Hip-Hop: Atlanta* may not get their wish, exactly. Most shoots are closed, though they're easily spotted by the caravan of white film trucks and star trailers.

Even if you don't stumble across a production in progress, you can still get a peek at the locations of many favorites. The **Georgia Film, Music and Digital Entertainment Office** (800/847-4842, http://cometourgeorgia.com/filmtv) keeps a comprehensive and up-to-date list of film and TV productions online. The fan-oriented site gives handy tips for scoping out sites from *The Hunger Games: Catching Fire*, *Anchorman 2*, several Tyler Perry productions, and many more. Best of all, it's free.

Atlanta Movie Tours (327 Nelson St., 855/255-3456, http://atlantamovietours.com, $65) offers the sweetest deal in town for a hands-on expedition of film sites. Launched by cinephiles Patti Davis and Carrie Sagel Burns in 2012, the guided tours hit a

CHASTAIN PARK AMPHITHEATER

Many seats here have built-in tables or room for picnic baskets, so concert-goers usually come with snacks and beverages, but loud conversations and clinking wineglasses can sometimes drown out the performance. The summer Classic Chastain series features a combination of pop and country acts, younger talents, and concerts by the Atlanta Symphony Orchestra. The best parking lots are reserved for season ticket holders, leaving other visitors to search for spots in the residential streets surrounding the venue.

MAP 7: 4469 Stella Dr., Atlanta, 404/233-2227, www.classicchastain.com; ticket prices vary

COBB ENERGY PERFORMING ARTS CENTRE

Atlanta's affluent northern suburbanites got the concert hall they'd long howled for with the arrival of the $145 million Cobb Energy Performing Arts Centre in 2007. The resplendent 2,750-seat venue is home to two of the city's most respected cultural institutions, the Atlanta Ballet and the

You might walk the tracks to Terminus on *The Walking Dead* Atlanta Movie Tour.

constantly updated list of locations. Its pair of Big Zombie tours hit spooky sites from *The Walking Dead* and *Zombieland*; some of the guides have even played walkers on the show. Other options include a more generalized Atlanta Film Sites tour and a *Gone With the Wind* tour.

Efforts to brand Atlanta as "Hollywood of the South" hit a slight snag: The slogan is already trademarked by nearby Covington, where countless movies and shows have been filmed. **Mystic Falls Tours** (2101 Clark St., 404/549-1489, Covington, www.mysticfallstours.com, $55) takes guests to the Salvatore brothers' haunted hangouts from *The Vampire Diaries* and locations from its supernatural spin-off, *The Originals*. For a cheaper outing, visit the **Covington/Newton Visitor Information Center** (2101 Clark St., Covington, 770/787-3868, http://gocovington.com) and grab a brochure for the self-guided Covington: On Location tour, which hits sites from *In the Heat of the Night*, *The Dukes of Hazzard*, and more than 60 feature films.

Atlanta Opera. The acoustically solid concert hall hosts big-name bands, comedians, and touring productions. The Cobb Energy Centre is about a 15-minute drive from Downtown, potentially much longer with traffic. **MAP 7:** 2800 Cobb Galleria Pkwy., Atlanta, 770/916-2800, www.cobbenergycentre.com; ticket prices vary

SPIVEY HALL

"Spivey Hall is to music what light is to painting," the late maestro Robert Shaw once declared, a hyperbolic testimony to the superior acoustics of the beloved venue. Clayton State University's warm, 400-seat theater is regularly ranked as one of the best small performing-arts venues in the country. Spivey Hall hosts a busy series of jazz and classical music concerts, which are often heard on American Public Media's *Performance Today* on NPR. **MAP 7:** 2000 Clayton State Blvd., Morrow, 678/466-4200, www.spiveyhall.org; ticket prices vary

MUSEUMS

★ DELTA FLIGHT MUSEUM

Atlanta-based Delta Air Lines is among the largest in the world. Vintage aircraft from the company's earliest days of transporting passengers are lovingly preserved at the Delta Flight Museum. The museum occupies two 1940s-era maintenance hangars north of Hartsfield-Jackson. Guests must show ID at a security station before admittance. Once inside, head first to Hangar 1 and watch the short documentary before browsing the display cases or Delta's first 767 next door.

MAP 7: 1060 Delta Blvd., Building B, Dept. 914, 404/715-7886, www.deltamuseum.org; Mon.,Tues., Thurs., Fri., Sat. 10am-4:30pm, Sun. noon-4:30pm; $12.50 adult, $7 child, $10 senior

MARIETTA/COBB MUSEUM OF ART

Even though its collection of 19th- and 20th-century American masters won't ever compete with other high-profile Atlanta institutions, the quaint Marietta/Cobb Museum of Art has other charms. The best asset may be the building itself, a grand Greek Revival monolith that opened as a post office in 1910. The museum hosts a full calendar of exhibitions by local and national artists, as well as popular martini nights once a quarter and a variety of art classes.

MAP 7: 30 Atlanta St., Marietta, 770/528-1444, www.mariettacobbartmuseum.org; Tues.-Fri. 11am-5pm, Sat. 11am-4pm, Sun. 1pm-4pm; $8 adult, $5 student and senior, free under 6

MARIETTA GONE WITH THE WIND MUSEUM: SCARLETT ON THE SQUARE

If the *Gone With the Wind* goodies at the Margaret Mitchell House left you craving more, this gracious suburban outpost takes Scarlett fever to the next level. Highlights include the original Bengaline honeymoon gown Vivien Leigh wore in the film and many rare volumes of the novel. A visit shouldn't take longer than 45 minutes. Don't miss the annual Memorial Day weekend picnic, which recreates the Twelve Oaks barbecue from the movie.

MAP 7: 18 Whitlock Ave. NW, Marietta, 770/794-5576, www.gwtwmarietta.com; Mon.-Sat. 10am-5pm; $7 adult, $6 student and senior

ZUCKERMAN MUSEUM OF ART

The unveiling of this dazzling museum in 2014 led to a good bit of astonishment locally—who expected a significant new arts institution to sprout in the far northern suburbs?—and national praise for its architectural appeal. Located on the campus of Kennesaw State University, the 9,200-square-foot museum designed by Atlanta-based architects Stanley Beaman & Sears features visiting exhibitions of work by contemporary artists, items from the university's permanent collection, and student showcases.

MAP 7: 492 Prillaman Way, Kennesaw, 470/578-3223, http://zuckerman.kennesaw.edu; Tues.-Thurs. 11am-4pm, Sat. 11am-4pm; free

Above: Marietta Gone With the Wind Museum. **Below:** hangar in the Delta Flight Museum.

PERFORMING ARTS

ATLANTA BALLET

It may be one of the oldest professional dance companies in America, but the Atlanta Ballet is definitely not acting its age. In recent years the ballet has enjoyed high-profile collaborations with artists such as hip-hop superstar Big Boi and local folk rockers the Indigo Girls—not the kind of fare typically associated with the *Swan Lake* set. Its annual *Nutcracker* production is an Atlanta holiday tradition that fills the Fox Theatre to capacity.

MAP 7: 1695 Marietta Blvd., 404/873-5811, www.atlantaballet.com; ticket prices vary

ATLANTA OPERA

Sometimes dismissed as a genre out of touch with modern listeners, opera enjoys a surprisingly passionate following here thanks to the efforts of the Atlanta Opera. Founded in 1979, the company has taken steps to update traditional opera for modern audiences, including providing digital subtitles and staging productions that often turn conventions on their ear. The annual season typically offers five productions at the Cobb Energy Performing Arts Centre.

MAP 7: 1575 Northside Cir. NW, Atlanta, 404/881-8801, www.atlantaopera.org; ticket prices vary

Sports and Activities

Highlights

★ **Best Ball Game:** Any outing to see the **Atlanta Hawks** dominate the court at Philips Arena is always an adrenaline-fueled evening (page 136).

★ **Best Walk Down Memory Lane:** To get a passionate lesson on local history, try one of the **Atlanta Preservation Center Guided Walking Tours**. Knowledgeable docents provide thought-provoking and often funny anecdotes about heritage sites (page 136).

★ **Best Urban Hike:** It's only 2.25 miles from Midtown to Inman Park via the **Atlanta BeltLine Eastside Trail,** but the walk feels longer due to path's art installations and buzz of activity (page 139).

★ **Best Skatepark:** Atlanta skateboarders had a say in the design of the concrete skatepark within **Historic Fourth Ward Park,** which features ramps and half-pipes for skaters of all skill levels (page 143).

★ **Best Tours:** While other companies focus mainly on the big attractions, **Bicycle Tours of Atlanta** takes visitors on well-planned expeditions into handsome intown neighborhoods (page 144).

★ **Best Amusement Park:** Who needs Mickey Mouse? Hang out with Batman, Superman, and Bugs Bunny at **Six Flags Over Georgia,** the state's largest theme park, featuring 12 roller coasters, several water rides, and much more (page 144).

★ **Best Boating:** The 48 miles of the **Chattahoochee River National Recreation** offers countless options for kayaking, canoeing, or rafting (page 145).

★ **Best Bike Trail:** The 61-mile **Silver Comet Trail** is a paved multiuse path that draws bicyclists from across the region (page 146).

How serious is Atlanta's obsession with sports? The numbers don't lie: $68 million for the College Football Hall of Fame, an estimated $672 million for a new baseball park, roughly $1.5 billion for a forthcoming football stadium. And that's only spectator sports. Each summer, 60,000 runners flood the streets of Buckhead for the Peachtree Road Race. The 80,000-member Atlanta Lawn Tennis Association is the largest community group of its kind—*in the world*. And more than a million annual hikers, bikers, and skateboarders are expected to make use of the Atlanta BeltLine Eastside Trail.

Sports fans, weekend warriors, and amateur athletes are spoiled with an embarrassment of riches here. Atlanta's many months of sunshine and relatively mild winters make options for outdoor recreation as varied as the cultural scene. Miles of walking paths reach from Midtown to Stone Mountain. Recent years have seen a major investment in bike lanes connecting key intown neighborhoods. The dozens of golf courses across the metro area stay busy almost year-round. For runners, the calendar packs in more than 7,000 footraces annually.

Neighborhood groups play the role of fierce defenders of nearby parks, as well as investors in the green spaces' maintenance and future. The city contains 343 parks that cover a total of 3,622 acres. It's actually one of the smallest park systems for any major American city, but a windfall of federal funding and voter-backed infrastructure projects may soon change that. If lacking in acreage, Atlanta's parks don't hurt for usage or loyalty.

Previous: walking along the Atlanta BeltLine; Six Flags Over Georgia.

Downtown

Map 1

SPECTATOR SPORTS

ATLANTA BRAVES

The only thing an Atlanta Braves fan loves more than cheering for the home team is griping about them. Many cried foul when the team announced plans to vacate **Turner Field** and abandon Atlanta proper. The forthcoming **SunTrust Park** sits outside city limits and is slated to open for the 2017 season. The much-loved but also much-maligned-baseball franchise came to Atlanta in 1966. The Braves rose from last place to win the World Series in 1995.

MAP 1: Turner Field, 755 Hank Aaron Dr. SE, 404/522-7630, http://atlanta.braves.mlb.com; $15-95

ATLANTA FALCONS

Atlanta's NFL franchise since 1965, the Falcons enjoyed a brief stint as the city's most admired sports team when they made it to the Super Bowl in 1999. Sadly, the years since have not been kind to the "dirty birds." Team owner Arthur Blank hopes to reverse the trend with a new, $1.5 billion stadium scheduled for completion in 2017. It's barely a stone's throw from the **Georgia Dome,** home to the Falcons since 1992.

MAP 1: Georgia Dome, 1 Georgia Dome Dr. NW, 404/223-4636, www.atlantafalcons.com; $35-135

★ ATLANTA HAWKS

While the Braves and the Falcons were busy squabbling over stadium deals and zoning laws, the city's underrated NBA team clinched its first division title in more than two decades in 2015. Experiencing an Atlanta Hawks basketball game may be one of the most adrenaline-inducing sports events in the city. Since 1999, the team has played in **Philips Arena,** a bright and loud sports complex that doubles as a concert venue.

MAP 1: Philips Arena, 1 Philips Dr., 404/878-3000, www.nba.com/hawks; $10-85

TOURS

★ ATLANTA PRESERVATION CENTER
GUIDED WALKING TOURS

Since 1980, the Atlanta Preservation Center has been an advocate for protecting local historic landmarks. It's credited with saving close to 200 threatened sites. The agency also offers some of the most insightful guided walking tours in town. Knowledgeable, professionally trained volunteers lead treks through eight areas, including Sweet Auburn, Druid Hills, and Ansley Park. Also on tap: a sacred spaces series and tours of the 1856 L.P. Grant Mansion. Tours last around 90 minutes.

MAP 1: 327 St. Paul Ave. SE, 404/688-3350, www.atlantapreservationcenter.com/walking_tours; $10 adult, $5 child and senior

Above: Philips Arena, home of the Atlanta Hawks. **Below:** Atlanta BeltLine Eastside Trail.

Five Ways to Beat the Heat

- Take a five-story drop down the world's first hybrid, zero-gravity water slide at **Hurricane Harbor** (561 Six Flags Pkwy., Austell, 770/948-9290, www.sixflags.com/overgeorgia; $63 adult, $43 child), the seven-acre water park inside Six Flags Over Georgia. The Caribbean-themed attraction opened in 2014 as part of the largest expansion ever for the longstanding amusement park.

- Grab a shady spot poolside at **Piedmont Park Aquatic Center** (Piedmont Park, 1345 Piedmont Ave., 404/875-7275, http://piedmontpark.org/do/swimming.html; $4 adult, $2 child, $2 senior), an inviting recreation facility that underwent a substantial renovation in 2009. The pool offers lap lanes, a "beach" area, current channel for floating, spacious changing rooms, and lockers

- Save cash while enjoying a lazy afternoon drifting down the Chattahoochee River with **$10 River Tubing** (4349 Abbotts Bridge Rd., Duluth, 678/349-6880, www.gorivertubing.com; $10). Trips range from 2-6 hours and include a life vest and transportation service.

- Stroll 40 feet in the air above one of the city's last remaining urban forests on the elevated **Canopy Walk** (1345 Piedmont Ave., 404/876-5859, www.atlantabg.org; $19 adult, $13 child) in the Atlanta Botanical Garden. The dense cover of foliage in Storza Woods helps keep the path light and breezy.

- Catch a summer blockbuster while floating in a 750,000-gallon wave pool at **Dive-In Movies** (250 Cobb Pkwy. N., Marietta, 770/948-9290, www.sixflags.com/whitewater), the popular film series at Six Flags White Water. Movies are shown at 7pm June-July on a 25-foot screen next to the park's massive Atlanta Ocean.

ATL CRUZERS

These fun, fast-moving tours take visitors on rolling itineraries through Downtown, Midtown, and east-side neighborhoods. Choose either the 90-minute, 15-mile electric car tour—not unlike seeing the city via supersized golf cart—or one of the 2.5-hour Segway tours. Each guest gets an i2 Segway Personal Transporter, which may sound intimidating, but controls are intuitive and there's a mandatory safety video, plus driving lessons. Segway drivers must be 14 or older. Reservations are required.

MAP 1: 160 Spring St. NW , 404/492/7009, www.atlcruzers.com/Atlanta; daily 11am-3pm; $29-59 adult

Midtown

Map 2

BIKE AND SKATE RENTALS
SKATE ESCAPE

You can't beat the location of this family-owned bike shop, which sits just across the street from one of Piedmont Park's busiest entrances. Come springtime, the place is always full. The funky, friendly little store rents bikes, inline skates, and even tandems by the hour or for the day at reasonable prices. The shop sells a wide line of skateboarding goods and safety equipment, and offers repair services for bikes and rollerblades.

MAP 2: 1086 Piedmont Ave. NE, 404/892-1292, www.skateescape.com; daily 11am-7pm; bikes $6 per hour/$35 per day, skates $6 per hour/$20 per day

GYMS AND HEALTH CLUBS
URBAN BODY FITNESS

Urban Body Fitness adds some much-needed local flavor to a town overrun with chain athletic clubs. The trendy gym features state-of-the-art equipment, comfortable locker rooms, and complimentary towel service. The slate of classes can't be beat: In addition to the spin, boot camp, and kickboxing classes offered at UBF, check out the affiliated **Urban Body Studios** (730 Ponce de Leon Pl., 404/201-7994, www.urbanbodystudios. com, Mon.-Thurs. 6am-9pm, Fri. 6am-8pm, Sat.-Sun. 8am-6pm) for a full lineup of yoga and pilates instruction.

MAP 2: 500 Amsterdam Ave. NE, 404/885-1499, www.urbanbodyfitness.com; Mon.-Fri. 5am-10pm, Sat. 8am-8pm, Sun. 8am-7pm, $15 daily guest pass, membership around $75/ month

HIKING, BIKING, AND JOGGING TRAILS
★ ATLANTA BELTLINE EASTSIDE TRAIL

The long-discussed redevelopment of the Atlanta BeltLine, an old railway loop surrounding the city, seemed to kick into warp speed with the 2012 unveiling of the Eastside Trail, its first finished section. The 2.25-mile multiuse trail and greenspace found immediate popularity among cyclists, joggers, dog walkers, and skateboarders. Easy trail access points link Midtown's Piedmont Park with Historic Fourth Ward Park and the Krog Street restaurant scene. Try early on a weekday morning for smaller crowds.

MAP 2: Monroe Dr. and 10th St., http://beltline.org/trails/eastside-trail; daily 6am-10pm; free

Buckhead Map 3

AMUSEMENT PARKS
LEGOLAND DISCOVERY CENTER

Rumors swirled for years that Legoland was eyeing Atlanta as the location for an interactive children's attraction, but nobody could have guessed that the concept would land at Phipps Plaza, probably the glitziest shopping mall in Georgia. One of only four such Legoland properties in the country, the immersive 32,000-square-foot complex gives kids a dozen distinctly themed play areas, including rides, building classes, and a 4-D cinema. Ideally suited for ages 3-10.

MAP 3: 3500 Peachtree Rd. NE, Ste. G-1, 404/848-9252, http://atlanta. legolanddiscoverycenter.com; Mon.-Fri. 10am-7pm, Sat. 10am-9pm, Sun. 10am-6pm; $19 adult, $15 child

BOWLING
MIDTOWN BOWL

It's clean, it's smoke-free, it's open late. No wonder Midtown Bowl attracts such a loyal following, making it the go-to place for bowling leagues in the heart of the city. The family-friendly venue features 32 lanes along with the standard bowling alley amenities (shoe rental, beer, fried food). Though the prices are a bit higher than at some of the other bowling alleys, the rates go down if you reserve your lane ahead of time.

MAP 3: 1936 Piedmont Cir. NE, 404/874-5703, www.midtownbowl.com; daily 9am-3am; lane rentals $12-40 per hour

GOLF
BOBBY JONES GOLF COURSE

In 1930, celebrated Atlanta athlete Bobby Jones won the golf Grand Slam: the British Amateur, U.S. Open, British Open, and U.S. Amateur. His namesake golf course, an 18-hole 71-par course positioned on an old Civil War battlefield, has been a Buckhead favorite since 1931. Though once derided for shoddy maintenance, the property has undergone renovations and installed new Champion Bermuda greens. It's not a particularly challenging course, but the location alone makes this a worthwhile destination.

MAP 3: 384 Woodward Way NW, 404/355-1009, http://bobbyjones.americangolf.com; $20-45.50 per 18 holes

TENNIS
BITSY GRANT TENNIS CENTER

Atlanta tennis legend Bryan M. Grant Jr.—nicknamed "Bitsy" because of his diminutive frame—enjoyed a long and illustrious career on the world stage. For years, he was also a fixture at the Buckhead tennis center that bears his name. The center today offers 13 clay courts (6 lighted) and 10 hard courts at reasonable prices. Courts are available on a first-come, first-served basis with no reservations. The center also offers lessons for players of all skill levels.

MAP 3: 2125 Northside Dr. NW, 404/609-7193, www.bitsytennis.com; Mon.-Thurs. 9am-10pm, Fri. 9am-7pm, Sat.-Sun. 9am-6pm; $3-7 per hour

Above: Skate Escape. **Below:** Midtown Bowl.

Virginia-Highland Map 4

HIKING, BIKING, AND JOGGING TRAILS
DANIEL JOHNSON NATURE PRESERVE

Along with adjoining **Herbert Taylor Park,** this natural floodplain makes for a thoroughly unexpected sliver of raw forest in an otherwise typical neighborhood. The 25-acre nature preserve is popular among trail runners and hikers. The main path follows a 1.5-mile circle along the banks of Rock Creek and South Fork Peachtree Creek. Though the area is maintained by the Rock Creek Watershed Alliance, the trails can be somewhat overgrown in places.

MAP 4: Beech Valley Rd. and Johnson Rd.; daily dawn-dusk; free

MORNINGSIDE NATURE PRESERVE

Concerned neighbors rallied in 2006 to stop the destruction of one of the last large urban forests inside city limits. The grassroots effort led to the Morningside Nature Preserve. Even though bustling Cheshire Bridge Road is just a few blocks away, this lush, 30-acre woodland offers one of the most serene and scenic hiking trails in the city. The path crosses the sandy banks of South Fork Peachtree Creek via a gorgeous wooden suspension bridge.

MAP 4: Wildwood Rd. and Wellbourne Dr.; daily dawn-dusk; free

PARKS
LULLWATER PARK

Hidden on the edge of Emory University's campus, Lullwater Park has a more natural ambience than some of the city's other parks. The 185-acre wooded green space is used most often by Emory students but is open to the public. The park features jogging trails, a pond, manicured gardens, and ducks and swans. The English Tudor mansion of Emory's president also sits on Lullwater's grounds. Enter near the intersection of Clifton Road and Haygood Drive.

MAP 4: 1463 Clifton Rd. NE, 404/875-7284; daily dawn-dusk; free

Little Five Points and East Atlanta

Map 5

GOLF

CANDLER PARK GOLF COURSE

This nine-hole course may be light on amenities, but it's heavy on a casual live-and-let-live outlook that fits the vibe of the surrounding Candler Park neighborhood. Devoid of the pretension found at some of the city's more exclusive golf clubs, Candler Park is a good option for beginners or those who love the game but hate its uppity trappings. The attractive course sits adjacent to Freedom Park and is just outside of Little Five Points.

MAP 5: 585 Candler Park Dr. NE, 404/371-1260, http://candlerparkgolf.com; $10-13 per nine holes

GYMS AND HEALTH CLUBS

CANDLER PARK YOGA

Although Candler Park Yoga offers a full range of instruction for advanced devotees, it's also known for being especially welcoming to newcomers. The informal studio has a soothing, understated atmosphere. The studio offers more than two dozen weekly classes devoted to the practices of Kripalu and Pranakriya Yoga, plus classes in breath work and meditation and advanced courses.

MAP 5: 1630-D DeKalb Ave. NE, 404/370-0579, www.jaishantiyoga.com; daily 8am-10pm; $10-16 per class

PARKS

FREEDOM PARK

Freedom Park marks a large green X in the center of Poncey-Highland. The open terrain draws a symbolic line from the Martin Luther King Jr. National Historic Site to the Jimmy Carter Presidential Library, with lots of jogging paths and rolling hills. As an official Atlanta Art Park, the six-mile corridor hosts several permanent installations of public art. Its northern arm connects with Candler Park, allowing for trails that run all the way to Fernbank Forest.

MAP 5: North Ave. and Freedom Pkwy., 404/875-7284, www.freedompark.org; daily 6am-11pm; free

★ HISTORIC FOURTH WARD PARK

Atlanta got its first public **skatepark** in 2011 with the opening of this 17-acre greenspace. Celebrity skateboarder Tony Hawk's foundation pitched in $25,000 toward costs of the concrete course, designed with ramps, half-pipes, and fun-boxes for skaters of all skill levels. A path finished in 2014 connects Historic Fourth Ward Park to the BeltLine's Eastside Trail near North Angier Avenue. The park includes an outdoor theater, several lawns, a playground, and a pond.

MAP 5: North Ave. and N. Angier Ave., 404/590-7275, www.h4wpc.com; daily 6am-11pm; free

TOURS
★ BICYCLE TOURS OF ATLANTA

Atlanta's investment in bike lanes is making life much easier for this company, established in 2009. The tour group offers well-planned bicycle expeditions that highlight lovely intown neighborhoods and hit historic sites such as Oakland Cemetery and Sweet Auburn. The leisurely 10-mile, three-hour Heart of the City Tour kicks off from Studioplex in the Old Fourth Ward and cycles through Inman Park, Grant Park, Little Five Points, and Cabbagetown. Cost includes helmets and bottled water.

MAP 5: 659 Auburn Ave. NE, 404/273-2558, www.biketoursatl.com; tour schedule varies, Mar.-Oct. daily; $59 adult and child

Decatur   Map 6

TOURS
DECATUR GHOST TOUR

Skeptics may sneer when the guide tells of ghostly wounded soldiers heard crying in the night or specters haunting the old train depot, but even non-believers go quiet during the moonlit walk through Decatur Cemetery. This fun and spooky evening ritual is led by Boo Newell, a clairvoyant ghost whisperer who brings lots of life to her stories of the unquiet dead. The two-hour tour begins at the bandstand in Decatur's town square.

MAP 6: 101 E. Court Sq., 404/296-7771, www.decaturghosttour.com; Fri.-Sat. 8pm; $15 adult, $12 child

Greater Atlanta   Map 7

AMUSEMENT PARKS
★ SIX FLAGS OVER GEORGIA

Georgia's favorite summertime escape since 1967 retains some of the Southern-fried flair from its early days, but Batman and Bugs Bunny now rule the roost. The property, 10 miles west from Downtown, features 12 roller coasters, including the gigantic Goliath and the Joker Chaos Coaster, plus a Caribbean-themed water park. The Monster Mansion is a psychedelic mind-trip. Crowds can be oppressive in summer. Save cash by parking in an unofficial lot across the interstate.

MAP 7: 275 Riverside Pkwy., Austell, 770/948-9290, www.sixflags.com/overgeorgia; Mar.-mid-May Sat. 10am-9pm and Sun. 10:30am-8pm, late May-late June Mon.-Fri. 10:30am-8pm and Sat.-Sun. 10am-9pm, late June-July Sun.-Fri. 10:30am-9pm and Sat. 10am-10pm, early Aug.-mid-Aug. Mon.-Fri. 10:30am-7pm and Sat.-Sun. 10am-8pm, mid-Aug.-late Aug. Sat.-Sun. 10am-8pm, Sept. Sat. 10am-8pm and Sun. 11am-7pm; $63 adult, $43 child

SIX FLAGS WHITE WATER

The 2014 addition of an expensive new water park to Six Flags Over Georgia seems like an odd diversion from its sister property, Six Flags White Water. This 69-acre attraction offers more than two dozen water rides for kids and adults. The daunting Cliffhanger, billed as one of the tallest freefall water slides in the world, hurls guests nine stories down into the drink below. Located 16 miles northwest of Downtown.

MAP 7: 250 Cobb Pkwy. N., Marietta, 770/948-9290, www.sixflags.com/whitewater; late May-July daily 10:30am-7pm, early Aug. daily 10:30am-6pm, mid-Aug.-early Sept. Sat.-Sun. 10:30am-6pm; $40 adult, $35 child

BIKE AND SKATE RENTALS
SILVER COMET CYCLES

As the name suggests, the handy bike shop offers easy access to the Silver Comet Trail. The helpful staff knows how to choose the right bike for any skill level. Child trailers and youth bikes are also available. For bike novices, the website includes a beginner's guide to shifting and common cycling blunders newbies make. Reservations for rental equipment are encouraged but not required.

MAP 7: 4342 Floyd Rd., Mableton, 678/945-6084, www.silvercometdepot.com; Sun.-Mon. 10:30am-5pm, Tues.-Fri. 10:30am-6pm, Sat. 9am-6pm; $10 per hour, $50 per day

CANOEING, KAYAKING, AND RAFTING
★ CHATTAHOOCHEE RIVER NATIONAL RECREATION AREA

The mind boggles that such an expansive national park can exist so close to the city. The Chattahoochee River National Recreation Area covers a 48-mile stretch of the Chattahoochee River, with 16 segments stretching from Lake Lanier to Peachtree Creek. Besides the hiking/jogging trails along the river, Chattahoochee offers 11 distinct areas for canoeing, kayaking, or rafting. Some are more accessible than others. Spend time online or visit the station to decide which area best suits your needs.

MAP 7: Island Ford Visitor Contact Station, 1978 Island Ford Pkwy., Sandy Springs, www.nps.gov/chat; daily 9am-5pm, $3 per day

HIGH COUNTRY OUTFITTERS

"Shooting the 'Hooch"—drifting down the Chattahoochee—has been a homegrown summertime tradition for years, sadly overshadowed in recent years by reports of pollution in the river. High Country Outfitters is one of a small handful of local companies that rent canoes, kayaks, or stand-up paddleboards for Chattahoochee adventures. The Sandy Springs rental shop is conveniently located on the river; it's open seasonally May through September. For more selection, check out the flagship store in Buckhead (3906B Roswell Rd., 404/814-0999, Mon.-Fri. 10am-8pm, Sat. 10am-6pm, Sun. noon-6pm).

MAP 7: 200 Morgan Falls Rd., Sandy Springs, 770/321-4780, www.highcountryoutfitters.com; May-Sept. Fri.-Sat. 9am-6pm, Sun. 10am-6pm; $55-75 per day

GYMS AND HEALTH CLUBS

ATHLETIC CLUB NORTHEAST

Fitness club or shopping mall? The echoing Athletic Club Northeast could single-handedly swallow up most other gyms in Atlanta and still have a locker room to spare. It incorporates six racquetball courts, a full-sized basketball gymnasium, two pools, a pilates studio, two weight rooms, and eight outdoor tennis courts—just to name a few of the amenities. The clientele tilts toward old-timers who've belonged to the club long enough to see their grandkids become members.

MAP 7: 1515 Sheridan Rd. NE, Atlanta, 404/325-2700, www.athleticclubnortheast.com; Mon.-Fri. 5am-10pm, Sat.-Sun. 8am-8pm; $20 daily guest pass, yearly membership varies

HIKING, BIKING, AND JOGGING TRAILS

CHASTAIN PARK TRAIL

It's a series of loops surrounding one of the city's most graceful public parks—but don't expect to have the Chastain Park Trail to yourself. An average of 250 walkers, joggers, cyclists, and inline skaters use this immensely popular circuit each *hour*. The trail is split between a three-mile course covering the vast majority of the park and two smaller paths north of West Wieuca Road.

MAP 7: West Wieuca Rd. and Lake Forest Rd., Atlanta, 404/875-7284, www.chastainpark. org; daily 6am-11pm; free

★ SILVER COMET TRAIL

Built over abandoned railroad lines, the Silver Comet Trail stretches 61 miles from suburban Atlanta to Alabama, where it connects with the Chief Ladiga Trail and continues for another 33 miles. The fully paved two-lane path provides an up-close encounter with the raw Georgia countryside, from the 25,000-acre Paulding Forest to forgotten farmland outside Cedartown. It's a great and unique option for walking, biking, inline skating, and even horseback riding.

MAP 7: Starts at S. Cobb Dr. and East-West Connector in Cobb County, 404/875-7284, www.silvercometga.com; daily dawn-dusk; free

PARKS

CHASTAIN PARK

Chastain Park, Atlanta's largest, often gets overshadowed by the more centrally located Piedmont Park, but this splendid 268-acre green space has plenty to offer. Once the site of a Creek Indian village, the land was first developed as North Fulton Park in the late 1930s and renamed in 1945 to honor a civic leader. Today it incorporates diverse options: amphitheater, arts center, jogging trails, horse park, ball fields, aquatic center, tennis courts, and golf course.

MAP 7: Powers Ferry Rd. and W. Wieuca Rd., Atlanta, 404/817-6744, www.chastainpark. org; daily 6am-11pm; free

TENNIS

ATLANTA LAWN TENNIS ASSOCIATION (ALTA)

One of the most popular sports organizations in Atlanta, this nonprofit started league play in 1971 with fewer than 1,000 members. Today ALTA has more than 80,000 members, assigned to leagues based on skill level, gender, and geography. Separate tiers exist for women, men, youth, and wheelchair-bound competitors. The tournaments, though cordial, can push the envelope on friendly competition to become heated battles with long-standing rivalries. Games pop up all over town.

MAP 7: 6849 Peachtree Dunwoody Rd. NE, tournaments in various locations, 770/399-5788, www.altatennis.org; annual membership adult $25, child $10

Shops

Any sentence that involves the words "shopping" and "Atlanta" often ends with "Buckhead"—which makes sense given that two of the city's largest upscale malls and some of the region's most chic designer boutiques are located there. But it would be a shame for anyone to devote an entire Atlanta visit to Lenox Square Mall and Phipps Plaza. The city offers loads of other options for shopaholics looking for more than the typical brand-name standards. Unlike in some other major cities, Atlanta's retail treasures may require a bit of footwork.

Certain shopping districts feature tempting clusters of must-see stores. Virginia-Highland is dotted with interesting boutiques, home stores, and gift shops, making it a destination for patrons seeking an alternative to Buckhead. West Midtown has enjoyed a steady trend of stylish businesses popping up in refurbished spaces and new shopping complexes. Nearby, the streets of Atlantic Station are never empty, thanks to the density of brand-name shops in an instant neighborhood whipped up from scratch.

Shoppers in search of more independent-minded options should make a beeline for the eccentric emporiums of Little Five Points, a mecca for thrift stores, record shops, and tattoo parlors. The neighborhoods of Decatur and East Atlanta Village offer a similar mix of offbeat urban outposts.

Atlanta's relatively low cost of living and potpourri of retail delights have helped create the Southeast's premier destination for racking up credit-card debt. The blend of sprawling department stores, funky flea markets, familiar chains, and elegant emporiums means there's something here for everyone—even window shoppers.

Previous: Macy's Pink Pig at Lenox Square Mall; Junkman's Daughter.

Highlights

★ **Best Gourmet Goodies:** A sister shop to be-seen restaurant Bacchanalia, **Star Provisions** is Atlanta's best high-end gourmet market (page 153).

★ **Best Men's Clothing:** Fashion guru **Sid Mashburn** has a reputation for his impeccable taste and diligent customer service (page 155).

★ **Best Spa: Blue MedSpa** is a go-to destination for a luxurious day of pampering (page 155).

★ **Busiest Art Store:** After 60 years in business, **Binders Art Supplies and Frames** does a lot more than sell paintbrushes. The cavernous Buckhead hideaway houses a framing shop, gallery space, and art school (page 157).

★ **Best Mall:** It was Georgia's first mall and one of the first enclosed shopping centers in the region. Today, **Lenox Square Mall** remains an in-demand retail palace, home to 250 shops (page 160).

★ **Best Toy Store:** It may look like a typical five-and-dime, but venture deeper into **Richard's Variety Store** to discover a cavalcade of nostalgic toys, retro costumes, and other half-forgotten treasures from childhood (page 160).

★ **Most Buzz-Worthy Boutique:** Virginia-Highland's ingenious **Henry & June** calls itself a "coffee and clothing gallery," a place to sip high-quality espresso drinks while discovering up-and-coming designers (page 164).

★ **Best Independent Record Store:** A Little Five Points fixture since 1991, **Criminal Records** soldiers on and gets better with age (page 166).

★ **Best Carnival of Kitsch:** Eccentric gift and clothing shop **Junkman's Daughter** could be called a pop-culture blender, garish knickknack store, and trippy sideshow all at once. No place sums up the spirit of Little Five Points better (page 166).

SHOPPING DISTRICTS
Atlantic Station

No single development in modern history has impacted intown Atlanta as thoroughly as Atlantic Station, which transformed an ugly and polluted steel-mill site into a dense 138 acres of retail, commercial, and residential space. Hailed as a model for the New Urbanist movement, the "city within a city" opened in 2005. Its central shopping district has the feeling of a small town—or else a massive outdoor mall perched atop an enormous parking deck. You'll find plenty of brand-name clothing stores here (Banana Republic, Express, H&M, and Dillard's), a multiplex movie theater with one of the few IMAX screens in the area, an athletic club, and a mixed bag of restaurants.

Buckhead Atlanta

The redevelopment of this former nightclub district into a high-end shopping destination finally reached fruition in late 2014. The mixed-use project covers six blocks stretching northeast from the intersection of East Paces Ferry and Peachtree roads. While the chic, pedestrian-friendly complex's name may be thoroughly boring, its roster of almost 20 luxury boutiques is anything but: Christian Louboutin, Helmut Lang, Hermès, Dior, and much more.

Decatur Square

Laid-back, colorful Decatur Square used to be one of greater Atlanta's best-kept secrets—a vibrant and progressive hangout that felt like a college town, as well as a fun locale for neighborhood festivals. These days, the news is definitely out. The rows of shops and restaurants around the old Decatur Courthouse sometimes get slammed on weekends, especially when the weather warms and the sidewalks clog with strollers. Shoppers will want to experience the square's eclectic collection of craft and jewelry stores, antiques shops, and gift galleries—not to mention a couple of popular independent booksellers.

Little Five Points

Little Five Points, Atlanta's enduring capital of all things alternative, remains a destination for visitors with eclectic, envelope-pushing tastes. The commercial district branches out from the intersection of Moreland and Euclid Avenues, with a diverse blend of new and vintage boutiques, novelty shops, indie bookstores and record stores, tattoo parlors, bars, and restaurants. A few blocks south, a new commercial development brings big-box shopping to the mix. Many locals cried foul when the mixed-use Edgewood strip mall went in, but its proximity hasn't stifled the anti-corporate Little Five Points attitude.

Midtown Mile

Atlanta's homage to Chicago's Magnificent Mile gives a glimpse into the ongoing transformation of Peachtree Street. Spurred by the outburst of new condo and office towers rising in this part of town, the shops of the

SHOPS

Midtown Mile tend to be cosmopolitan and on the expensive side, a mix of designer furniture galleries, ritzy boutiques, and specialty stores. It offers a nice blend of food options, from casual noodle houses to four-star restaurants. Officially, the Midtown Mile runs from North Avenue to 15th Street, but the term more frequently describes the businesses north of 10th Street.

North Highland Avenue

North Highland Avenue isn't home to just one interesting commercial district but, depending on how you slice it, four or five strips of noteworthy shops spread out over a couple of miles. Start in the Old Fourth Ward around Sampson Street and head east to experience the newest segment of the extensive retail corridors. As the street curves north, the intersection of North Highland and Ponce de Leon Avenue ("Poncey-Highland" to locals) features another group of interesting storefronts, including a few bars and restaurants. The biggest commercial district of all lies at the intersection with Virginia Avenue, ground zero for frilly boutiques, gift stores, and miscellaneous shops. More options pop up here and there as the avenue carries on into Morningside.

Downtown   Map 1

MARKETS
SWEET AUBURN CURB MARKET

Though it was founded in 1923, the Sweet Auburn Curb Market has the amenities of a modern food court mixed with a deli counter—plus a dash of flea market thrown in for extra flavor. Stands sell fresh produce, cheeses, baked goods, and seafood. Its 11 cafés run the gamut. The complex includes a florist, pharmacy, and gift store. Parking is free for the first hour in the nearby lot on Jessie Hill Jr. Drive.

MAP 1: 209 Edgewood Ave. SE, 404/659-1665, www.thecurbmarket.com; Mon.-Sat. 8am-6pm

Midtown   Map 2

CHILDREN'S CLOTHING
SEED FACTORY

If you're grooming a toddler to be a budding fashionista, dig no further. This popular west-side baby boutique (previously known as Sprout) has blossomed into a playground for Atlanta's most pampered tots and their choosy parents. The meticulous, well-groomed children's shop sells clothing, toys, games, and furniture—and steers clear of blatantly corporate products. The aesthetic feels modern and timeless, offering accessories for childhood that are playful and understated.

MAP 2: 1170 Howell Mill Rd. NW, 404/355-2043, www.seedfactoryatlanta.com; Mon.-Sat. 10am-6pm

GOURMET TREATS

★ STAR PROVISIONS

Foodies go gaga over the delectable selection of meats, cheeses, wines, and pastries at Star Provisions, the market and deli storefront that doubles as the entryway for five-star restaurant Bacchanalia. Star Provisions sells charming tableware and a handsome hodgepodge of culinary gifts and home accessories. Hit the takeout counter, or enjoy a heaping deli sandwich at one of the picnic tables. Not for penny-pinchers, the sweet extravagances at Star Provisions attract gourmands with dough to spare.

MAP 2: 1198 Howell Mill Rd. NW, 404/365-0410, www.starprovisions.com; Mon.-Sat. 10am-midnight

HOME FURNISHINGS

INTAGLIA HOME COLLECTION

This perpetually tasteful furniture store has been a fixture in Midtown since 1999. Its current Ansley Mall incarnation features the largest showroom yet, a relaxed gallery known for bargain finds. Intaglia is the kind of place where the furniture whispers and never screams, a purveyor of sleek, comfortable sofas and elegant dining room tables aimed at a Martha Stewart market. Don't miss the fun display of greeting cards.

MAP 2: 1544 Piedmont Ave. NE, Ste. 105, 404/607-9750, www.intagliahome.com; Mon.-Fri. 11am-7pm, Sat. 10am-6pm, Sun. noon-5pm

MARKETS

GREEN MARKET FOR PIEDMONT PARK

The movement to buy organic, locally grown produce has helped Piedmont Park's farmers market flourish into a mandatory weekend destination. It started in 2004 with a handful of sleepy-eyed neighbors browsing the booths; now, the market has evolved into one of Midtown's Saturday morning traditions. Beyond the veggies, vendors also sell a variety of "natural products," a term that apparently applies to everything from pet collars to greeting cards.

MAP 2: 14th St. and Piedmont Ave., 404/876-4024, www.piedmontpark.org; Mar.-Dec. Sat. 9am-1pm

MEN'S CLOTHING

BOY NEXT DOOR

Boy Next Door sells casual and club-ready menswear in a compact boutique always throbbing with a heavy house beat. Intimate without feeling cramped, it's a great destination for designer undies, jeans, and swimsuits. The prices sometimes shock, but the store's roomy clearance area is usually ripe for bargains. The sales clerks are some of the most helpful in town, though be forewarned: The transparent curtains of the "changing rooms" leave little to the imagination.

MAP 2: 1447 Piedmont Ave. NE, 404/873-2664, www.boynextdoormenswear.com; Mon.-Sat. 11am-8pm, Sun. noon-6pm

Above: Krog Street Market. **Below:** Sid Mashburn.

Think of it as a fashion concierge—equal parts gracious tailor's shop, off-the rack boutique, and gentlemen's club. Sid Mashburn, a former design director for Ralph Lauren and J. Crew, sells both trendy labels and his own classically inspired creations, clothes with a whiff of New England privilege but tempered by a friendly, down-to-earth sales floor. The offbeat accessories and Sid's gasp-worthy attention to detail have made the shop yet another West Midtown success story.

MAP 2: 1198 Howell Mill Rd. NW, 404/350-7135, www.sidmashburn.com; Mon.-Sat. 10:30am-6:30pm

PETS
PIEDMONT BARK

Atlanta's most pampered pooches get to spend weekdays at Piedmont Bark. Its doggy daycare offers 8,000 square feet of exercise space in a simulated outdoor setting, complete with trees and park benches. Designated run areas separate out the small, medium, and large dogs, with a similar categorical approach to the kennels. Piedmont Bark's walk-in dog wash is also a popular draw. You can even throw your puppy a private birthday party here.

MAP 2: 501 Amsterdam Ave. NE, 404/873-5400, www.piedmontbark.com; Mon.-Fri. 7am-7:30pm, Sat. 8am-5pm, Sun. noon-6pm

SALONS, SPAS, AND BEAUTY
★ BLUE MEDSPA

Wedged in an unlikely 10th Street building with funky geometric windows, Blue MedSpa makes for a welcome retreat from the bustle of Midtown. Visitors pass a gushing outdoor water wall before entering the hushed, all-white world of the spa's interior. Services range from massage and manicures to facials and Botox. The locker rooms may be on the small side, but the interior ambience feels posh and tranquil. The treatments never disappoint. Call early for reservations.

MAP 2: 190 10th St. NE, 404/815-8880, www.bluemedspa.com; Mon. 9am-6pm, Tues.-Sat. 9am-9pm, Sun. noon-6pm

HELMET HAIRWORX

Too many stylish hair salons ooze a subtle attitude of derision, but not Helmet. Located on two floors of a renovated Midtown bungalow, the salon retains a gracious Southern charm mixed with cosmopolitan sophistication. The stylists are both hip and approachable. Even though the place always seems to be full, it's usually easy to get an appointment. Men's haircuts range $45-65; women's cuts run higher. The salon offers color services, manicures, pedicures, and eyebrow waxing.

MAP 2: 970 Piedmont Ave. NE, 404/815-1629, www.helmethairworx.com; Mon. 10am-8pm, Tues.-Fri. 9am-8pm, Sat. 9am-7pm, Sun. 10am-6pm

SHOPS
MIDTOWN

Homing in on Home Goods

As a rule, Atlanta businesses don't usually congregate into areas dedicated to a single category of goods, like New York's Diamond District or L.A.'s Fashion District. But there are always exceptions: The city has no shortage of high-end home stores selling everything from fashionable furniture and accessories to upmarket antiques and art. Some of the best shops are folded into out-of-the-way pockets of the city. The best example may be the **Miami Circle Art and Design District** (www.miamicircleshops.com), an easily overlooked commercial cul-de-sac that branches off Piedmont Road a block north of the Lindbergh Plaza shopping center. Businesses on the meandering street specialize in tasteful, traditional home decor aimed at the luxury market, with a concentration of exclusive European and Asian antiques, classic furniture, fine fabrics, and rugs. More recently, the street has seen an influx of art galleries. It's a fun drive for window shopping no matter what your budget is.

A couple of miles west, **Bennett Street** is a great destination for discerning home goods. Unlike Miami Circle, this former warehouse row has a quirky post-industrial vibe; it saw a stint as a nightlife district in the 1970s before morphing into its current mix of art galleries and antiques shops. The 48,000-square-foot TULA Art Center is by far the biggest draw, featuring the Museum of Contemporary Art of Georgia. Bennett Street sits in South Buckhead and intersects with the 2100 block of Peachtree Road.

Meanwhile, **West Midtown** keeps gaining momentum as a hot spot for chic home accessories. The tastes you'll find here tend to be more modern, with contemporary furniture stores and cutting-edge art galleries. Though the businesses are spread out, there's an obvious critical mass on Huff Road, Ellsworth Industrial Boulevard, and Howell Mill Road near Marietta Street.

LOOK YOUNG ATLANTA

Forget the double-speak heard at other med spas. Look Young Atlanta puts its priorities front and center and does exactly what the name promises, offering services designed to keep patrons looking fresh and vivacious. Using state-of-the-technology for an evolving menu of treatments, the spa specializes in laser hair removal, wrinkle removal injections, photo facials, and even B12 vitamin shots. The on-site hair salon delivers impeccable services. It's in an almost-hidden Midtown loft.

MAP 2: 165 6th St. NE, 404/239-3911, www.lookyoungatlanta.com; Mon.-Fri. 9am-5pm, Sat. 9am-noon

SHOES
PHIDIPPIDES

No place in town knows running shoes like Phidippides. Named for the ancient Athenian whose sprint to Sparta inspired the modern marathon, this cozy Midtown favorite opened in 1974 as one of the first running specialty stores in the world. Its customer service can't be topped: An experienced sales associate will watch you take a quick jog around the store before finding exactly the right sneaker for your gait and stride.

MAP 2: 1544 Piedmont Ave. NE, 404/875-4268, www.phidippides.com; Mon.-Wed. and Fri. 10am-7pm, Thurs. 10am-8pm, Sat. 10am-6pm

157

WOMEN'S CLOTHING
ANN MASHBURN

Ann Mashburn is married to local style guru Sid Mashburn. In 2010, Ann opened her own feminine equivalent to her hubby's white-hot haberdashery, a few paces away in the same complex. A veteran of *Vogue* and *Glamour,* Ann favors fashions that are comfortable and classic, with just a hint of spice. The store, known for its impeccable service, is worth checking out even if the price tags can be gasp-worthy.

MAP 2: 1198 Howell Mill Rd. NW, 404/350-7135, www.annmashburn.com; Mon.-Sat. 10am-6:30pm

FAB'RIK

Atlanta native Dana Spinola opened her stylish yet affordable women's boutique in 2002. The concept has since spread to 30 spots across the Southeast. Fab'rik's chic, minimalist Atlantic Station showroom touts high-fashion finds without the Paris prices. Most pieces are less than $100 (with the exception of the excellent denim selection). The Buckhead location (3400 Around Lenox Rd., 404/816-6221, Mon.-Sat. 10am-7pm, Sun. noon-5pm) caters more to the luxury market, while the former flagship in Midtown has been converted into **Free Fab'rik Boutique** (1114 W. Peachtree St., 404/881-8223, www.freefabrik.org, Tues.-Sat. 11am-7pm), a charity shop that sells donated clothing to benefit young women in need.

MAP 2: 265 18th St. NW, Ste. 4170, 404/685-8595, www.fabrikstyle.com; Mon.-Wed. 10am-8pm, Thurs.-Sat. 10am-9pm, Sun. noon-6pm

Buckhead
Map 3

ANTIQUES
BELVEDERE FURNITURE, LIGHTING & DECORATIONS

You could say that Julia-Carr Bayler is stuck in the past—in a very good way. Since 1999, she's been hyping her love for stylish mid-20th-century designs at Belvedere, her Buckhead furniture gallery that sells both vintage and new goods. The store specializes in hard-to-find pieces from the 1930s through the 1960s, though its sense of style mixes modern accents in seamlessly with the vintage items. Also on the menu: accessories, jewelry, and artwork.

MAP 3: 721 Miami Cir. NE, Ste. 105, 404/352-1942, www.1stdibs.com; Mon.-Thurs. 11am-5pm

ARTS AND CRAFTS
★ BINDERS ART SUPPLIES AND FRAMES

This legendary Atlanta success story began way back in 1955, when a tiny gift shop started selling paints. Today, Binders isn't so easily pigeon-holed. The cavernous, 18,000-square-foot store beneath a Buckhead strip mall carries a stockpile of art supplies. It's also a gallery that shows work by local and emerging artists, *and* an art school teaching students of all skill levels painting, drawing, comic illustration, and more. Did we mention the custom framing shop? In 2014, Binders opened a smaller but just as lively location in **Ponce City Market** (650 North Ave., Suite S 102, 404/682-6999, Mon.-Sat. 9am-6pm, Sun. 11am-6pm).

MAP 3: 3330 Piedmont Rd. NE, Suite 18, 404/237-6331, www.bindersart.com; Mon.-Fri. 9am-8pm, Sat. 10am-7pm, Sun. 11am-6pm

SAM FLAX ATLANTA

After years in a dreary West Midtown warehouse, Sam Flax's relocation to south Buckhead feels like a creative dream come true. The bright and spirited space has the ambience of an artsy supermarket (perhaps because it really is a former supermarket), a one-stop-shop for brushes, paint, canvases, and frames. Non-artists can appreciate the office furniture, funny desk accessories, and fine paper goods. Check out Sam Flax for off-the-wall gift shopping during the holidays.

MAP 3: 1745 Peachtree St., 404/352-7200, www.samflaxsouth.com; Mon.-Fri. 8:30am-7:30pm, Sat. 10am-7pm, Sun. 11:30am-6pm

BOOKS AND MUSIC
OXFORD COMICS & GAMES

Atlanta's most popular comic, manga, and anime shop is a paradise for fanboys and fangirls. With a colossal display of current and past titles and a super-sized selection of graphic novels, the 30-year-old store is the only surviving member of a once-cherished local chain. The hometown vibe lives on in the friendly staff and chatty atmosphere. The front of the store features action figures, trading cards, games, anime and cult film DVDs, T-shirts, and an adults-only section.

MAP 3: 2855 Piedmont Rd. NE, 404/233-8682, www.oxfordcomics.com; Mon.-Sat. 10am-10pm, Sun. 11am-7pm

HOME FURNISHINGS
JONATHAN ADLER

Atlanta's most capricious home accessories shop is part of a national chain from design guru Jonathan Adler, but let's not hold that against it. Adler describes the concept as "everything you'd need to furnish a groovy, happy home." His signature "Happy Chic" aesthetic can be found on everything from lavish bedding and throw pillows to playing cards and coasters. Expect an inventory heavy on whimsy, aimed at an upscale clientele who won't flinch at the designer prices.

MAP 3: 3065 Peachtree Rd., Space B208, 404/367-0414, www.jonathanadler.com; Mon.-Sat. 10am-7pm, Sun. 11am-5pm

MEN'S CLOTHING
MODA404

Moda404 sets itself a step above the rest with its propensity for attracting Atlanta's hip-hop royalty and big-spending sports gods. Owners Lee Brockwell and Kwassi Yves Byll-Cataria seem to have snagged lightning in a champagne bottle with their spare, sophisticated space that sells high-end designer labels, European casual wear, exclusive sneakers, vintage sunglasses, and accessories. It's perfect for pop stars and aspiring DJs, with prices that range from rational to ridiculous.

MAP 3: 3145 Peachtree Rd. NE, 404/869-3310, www.moda404.com; Mon.-Sat. noon-10pm

ONWARD RESERVE

Southern gentility lives on at Onward Reserve. The boutique opened in 2013, two years after the company's launch in Athens—which may help explain the decor's intoxicating blend of frat house man cave and hunting lodge. Lucky customers can sip free beer (offered sporadically) while browsing the shop's preppy polos, khakis, and bowties. Onward Reserve is a go-to spot to gear up for the Kentucky Derby or replace your boat shoes before the Georgia-Florida game.

MAP 3: 3072 Early St. NW, 404/814-8997, www.onwardreserve.com; Mon.-Sat. 10am-6pm, Sun. noon-5pm

SALONS, SPAS, AND BEAUTY
GLOWDRY

Unlike certain Buckhead salons that seem to spike their prices based solely on the location, Glowdry delivers exceptional services that won't break your budget. It opened in 2013 and soon attracted a loyal following thanks to its one-stop-shop approach to pampering. Clients get comfy in one of 12 salon chairs and are handed iPads to browse. Services come with a complimentary flute of champagne, plus a scalp massage—not a bad deal for $45.

MAP 3: 3722 Roswell Rd. NE, 404/549-8007, www.myglowdry.com; Mon.-Wed. 7am-7pm, Thurs.-Fri. 7am-8pm, Sat. 8am-8pm

ONA ATLANTA

The name means "she" in Polish, an appropriate shorthand for this girly luxury boutique run by a pair of sisters. Owners Sarah and Jenny Bronczek bring style and lighthearted sophistication to the shop's assortment of beauty products, home accessories, and gifts. It's a great place to pamper yourself with deluxe bubble bath or artisan body oil, or find a unique present for a new mom (stuffed animals, picture frames, scented candles).

MAP 3: 3400 Around Lenox Rd., 404/812-0002, www.onaatlanta.com; Mon.-Sat. 10am-6pm

SUGARCOAT

An explosion of girly pink and white furnishings accented by a crystal chandelier, Sugarcoat pampers its clients with manicure and pedicure services that feel lifted straight out of a chick flick. First-time clients are given their own personal pouch of nail tools—files, toe separators, pumice stones—that they bring back on subsequent visits, a testament to the shop's obsession with sanitation. The store also sells scents, bath goods, and small gift items. Sugarcoat also has a Virginia-Highland location (1062 St. Charles Ave., 404/249-0013, Tues.-Sat. 10am-7pm, Sun. noon-6pm).

MAP 3: 256 Pharr Rd. NE, 404/814-2121, www.sugarcoatbeauty.com; Tues.-Sat. 10am-7pm, Sun. noon-6pm

SHOES
JEFFREY ATLANTA

Jeffrey Kalinsky, a former buyer for Barneys, built his fashion fiefdom with boutiques in Atlanta and New York's Meatpacking District. His Phipps Plaza location showcases high-end footwear from the likes of Manolo Blahnik, Gianvito Rossi, and Saint Laurent. The strikingly minimal store-front is heavy on attitude and selective about merchandise. Beyond shoes, the boutique carries ready-to-wear accessories, handbags, jewelry, and fra-grances by top designers. The staff can be standoffish to customers who aren't dressed to impress.

MAP 3: Phipps Plaza, 3500 Peachtree Rd. NE, 404/237-9000, www.jeffreynewyork.com; Mon.-Wed. and Fri. 10am-8pm, Thurs. 10am-9pm, Sat. 10am-7pm, Sun. 12:30pm-6pm

SHOPPING MALLS
★ LENOX SQUARE MALL

Lenox Square Mall has been one of the city's premier gathering places for half a century. Originally an open-air shopping center, it was enclosed in the early 1970s and has gone through many renovations, including a 2014 revamp that greatly improved the ground-floor food court. The result is a sprawling, upscale urban mall with 250 shops spread out over four levels. Anchor stores include Macy's, Bloomingdale's, and Neiman Marcus; you'll also find Burberry, Cartier, and Prada.

MAP 3: 3393 Peachtree Rd. NE, 404/233-6767, www.lenoxsquare.com; Mon.-Sat. 10am-9pm, Sun. noon-6pm

PHIPPS PLAZA

Diagonally across Peachtree Road from Lenox Square Mall sits its sibling property, Phipps Plaza. The playing field between these two shopping malls has leveled over the years, though Phipps retains the edge in terms of upmarket atmosphere and clientele. Specialty shops include Kate Spade, Gucci, and Giorgio Armani. Saks Fifth Avenue, Nordstrom, and Belk are the largest tenants. In 2012, Phipps Plaza scrapped its food court and re-placed most of the top level with Legoland Discovery Center.

MAP 3: 3500 Peachtree Rd. NE, 404/262-0992, www.phippsplaza.com; Mon.-Sat. 10am-9pm, Sun. noon-5:30pm

TOYS
★ RICHARD'S VARIETY STORE

While some aisles feature stuff found in most any pharmacy (light bulbs, reading glasses), Richard's Variety can't conceal its true colors as an unpre-dictable menagerie of toys, provocative gifts, costumes, and party supplies. The family-owned store opened in 1951—which may explain its affinity for all things retro. From Baby Boomer lunch boxes to Halloween costumes you might remember from childhood, Richard's offers a fun flashback to the five-and-dime era with prices that are still competitive. A second

location in Midtown (931 Monroe Dr., Ste. 113, 404/879-9877, Mon.-Sat.
10am-8pm, Sun. noon-6pm) carries similar kitschy goods and home accessories in a larger space.

MAP 3: 2347 Peachtree Rd., 404/237-1412, www.richardsvarietystore.com; Mon.-Sat. 10am-6pm, Sun. 12:30pm-5:30pm

Virginia-Highland   Map 4

ANTIQUES
PARIS ON PONCE

A visit to this 46,000-square-foot complex evokes a lazy afternoon exploring the shops of the Montmartre, sans tourists. The maze of showrooms divided into multiple small (and always surprising) chambers displays a menagerie of antiques, vintage furniture, offbeat art, and various other oddities from Europe and America. The selection turns over frequently, making each visit a fresh adventure into a foreign land. Its events space, Le Maison Rouge, hosts private parties and occasional performances.

MAP 4: 716 Ponce de Leon Pl. NE, 404/249-9965, www.parisonponce.com; Mon.-Sat. 11am-6pm, Sun. noon-6pm

GOURMET TREATS
ALON'S

Part café, part gourmet market, Alon Balshan's original Virginia-Highland bakery opened in 1992 and quickly expanded to include prepared foods, wine, flowers, and an artisan cheese selection with more than 120 varieties from local and international producers. The mouthwatering sandwiches and soups bring in a full lunch business, but Alon's is probably still best known as a bakery, with fresh breads made daily and some of the most delicious cakes and cookies in the city.

MAP 4: 1394 N. Highland Ave. NE, 678/397-1781, www.alons.com; Mon.-Fri. 7am-9pm, Sat. 8am-9pm, Sun. 9am-7pm

TOSCANO & SONS ITALIAN MARKET

Authentic Italian delis may be neighborhood fixtures in New York or Philadelphia, but a place like Toscano & Sons feels like a novelty in Atlanta. This busy, family-run grocery and deli is a welcoming wonderland for foodies thanks to its assortment of fine meats, cheeses, dried pastas, sauces, and sweets. The panini are known as some of the best in town. Open since 2007, Toscano & Sons relocated to the heart of Virginia-Highland in 2013.

MAP 4: 1050 N. Highland Ave. NE, 404/815-8383, www.toscanoandsons.com; Mon.-Sat. 11am-7pm, Sun. noon-6pm

MARKETS
MORNINGSIDE FARMERS MARKET

Morningside's year-round produce market has been a favorite in since the late 1980s. It's held every Saturday, rain or shine, and features only local vendors (who live no more than two hours outside the city). Look for certified organically grown fruits and vegetables, freshly baked breads, handmade soaps, floral arrangements, and seasonal surprises. The small market can be very crowded; arrive early to catch the cooking demonstrations by local chefs held at 9:30am.

MAP 4: 1393 N. Highland Ave. NE, 404/313-5784, www.morningsidemarket.com; Sat. 8am-11:30am

PETS
HIGHLAND PET SUPPLY

Animal lovers purr over the huge selection of high-end accessories, organic pet foods, and treats at this locally owned pet emporium. The store's crafty do-it-yourself dog-wash area is another a crowd-pleaser, featuring elevated tubs, shampoos, towels, and blow dryers. Known for friendly customer service, Highland Pet Supply offers a five-week off-site training program designed to change unruly pups into courteous canines.

MAP 4: 1186 N. Highland Ave. NE, 404/892-5900, www.highlandpet.com; Mon.-Fri. 9am-8pm, Sat. 9am-7pm, Sun. 10am-6pm

TOYS
BLABLA

The sheer variety of knitted goodies at Blabla is noteworthy: plush toys, crib mobiles, pillows, rattles, and more. In business since 2001, this imaginative Virginia-Highland doll house keeps updating its line of Peruvian hand-crafted wares. The real stars of the show come from the endearing collection of knitted animal buddies with names like Mcnuttie the Squirrel and Sardine the Cat. The products are aimed for the pre-school set; the price tags can be anything but pint-sized.

MAP 4: 1189 Virginia Ave. NE, 404/875-6496, www.blablakids.com; Mon.-Fri. 10am-6pm, Sat. 11am-4pm

WOMEN'S CLOTHING
BILL HALLMAN

Almost two decades ago, Bill Hallman helped introduce a certain flavor of fashion-forward looks to Atlanta. These days the number of rival shops has exploded, but Hallman's boutiques keep current via constant reinvention. The flagship Virginia-Highland store features up-to-the-minute collections of midrange designer labels, denim, shoes, and accessories (including killer sunglasses) for women and men. The emphasis is on a young, well-heeled clientele; the prices can be anything but budget-friendly. In 2015, Hallman closed his Buckhead outpost and launched a new hybrid location in Inman Park (299 N. Highland Ave., Suite Q, 404/814-0030), offering more moderately priced goods for women and men, along with custom tailoring services.

MAP 4: 792 N. Highland Ave. NE, 404/876-6055, www.billhallman.com; Mon.-Tues. noon-8pm, Wed.-Thurs. 11am-9pm, Fri.-Sat. 11am-10pm, Sun. noon-7pm

Clockwise from top left: Psycho Sisters Consignment; Henry and June; Paris on Ponce.

It didn't take long for this new kid on the block to create a buzz in Virginia-Highland—a caffeine buzz. The unconventional boutique's in-house espresso bar serves hand-picked coffees from micro-roasters and home-made baked goods. This perk may seem like a gimmick, but it's an integral part of the vision. The café-meets-fashion gallery sells modern, high-end casual wear for women and men sourced from independent designers. The price tags on certain items may provide an extra jolt.

MAP 4: 784 N. Highland Ave. NE, 470/355/9751, www.henryandjuneatl.com, Mon.-Wed. 8am-6pm, Thurs.-Fri. 8am-7pm, Sat. 9am-8pm, Sun. 9am-6pm

310 ROSEMONT

In case of a fashion emergency, 310 Rosemont has your back. The chic Virginia-Highland boutique prides itself on outstanding customer service and a policy of opening early or staying late in case of a couture crisis. The inventory is selective and covers a lot of bases: flirty skirts, cocktail attire, and accessories for women; blazers, bowties, and cufflinks for men; high-end denim for both. This is one shop best enjoyed if money isn't an object.

MAP 4: 1038 N. Highland Ave. NE, 404/249-5326, www.310rosemont.com; Mon.-Sat. 11am- 7pm, Sun. noon-6pm

Little Five Points and East Atlanta

Map 5

ACCESSORIES
THE BEEHIVE

The alarmists who howled that an invasion of chain stores would destroy the indie spirit of Little Five Points should make a beeline for the Beehive, a shop about as homegrown and unique as they come. This "boutique collective" only carries products created by independent designers, transforming the Etsy ethos into brick-and-mortar reality. Apparel, accessories, and jewelry make up a big portion of the inventory, though there are also bath products, pet foods, and paper goods.

MAP 5: 1250 Caroline St. NE, Ste. C120, 404/581-9261, www.thebeehiveatl.com; Mon.-Sat. 11am-7pm, Sun. noon-5pm

YOUNG BLOOD BOUTIQUE

The name says plenty: Young Blood Boutique channels a youthful, in-your-face attitude with its quirky, urban-inspired goods. The Poncey-Highland boutique is the spin-off of a longstanding art gallery. When new owners Rebecca Hanna and Jessie White took over in 2013, they retained plenty of the former space's hipster cred while focusing on handcrafted wares such as jewelry, fragrances, home accessories, and a cornucopia of other one-of-a-kind creations from local artists.

MAP 5: 636 N. Highland Ave. NE, 404/254-4127, www.youngbloodgallery.com; Sun.-Thurs. noon-8pm, Fri.-Sat. noon-9pm

Antiques Heaven

The sprawling Lakewood Antiques Market was an Atlanta tradition for more than 20 years, drawing upwards of 12,000 customers to its monthly wonderland of vintage treasures. Held in the Spanish colonial livestock exhibition halls at the historic Lakewood Fairgrounds near the airport, the acclaimed event shut down in 2006.

The good news for antiques addicts is that the show continues north of the city near the tiny town of Cumming. **Lakewood 400 Antiques Market** (1321 Atlanta Hwy., 770/889-3400, www.lakewoodantiques.com; Fri. 9am-5pm, Sat. 9am-6pm, Sun. 10am-5pm; $3) takes place the third weekend of each month in a 75,000-square-foot showroom with more than 500 dealer spaces and an on-site restaurant. The featured merchandise tends to be a captivating hodgepodge of high-end furniture, classic jewelry, pop-culture artifacts, and bizarre bric-a-brac. Reaching the Lakewood 400 Antiques Market requires at least a 40-minute drive from the city center up Georgia State Route 400, but it's well worth the effort.

ANTIQUES
CITY ISSUE

It seems strange to call City Issue an "antiques store." Though the inventory of furniture and home accessories is totally vintage, don't expect the dust-covered lamps or gaudy glass doodads found in other stores around town. City Issues specializes in midcentury modern pieces for the home and office: 1970s swivel chairs, tuxedo-style 1960s sofas, groovy credenzas, moody oil paintings. Not a destination for bargain hunters, but a must for anyone with an interest in classic furniture.

MAP 5: 325 Elizabeth St. NE, 678/999-9075, www.cityissue.com; Sun.-Mon. noon-5pm, Tues. and Thurs.-Sat. 11am-7pm

KABOODLE

Kaboodle, a combination furniture gallery and gift shop, is on a mission to bring urban tastemakers back to East Atlanta Village's hit-or-miss retail strip. The locally crafted furniture evokes a casual style that's edgy enough to be interesting without being outlandish. The shop deserves props for its clever accessories and gifts, from candles and picture frames to cheeky magnets and retro glassware. Check out the cool line of nostalgic Atlanta artwork.

MAP 5: 485B Flat Shoals Ave. SE, 404/522-3006, Tues.-Fri. noon-8pm, Sat. 11am-9pm, Sun. noon-6pm

BOOKS AND MUSIC
A CAPPELLA BOOKS

A Cappella Books is a proud survivor of the ongoing war between big-box retailers and independent booksellers. The closet-sized shop almost overflows with new, used, and rare titles. Owner Frank Reiss pays particular emphasis to Southern and local authors, though he confesses that his interests in ancient history, baseball, and country music also inform the inventory. A Cappella's impact on the local literary community is gigantic, thanks to an exceptional series of author appearances.

MAP 5: 208 Haralson Ave., 404/681-5128, www.acappellabooks.com; Mon.-Sat. 11am-7pm, Sun. noon-6pm

CHARIS BOOKS AND MORE

Hailed as the South's oldest and largest feminist bookstore, Charis Books has served as a de facto community center for Little Five Points since 1974. The homey, accommodating shop offers a full line of fiction and nonfiction titles of interest to women, including a comprehensive catalog of progressive and lesbian literature. It also carries children's books and music by independent artists. **Charis Circle** (www.chariscircle.org), the nonprofit programming arm of the bookstore, hosts frequent events, including writing groups, social justice seminars, poetry readings, and author appearances.

MAP 5: 1189 Euclid Ave. NE, 404/524-0304, www.charisbooksandmore.com; Mon.-Sat. 11am-7pm, Sun. noon-6pm

★ CRIMINAL RECORDS

Criminal Records sells new albums, vintage vinyl, underground comics, offbeat periodicals, bizarre toys, and artwork to a discerning, hip clientele. The store opened in 1991 and has weathered the odds to become one of Atlanta's last independently owned record shops. It's the kind of place where you'll find obscure indie gold, turntable accessories, punk rock T-shirts, and graphic novels. Criminal features an unrivaled series of in-store events, ranging from concerts to some raucous book signings.

MAP 5: 1154A Euclid Ave. NE, 404/215-9511, www.criminalatl.com; Mon.-Sat. 11am-9pm, Sun. noon-7pm

WAX 'N' FACTS

Fact: Wax 'N' Facts is one of the city's oldest record stores. Opinion: It's also among the best. This dusty Little Five Points vinyl shop must be doing something right to have stayed in business since 1976. Much of the clientele consists of hardcore vinyl junkies obliviously digging through the stacks. The store specializes in used and hard-to-find vinyl, organized in a system that might make you snap were it not for the staff's encyclopedic knowledge.

MAP 5: 432 Moreland Ave. NE, 404/525-2275, www.waxnfacts.com; Mon.-Sat. 11am-8pm, Sun. noon-6pm

GIFTS AND SPECIALTY
★ JUNKMAN'S DAUGHTER

Junkman's Daughter has been peddling tacky knickknacks, obscure collectibles, and pop-culture detritus since 1982. The 10,000-square-foot bazaar includes rack after rack of hipster apparel for guys and girls, crass housewares, offbeat picture books, and more *A Nightmare Before Christmas* goodies than anyone other than Tim Burton knew existed. Browse the shoe department upstairs, or peek inside the fully stocked tobacco shop in back. Just be careful not to provoke the sales staff, who are notoriously surly.

MAP 5: 464 Moreland Ave. NE, 404/577-3188, www.thejunkmansdaughter.com; Mon.-Fri. 11am-7pm, Sat. 11am-8pm, Sun. noon-7pm

167

MARKETS
KROG STREET MARKET

Opened in 2014, the updated 1920s warehouse offers a range of homegrown restaurants and watering holes, as well as a mix of market stalls selling wares such as artisan soaps, greeting cards, and one-of-a-kind chocolates.

MAP 5: 99 Krog St. NE, 770/434-2400, www.krogstreetmarket.com; Mon.-Thurs. 7am-9pm., Fri. 7am-10pm, Sat. 8am-10pm, Sun. 8am-9pm

SALONS, SPAS, AND BEAUTY
FIG & FLOWER

Fig & Flower saves customers the hassle of researching the additives that go into beauty products. Founded on a passion for clean living and green consciousness, this welcoming "eco-beauty bar" only carries goods that use natural, non-toxic environmentally friendly ingredients and haven't been tested on animals. The broad inventory offers much more than makeup: fragrances, shampoos, shave soap for men, even natural dishwasher gels—with prices that are usually only a bit higher than pharmacies.

MAP 5: 636 N. Highland Ave. NE, 404/998-8198, www.shopfigandflower.com; Mon.-Sat. 11am-7pm, Sun. 11am-5pm

SHOES
ABBADABBA'S

Abbadabba's has grown into a local chain of casual footwear warehouses with four Atlanta locations. The original Little Five Points store has been a treasure trove of offbeat fashions since 1981. Though brands such as Toms, Clarks, and Dansko are represented heavily, Abbadabba's is best known for sandals. The Buckhead location (4389 Roswell Rd., 404/262-3356) became Georgia's first Birkenstock Specialty Store in 1998, with the other locations quickly following suit, a designation that gives the chain a greater selection than other dealers.

MAP 5: 421B Moreland Ave. NE, 404/588-9577, www.coolshoes.com; Mon.-Sat. 10am-7:30pm, Sun. noon-6pm

VINTAGE CLOTHING
THE CLOTHING WAREHOUSE

This homegrown emporium of gently used threads has been luring college students and aspiring hipsters to Little Five Points since 1992. The always-busy Moreland Avenue cornerstone carries a huge inventory of classic T-shirts, dresses, and denim. It probably won't ever win customers based on bargain prices—you'll find similar stuff much cheaper at most any large thrift store—but the Clothing Warehouse culls out the fashion don'ts for a selection that's suitably ironic and trendy.

MAP 5: 420 Moreland Ave. NE, 404/524-5070, www.theclothingwarehouse.com; Mon.-Thurs. 11am-8pm, Fri.-Sat. 11am-8:30pm, Sun. noon-7pm

PSYCHO SISTERS CONSIGNMENT

Psycho Sisters can't resist clothes on the crazy side. The tiny Little Five Points consignment shop buys and sells rockstar-ready fashions as well as miscellaneous casual duds, from vintage polyester disco pants to 1980s miniskirts and top hats. The store gets wild around Halloween, when seemingly every would-be hippie, pimp, and go-go kitten in town crams inside searching for the fullest pink boa. Check out the concert T-shirts and always eye-catching display of sunglasses. Its sister location in Sandy Springs (5964 Roswell Rd.,404/255-5578, Mon.-Sat. 11am-7pm) delivers a similar but slightly more tame selection.

MAP 5: 428 Moreland Ave. NE, 404/523-0100, www.psycho-sisters.com; Sun.-Tues. 11am-8pm, Wed.-Thurs. 10am-8pm, Fri. 10am-9pm, Sat. 10am-10pm

WOMEN'S CLOTHING
WISH

Remember the late 1990s, when you prowled thrift stores searching for just the right baby-T and track pants to wear to the next rave? Wish recalls those halcyon days of dancing until dawn, the era when this Little Five Points boutique established its reputation for envelope-pushing club gear. The shop carries fashions for women and men, watches, belts, bags, and offbeat home accessories. The aesthetic feels more hip-hop than hipster.

MAP 5: 447 Moreland Ave. NE, 404/880-0402, www.wishatl.com; Mon.-Sat. noon-8pm, Sun. 1pm-7pm

Decatur   Map 6

BOOKS AND MUSIC
LITTLE SHOP OF STORIES

This too-cute-for-words neighborhood hideaway is guaranteed to put smiles on the faces of readers no matter if they're 9 or 90. The warmly lit independent bookseller specializes in children's books, including activity kits, toys, funky gadgets, puzzles, and much more. While titles aimed at young readers dominate the shelves, you'll also notice a smattering of general-interest books. The bookstore maintains a full calendar of story readings, book clubs, theme parties, and author events.

MAP 6: 133A East Court Square, Decatur, 404/373-6300, www.littleshopofstories.com; Mon.-Wed. 10am-8pm, Thurs.-Sat. 10am-9pm, Sun. noon-8pm

GIFTS AND SPECIALTY
HELIOTROPE

"Good things for good people," says the motto of Heliotrope, a fanciful bazaar that doesn't land into any one category. Items on hand range from zany gag gifts, kitchen tools, and stylish home accessories to watches, jewelry, and heaps of miscellanea. It's perfect for grownups who never quite parted ways with their middle-school selves, a fun source for drumstick pencils, heat-sensitive coffee mugs, and Uglydoll plush toys. Heliotrope fits well into the crazy quilt of Decatur storefronts.

MAP 6: 248 W. Ponce de Leon Ave., Decatur, 404/371-0100, www.heliotropehome.com; Mon.-Sat. 10am-9pm, Sun. 11am-7pm

WILD OATS AND BILLY GOATS

Actual billy goats are not included. However, furry and feathered barnyard animals do figure prominently in this endearing Decatur gallery/gift store. The shop deals in handcrafted works created by local and regional folk artists, everything from ceramics and paintings to jewelry and hand-sewn plush toys. Its DIY aesthetic tends to have a rugged, self-taught vibe, with pieces designed with plenty of humor and whimsy. The store hosts painting classes for adults and art-making parties for kids.

MAP 6: 112 E. Ponce de Leon Ave., Decatur, 404/378-4088, www.wildoatsandbillygoats. com; Mon.-Thurs. 11am-7pm, Fri. 11am-8pm, Sat. 11am-9pm, Sun. 1pm-6pm

SALONS, SPAS, AND BEAUTY
SALON RED

This local chain of salons strives to offer a "creative, compassionate environment" (according to its mission statement) to bring out the best in clients, which means a full selection of professional beauty services in a clean, modern environment. The Candler Park location (1642 DeKalb Ave., 404/373-2868, Tues.-Thurs. 10am-8pm, Fri. 9am-8pm, Sat. 8am-7pm, Sun. 10am-6pm) includes a day spa, offering massage and reflexology, while **Salon Red Kids** (123 E. Ponce de Leon Ave., 404/377-6230, Tues.-Wed., Fri., Sun. 10am-6pm, Thurs. 10am-7pm, Sat. 9am-6pm) is a true rarity: a barber shop designed for the squirming set.

MAP 6: 119 E. Ponce de Leon Ave., Decatur, 404/377-3164, www.salonred.com; Mon.-Thurs. 10am-8pm, Fri. 9am-7pm, Sat. 8am-7pm, Sun. 10am-6pm

Hotels

PRICE KEY
⑤ Less than $150 per night
⑤⑤ $150–250 per night
⑤⑤⑤ More than $250 per night

Atlanta consistently ranks in the top tier of U.S. cities in terms of hotel inventory. Of the nearly 100,000 hotel rooms in the metropolitan area, almost 12,000 are within an eight-block area of Downtown. The apparent surplus in the lodging category isn't an accident: The city's robust conven-

tion industry brings more than a million business travelers to the Georgia World Congress Center each year—and that's only one of several large exhibition halls around town. The Downtown tourist district offers a surplus of brand-name chain hotels and luxury high-rises. Urban explorers coming to Atlanta for pleasure should look beyond the skyscrapers to get an authentic, street-level view of the city.

Buckhead abounds with luxurious high-rises representing some of the most sophisticated accommodations in the South, and also some of the most expensive. Even if your budget won't allow a stay in one of these lavish glass towers, the hotels can be worth a visit for their swanky bars, restaurants, and day spas. The same is true for the high-end properties in Midtown. The neighborhood offers a mixed range of options.

As in other cities, Atlanta has seen a bump in boutique hotels, designer properties that tend to be smaller and dripping with a heady sense of style. A few international hotel brands have attempted to get in on the action, offering their own answers to the concept. Atlanta has also experienced an influx of properties that are mixed-use: posh condo towers with a designated number of hotel rooms included. It's a harder task to locate a well-regarded bed-and-breakfast in the city; intown options have long been limp in the category, especially for budget-minded travelers. With a few

Previous: Shellmont Inn; Westin Buckhead Atlanta.

Highlights

★ **Best New Hotel:** A pricey renovation transformed a once-drab property into the chic (yet affordable) **Aloft Atlanta Downtown**, aimed at younger, tech-savvy travelers. (page 174).

★ **Most Dramatic Lobby:** The dramatic 47-story atrium at the **Atlanta Marriott Marquis** has been a much-photographed Downtown landmark since 1985 (page 174).

★ **Best Hotel for Kids:** With plenty of room for the family to spread out, **Embassy Suites Atlanta at Centennial Olympic Park** is convenient to some of the city's main kid-friendly attractions, including the Georgia Aquarium and the World of Coca-Cola (page 174).

★ **Best Spot for Sports Fans:** The **Omni Hotel at CNN Center** connects to Philips Arena (home of the Hawks and the Thrashers) and is an easy walk to the Georgia Dome (home of the Falcons) and the College Football Hall of Fame and Fan Experience (page 176).

★ **Most Historic Hotel:** Dating back to 1911, the **Georgian Terrace** famously hosted Vivien Leigh and Clark Gable for the 1939 *Gone With the Wind* premiere (page 179).

★ **Best Spa:** Midtown's **Loews Atlanta Hotel** stands out not only for its refined style and convenient location, but also for its access to the classes and services at Exhale spa (page 179).

★ **Best Bed-and-Breakfast:** Historic **Stonehurst Place** has become one of Atlanta's most poised and welcoming inns (page 180).

★ **Best Place to Film a Reality Show:** It's tempting to party like a champagne-swilling "real housewife" at the sexy **W Atlanta Midtown** (page 180).

★ **Best Suburban Hotspot:** Though it's geared toward high-end business travelers, Dunwoody's **Le Méridien Atlanta Perimeter** is a pleasure for anyone (page 184).

CHOOSING A HOTEL

It may seem like a no-brainer, but selecting the best hotel has everything to do with location—or, more specifically, transportation. If you're planning to visit Atlanta and not rent a car, it's essential to find a property with effortless access to public transit or within walking distance of the sights you want to experience. Travelers on a mission to take in the city's most obvious tourist attractions—including the Georgia Aquarium, CNN Center, and the Martin Luther King Jr. National Historic Site—will probably want to stick with a hotel in pedestrian-friendly Downtown. Keep in mind that the availability of rooms downtown can depend greatly on what conventions are going on around town. Add to that the usual weekday business travelers and you may find that some properties have limited availability for certain dates. Downtown hotels run the full gamut from budget-busters to bare-bones options.

A hotel in Midtown can be a great choice for folks whose itineraries will take them to several different areas of town, thanks to the neighborhood's central location. Visitors out to get a taste of Atlanta's arts scene should consider staying here. Many properties in Midtown are within walking distance of the High Museum of Art, Piedmont Park, and the Atlanta Botanical Garden. The area's three MARTA stations can connect you to parts of the rest of the city.

Staying in Buckhead can be an unforgettable and extravagant experience, and it will also land you in the lap of Atlanta's ritziest shopping and dining district. At the same time, the neighborhood is removed from the best museums and sights. Though MARTA runs along Peachtree Road, the subway isn't necessarily an ideal choice for getting to other areas of town.

For the cheapest, no-frills hotels, the district around Hartsfield-Jackson Atlanta International Airport is overflowing with familiar chain properties. Tempting as it might be to try to save a few bucks, staying near the airport can make getting in and out of the city a major hassle.

Because Atlanta has no lack of ubiquitous chain hotels, this chapter attempts to focus on more distinctive properties, including brand-name hotels that qualify as iconic Atlanta institutions. All rates listed here are based on double occupancy in the high season (June-August). Many hotels include parking services, with prices around $15-20 per day.

HOTELS

Downtown

Map 1

★ ALOFT ATLANTA DOWNTOWN ❸

Aloft Atlanta Downtown bills itself as a "tech-forward innovation hub for millennial-minded travelers." Sounds pretty fancy for a former Days Inn, but it's obvious that big money went into the sweeping makeover of the 258-room property in 2014. Aloft's technology options live up to the hype: free Wi-Fi throughout the hotel, high-end AV equipment in conference rooms, plug-and-play connectivity in rooms. The vibrant **Re:mix** lounge features a pool table and a fun atmosphere for mingling.

MAP 1: 300 Spring St. NW, 678/515-0300, www.aloftatlantadowntown.com

★ ATLANTA MARRIOTT MARQUIS ❸❸

The graceful Marriott Marquis may be familiar to younger guests thanks to its appearances in the second and third *Hunger Games* films. The John Portman-designed 50-story convention hotel remains one of the city's architectural gems, with a jaw-dropping atrium that spans the height of the building. A much-needed $138 million renovation updated all of the 1,663 guest rooms back in 2007; the hotel is due for another brush-up. The main bar, **Pulse** (404/586-6081, www.pulsebaratlanta.com, Mon.-Sun. 3pm-1am), is particularly metropolitan and sexy.

MAP 1: 265 Peachtree Center Ave. NE, 404/521-0000, www.marriott.com

ELLIS HOTEL ❸❸

On a busy stretch of Peachtree Street, a short walk to the neighborhood's attractions, the intimate Ellis features 127 rooms and suites appointed with 32-inch LCD televisions and beds with ritzy ostrich-leather headboards. The hotel brings something unusual to the Atlanta market: a women's-only floor with extra security and private spa access. There's also a "fresh-air floor," featuring rooms treated to cut allergens and with air-filtering machines. The property is definitely geared toward business travelers.

MAP 1: 176 Peachtree St. NE, 404/523-5155, www.ellishotel.com

★ EMBASSY SUITES ATLANTA AT CENTENNIAL OLYMPIC PARK ❸❸

This eight-story all-suite property gets high marks for its location next to Centennial Olympic Park and near other popular tourist spots. All suites come with a separate living room with sleeper sofa, refrigerator, microwave, coffeemaker, and two televisions. It's a great option for families. Don't miss the view of the skyline from the rooftop pool. Plan ahead if you want to check out **Ruth's Chris Steak House** (404/223-6500, www.ruthschris.com, daily 11am-11pm) in the hotel lobby; reservations are definitely encouraged.

MAP 1: 267 Marietta St. NW, 404/223-2300, www.atlantacentennialpark.embassysuites.com

Downtown Deals

The average cost of a hotel room in metro Atlanta is around $98 per night. The key word here is "metro": Finding a reasonably priced room—that is, less than $150 per night, can be a tall order in the inner city. Even Downtown with its lion's share of lodging has a tendency to inflate prices depending upon demand, which fluctuates wildly with the convention calendar.

Visitors bent on staying downtown but who don't want to spend a month's salary on accommodations aren't completely out of luck. A little digging will usually turn up decent deals at some of the nearby chain properties. One standout is the **Hilton Garden Inn Atlanta Downtown** (275 Baker St., 404/577-2001, www.hiltongardeninn.hilton.com), a polite 242-room midrise in a prime location near Centennial Olympic Park.

The **Hyatt Place Atlanta Downtown** (330 Peachtree St., 404/577-1980, http://atlantadowntown.place.hyatt.com) has benefited from room updates in recent years. The 10-floor property may be especially attractive for budget travelers headed to AmericasMart.

It can also be a good idea to widen your search for bargains beyond the core of the tourist district. **Hampton Inn Atlanta Georgia Tech Downtown** (244 North Ave., 404/881-0881, http://hamptoninn.hilton.com) delivers a lot of bang for the buck in a location that's handy to the Georgia Tech campus and a quick MARTA hop to Downtown's attractions.

Heading south, the independent **Castleberry Inn** (186 Northside Dr. SW, 404/893-4663, www.castleberryinn.com) promises no-frills guest rooms for less than $100 per night. Located on the less desirable side of the Georgia Dome, the hotel may be one of Downtown's best-kept secrets. (Just don't go wandering into Vine City after dark.)

GLENN HOTEL ⊙⊙

The Glenn Hotel, billed as Downtown's "first boutique hotel," is tucked in a historic building near Centennial Olympic Park. The Marriott property's 110 rooms can be on the cramped side but make up for their lack of space with unique details, such as Herman Miller Aeron chairs and soothing rain showerheads. Be aware that the streets around the hotel see considerable traffic when there are major events at Philips Arena or the Georgia Dome.
MAP 1: 110 Marietta St. NW, 404/521-2250, www.glennhotel.com

HYATT REGENCY ATLANTA ⊙⊙

You can't miss the Hyatt Regency in photos of the Atlanta skyline: It's the building with the funny blue flying saucer up top (actually the rotating **Polaris** restaurant). The property benefited greatly from a sweeping $65 million renovation in 2012. The Hyatt Regency may be one of the best bargains among the big-box convention hotels in Downtown. The 22-story giant features 1,260 guest rooms, three restaurants, and Georgia's largest ballroom.
MAP 1: 265 Peachtree St. NE, 404/577-1234, www.atlantaregency.hyatt.com

★ OMNI HOTEL AT CNN CENTER ❸❸

This 28-story four-star property located within CNN Center is the closest Atlanta comes to Las Vegas-style lodging, with a massive food court, upscale restaurants, convention center, and sports arena all seconds outside your door. The two towers house 1,070 guest rooms with appropriately modern amenities (Chinese granite countertops, Italian marble floors, boutique toiletries, and flat-screen televisions), though rooms in the newer tower, completed in 2003, tend to be better than those in the original building.

MAP 1: 100 CNN Center NW, 404/659-0000, www.omnihotels.com

SOCIAL GOAT BED AND BREAKFAST ❸

This goat farm welcomes guests into six housing options spread out over three buildings. The Grant Park bed-and-breakfast doubles as a sort of petting zoo with resident Nigerian goats (of course), chickens, rabbits, and turkeys—plus three house cats, who must be masters of restraint in the face of such delicious temptation. It's a good value and plenty of fun for kids. Located south of Zoo Atlanta, a 10-minute drive from Downtown.

MAP 1: 548 Robinson Ave. SE, 404/626-4830, http://thesocialgoatbandb.com

TWELVE HOTEL CENTENNIAL PARK ❸❸

Don't let the name fool you: The hotel is actually several blocks from Centennial Olympic Park. Opened in 2007, the 39-story glass tower features 102 hotel suites with full-sized kitchens, 10-foot ceilings, complimentary wireless Internet, and multiple flat-screen TVs. The biggest perk—other than the spectacular views from most balconies—may well be the large size of each room, especially noteworthy given the prices. Twelve's elevated pool deck is also larger than those at most other hotels.

MAP 1: 400 W. Peachtree St. NW, 404/418-1212, www.twelvehotels.com

WESTIN PEACHTREE PLAZA ❸❸❸

The Downtown skyline wouldn't be the same without the Westin Peachtree Plaza, a shining black-glass cylinder that towers 73 stories above the city. The building opened as the tallest hotel in the world in 1976 and was Atlanta's tallest skyscraper for the next decade. Expect the signature features of the Westin brand, including better-than-average bedding and bathroom supplies. The revolving **Sun Dial Restaurant** (404/935-5279, www.sundialrestaurant.com) has been a popular tourist attraction for generations due to its jaw-dropping views.

MAP 1: 210 Peachtree St. NW, 404/881-9898, www.westin.com/peachtree

Midtown

Map 2

ARTMORE HOTEL ATLANTA ❸❸

This multicolored three-story boutique hotel, the reinvention of a historic 1924 apartment building with Spanish accents, appears unassuming from the street, but the interior is a must-see. Featuring 102 rooms, the Artmore has become a popular choice for events thanks partly to its pleasant courtyard and one-of-a-kind fiery fountain. It's a short walk away from Midtown's many museums, including the High Museum of Art, the Museum of Design Atlanta, and the Center for Puppetry Arts.

MAP 2: 1302 W. Peachtree St. NW, 404/876-6100, www.artmorehotel.com

CROWNE PLAZA ATLANTA MIDTOWN ❸❸

The signage at this 501-room Midtown high-rise (the 11th largest hotel in the city) changes with alarming frequency. The former Marriott Renaissance got a swanky makeover to become the Hotel Melia in 2010. Four years later, Crowne Plaza assumed control and launched a major renovation, bringing much-needed updates to the rooms and steering the property toward business travelers. Even more changes are in store for 2016, with 102 rooms being converted to the extended-visit Staybridge Suites brand.

MAP 2: 590 W. Peachtree St. NW, 404/877-9000, www.cpatlantamidtown.com

FOUR SEASONS HOTEL ❸❸❸

For luxury without limits, you can't top the Four Seasons, located near the Woodruff Arts Center, Crescent Avenue's restaurant row, and MARTA. Though the Four Seasons received a five-diamond designation from AAA, its atmosphere and attitude are less stuffy and more casual than you might expect. The service is impeccable. Its celebrated restaurant, **Park 75** (404/253-3840, Mon.-Sat. 6:30am-10pm, Sun. 7am-4pm), does a brisk business independent of hotel guests, with an especially popular afternoon tea. Check out the well-appointed day spa.

MAP 2: 75 14th St. NE, 404/881-9898, www.fourseasons.com/atlanta

GEORGIA TECH HOTEL AND CONFERENCE CENTER ❸

The Georgia Tech Hotel deserves props as a welcome change of pace from the massive glass palaces rising over the city. It's the cornerstone of Georgia Tech's Technology Square, a well-planned urban revitalization project that has brought new life to a once-empty corner of Midtown. The state-of-the-art facility offers pleasant and affordable accommodations. The 252-room property includes an indoor pool, a billiards room, and easy pedestrian access to nearby restaurants, shops, and Georgia Tech's campus.

MAP 2: 800 Spring St. NW, 404/347-9440, www.gatechhotel.com

Clockwise from top left: Westin Peachtree Plaza; The Georgian Terrace; Twelve Hotel Atlantic Station.

★ THE GEORGIAN TERRACE 💲💲

The Georgian Terrace qualifies as a bona fide Atlanta landmark. Built in 1911, the Beaux Arts building was for decades one of the city's grandest hotels, host to Vivien Leigh and Clark Gable for the 1939 *Gone With the Wind* premiere. The **Livingston Restaurant and Bar** (404/897-5000, www.livingstonatlanta.com, Mon.-Thurs. 11am-2:30pm and 5pm-10pm, Fri. 11am-2:30pm and 5pm-11pm, Sat. 10am-3pm and 5pm-11pm, Sun. 10am-3pm and 5pm-10pm) in the lobby draws a crowd of young professionals and theater-goers. The guest rooms, however, can be unpredictable in terms of size and fresh furnishings. Don't miss the stunning view from the rooftop pool.

MAP 2: 659 Peachtree St. NE, 800/651-2316, www.thegeorgianterrace.com

HOTEL INDIGO ATLANTA MIDTOWN 💲💲

Midtown's Hotel Indigo gets high marks for its playful interior design and commitment to using environmentally friendly materials. The rooms tend to be smaller than in some other hotels in the area. The whimsical bar often fills up with a busy pre-show crowd heading to the Fox Theatre. The Indigo is also known as one of the city's most pet-friendly hotels, with a weekly Canine Cocktail Hour for four-legged visitors (and their owners).

MAP 2: 683 Peachtree St. NE, 877/270-1392, www.hotelindigo.com

★ LOEWS ATLANTA HOTEL 💲💲

The development of the Midtown Mile, the bumper crop of flashy glass towers along Peachtree Street south of 14th Street, reached a crescendo with the completion of this 35-story monolith in 2010. The four-star property takes service seriously and offers an unbeatable location near Midtown's best attractions. With 414 rooms and 44 suites, the Loews Atlanta aims for a style that's refined and perhaps more understated than some of the other high-end hotels around town. Its spa, **Exhale** (404/720-5000, www.exhalespa.com, Mon.-Fri. 6am-10pm, Sat.-Sun. 8am-8pm), on the seventh floor is a must-see: posh and pricey.

MAP 2: 1065 Peachtree St. NE, 888/563-9736, www.loewshotels.com/atlanta-hotel

RENAISSANCE ATLANTA MIDTOWN HOTEL 💲💲

The short-lived Palomar Hotel, an opulent high-rise that shot up in 2009, went through only a moderate makeover two years later to become to the Renaissance Atlanta Midtown Hotel. The 21-floor Marriott property retains plenty of the swanky atmosphere of its previous concept, with a contemporary lobby area, lovely rooftop deck, and designer-inspired decor. Its rates can be a bit more down-to-earth than nearby hotels. Located on the Georgia Tech trolley stop for easy access to campus.

MAP 2: 866 W. Peachtree St. NW, 678/412-2400, www.renaissanceatlantamidtown.com

HOTELS
MIDTOWN

SHELLMONT INN 💲💲

The Shellmont Inn, a lovingly restored 1891 Victorian home on the National Register of Historic Places, looks like a photo spread from *Southern Living* brought to life. The six-room inn drips with antiques and authentic Southern charm. Shared meals are served twice daily, and the property features multiple porches for relaxing, as well as a Victorian fishpond out back. The innkeepers, Debbie and Ed McCord, are gracious without being overbearing and treat guests more like friends than strangers.

MAP 2: 821 Piedmont Ave. NE, 404/872-9290, www.shellmont.com

★ STONEHURST PLACE 💲💲💲

This charming 1896 estate was the home of a prominent Atlanta family for more than 100 years before becoming a bed-and-breakfast. A $1 million renovation brought the home back to its former grandeur in 2008. Stonehurst Place has established itself as one of the more plush—and pricey—inns in the city, with five lavishly appointed rooms and amenities aimed at the boutique hotel clientele (free wireless Internet, flat-screen televisions, iPod charging stations, luxury linens).

MAP 2: 923 Piedmont Ave. NE, 404/881-0722, www.stonehurstplace.com; MARTA: Midtown

TWELVE HOTEL ATLANTIC STATION 💲💲

The 26-story Twelve Hotel is split between residential units and hotel rooms, giving each of the 101 suites a homey, condominium feel, with large kitchens, comfortable bathrooms, and flat-screen televisions in every room. Wide balconies deliver splendid views of the city skyline, though recent construction has obscured the sight lines of some units. The hotel's prime location puts the restaurants and shops of Atlantic Station within a four-block radius, including a grocery store, gym, and cinema.

MAP 2: 361 17th St. NW, 404/961-1212, www.twelvehotels.com

★ W ATLANTA MIDTOWN 💲💲

The W Atlanta Midtown feels like a slice of South Beach had been transplanted to 14th Street. The 28-story black box features no lack of amenities aimed at a fun-loving younger clientele, from 37-inch flat-screen TVs with laptop plug-ins to iPod-ready clock radios. The pricey lobby bar, **Whiskey Park** (404/724-2550, daily 11am-2am), brings in an attractive, sometimes unruly crowd, though weekends are not the mob scene they used to be. While the standard rooms are cozy and cool, the expensive Wow Suite is truly a spectacle, with a built-in bar, two-person bathtub, and a den ready for *Love & Hip Hop Atlanta*.

MAP 2: 188 14th St. NE, 404/892-6000, www.whotels.com/atlantamidtown

Buckhead
Map 3

GRAND HYATT ATLANTA $$

Buckhead's Grand Hyatt Atlanta features 439 rooms in two 25-story towers on Peachtree Road. The Grand Hyatt knows from comfort: The rooms offer luxurious linens, down comforters, and plush pillow-top mattresses. Some rooms overlook a soothing Japanese Zen garden, part of **Onyx at the Grand** (404/995-4212, Mon.-Thurs. noon-12:30am, Fri.-Sat. noon-1:30am, Sun. noon-midnight), the lobby bar and coffee shop. The swanky Terminus office tower nearby adds fine-dining options to the equation; a complimentary shuttle service will take you to any destination within two miles of the hotel.

MAP 3: 3300 Peachtree Rd. NE, 404/237-1234, www.grandatlanta.hyatt.com

INTERCONTINENTAL BUCKHEAD $$$

The 22-story InterContinental Buckhead has a big-city vibe, with a ritzy pool deck that feels more like Boca Raton than Buckhead. It's known as one of the city's most opulent hotels and a favorite gathering spot for runners and spectators participating in the annual Peachtree Road Race 10K. The high-end restaurant, **Southern Art and Bourbon Bar** (404/946-9070, www.southernart.com, Mon.-Thurs. 6:30am-10pm, Fri. 6:30am-11pm, Sat. 7:30am-11pm), delivers classic comfort food in a sophisticated setting. The 422 spacious guest rooms feature whirlpool tubs, wireless Internet, and work desks with speakerphones.

MAP 3: 3315 Peachtree Rd. NE, 404/946-9000, www.intercontinentalatlanta.com; MARTA: Buckhead

MANDARIN ORIENTAL, ATLANTA $$$

The Mandarin Oriental looks like a fashion model: impossibly thin and effortlessly stylish. The 42-story designer hotel has become one of the city's signature hotels. The international boutique chain Mandarin Oriental assumed operation of the property in 2011, upping the ante on the already impeccable service and amenities—and raising the prices. With 127 high-end rooms and 45 residences, the hotel also features one of the neighborhood's most gorgeous spas, which is open to the public.

MAP 3: 3376 Peachtree Rd. NE, 404/995-7500, www.mandarinoriental.com/atlanta

RITZ-CARLTON BUCKHEAD $$$

It's a real shame that such an exquisite hotel has to make do with such an unattractive building, a sulking box that represents the worst of early-1980s architecture. The Ritz-Carlton Buckhead overcompensates for the drab exterior by sparing no expense on its elegant, fussy decor inspired by classic European nobility. All rooms are appointed with custom-designed furnishings, including marble-topped cabinets and roomy walk-in showers. The hotel's restaurant, **The Café** (404/240-7035, daily 6:30am-10pm), serves a popular Sunday brunch.

MAP 3: 3434 Peachtree Rd. NE, 404/237-2700, www.ritzcarlton.com/buckhead

WESTIN BUCKHEAD ATLANTA ⑤⑤

Compared with neighboring high-end hotels, the Westin Buckhead Atlanta deserves a prize for giving guests the most bang for their buck. The shining white 22-story building looks like it might be a second cousin to the High Museum; its lobby and common areas whisper of sleek European design. The 376 rooms feature contemporary-style furnishings, with freshly cut flowers, floor-to-ceiling windows, and marble bathrooms. The popular **Palm Restaurant** (404/814-1955, www.thepalm.com, Mon.-Fri. 6:30am-10:30pm, Sat. 7am-11pm, Sun. 7am-10pm) draws an energetic blend of locals and hotel guests.

MAP 3: 3391 Peachtree Rd. NE, 404/365-0065, www.westin.com/buckhead

Virginia-Highland

Map 4

EMORY CONFERENCE CENTER HOTEL ⑤

The mega-hotels of Downtown, Midtown, and Buckhead may get most of the attention, but there's more to Atlanta lodging than expensive high-rises and cheap chains. The Emory Conference Center Hotel rests in a comfortable middle ground between the two, a tasteful urban retreat surrounded by forest preserve. The building itself has an architectural style inspired by Frank Lloyd Wright, with 198 guest rooms that are classic, if a bit bland. Its location is handy to Emory University.

MAP 4: 1615 Clifton Rd., 800/933-6679, www.emoryconferencecenter.com

UNIVERSITY INN AT EMORY ⑤⑤

The best thing about this small, family-owned hotel is its proximity to the Emory University campus and medical facilities. The property offers 60 rooms split among three buildings; the main building is probably your best bet, with rooms including kitchenettes and Wi-Fi. The Guest House and Oxford Hall are aimed at guests who plan longer visits. The size and quality of accommodations vary greatly; some units have shared bathrooms. Don't be afraid to ask for an upgrade.

MAP 4: 1767 N. Decatur Rd., 800/654-8591, www.univinn.com

VIRGINIA HIGHLAND BED AND BREAKFAST ⑤

This tiny bed-and-breakfast in a restored 1920s Craftsman bungalow hasn't been modified much from its days as a private home and features four guest rooms, one a suite with its own entrance. Innkeeper Adele Northrup pays particular attention to the property's gardens, which are in bloom year-round. A lovely screened porch with a hammock makes for a sweet respite. The Virginia-Highland commercial district is a 15-minute walk away; Piedmont Park is less than 10 minutes on foot.

MAP 4: 630 Orme Cir. NE, 404/892-2735, www.virginiahighlandbb.com

Little Five Points and East Atlanta

Map 5

HIGHLAND INN $

The Highland Inn is, if nothing else, true to the bohemian character of its neighborhood: quirky, charming, and capricious. The hotel's biggest perk—its prime location in a busy part of Poncey-Highland's shops and restaurants—may also be its biggest weakness, due to the potential noise factor. The upside is its value, with rooms starting under $90 per night. The modest inn is housed in a historic two-story 1927 building that was refurbished for the 1996 Olympics. Its downstairs lounge, **Highland Ballroom** (404/874-5756, Thurs.-Sat. 8pm-2am) hosts various music acts and other eclectic events.

MAP 5: 644 N. Highland Ave. NE, 404/874-5756, www.thehighlandinn.com

INMAN PARK BED AND BREAKFAST $

Travelers thirsty for Atlanta history will marvel at the story behind this gracious Inman Park property; the 1912 home was built as a honeymoon residence for Coca-Cola king Robert Woodruff. It features heart-of-pine floors, 12-foot ceilings, and enough antiques to fill a small museum. A Charleston-style private garden in back feels like a private park in the city. The three guest rooms are furnished with either queen or twin beds; all offer private restrooms.

MAP 5: 100 Waverly Way NE, 404/688-9498, www.inmanparkbandb.com

SUGAR MAGNOLIA $$

Bed-and-breakfast Sugar Magnolia is an ideal choice for nostalgic dreamers and hopeless romantics. The three-story Victorian manor shines like a yellow beacon among the historic homes along Edgewood Avenue. The interior features four guest rooms, the best being the enormous Royal Suite with two balconies, a whirlpool tub, and a king-size bed in a recessed alcove. Highlights of the 1892 home include its grand three-story turret and staircase, oval beveled windows, and amazing crystal chandelier.

MAP 5: 804 Edgewood Ave. NE, 404/222-0226, www.sugarmagnoliabb.com

URBAN OASIS BED AND BREAKFAST $

The decor of bright and playful Urban Oasis goes overboard with contemporary accents: lime green walls, bold blue stripes, geometric patterns everywhere. The palette gets toned down in the comfortable guest rooms. This spacious, 5,400-square-foot Inman Park loft has four bedrooms and sits on the Atlanta BeltLine Eastside Trail, providing a handy pedestrian path that runs all the way to Piedmont Park. Be prepared to mingle with the resident dogs and cats.

MAP 5: 130A Krog St. NE, 770/714-8618, www.urbanoasisbandb.com

COURTYARD ATLANTA DECATUR ⑤

Visitors itching to explore Decatur's town square aren't likely to find a better option than this Courtyard, two blocks north of the Old Courthouse. The property was renovated in 2012, transforming what was a dull Holiday Inn into a sunny and modern suburban-style hotel with 175 rooms, an attractive five-story atrium, and modern conference center. Guest rooms are warm and inviting, if a little small, but the indoor pool almost makes up for other shortcomings.

MAP 6: 130 Clairemont Ave., Decatur, 404/371-0204, www.marriott.com; MARTA: Decatur

MILEYBRIGHT FARMHOUSE BED & BREAKFAST ⑤⑤

Close enough to Atlanta to be convenient, yet far enough to feel like the countryside, this 1900 residence was built as a dairy farm. Restored to a classic 1930s Southern character, the pleasant bed-and-breakfast is split into one guest room and a one-, two-, or three-bedroom apartment. Modern amenities include wireless Internet, a gas log fireplace, satellite TV, 11-foot ceilings, hardwood floors, large private terraces, and an outdoor spa tub.

MAP 6: 3244 Covington Hwy., Decatur, 404/508-6060, www.mileybright.com

Greater Atlanta   Map 7

★ LE MÉRIDIEN ATLANTA PERIMETER ⑤⑤

Business travelers bound for Dunwoody's commercial district have made Le Méridien Atlanta Perimeter a prime meeting place for deal-making and networking. The ambience, though, is more pleasure than business, with crisp, modern accents that would suit an upscale Mediterranean resort. The 275-room hotel underwent a $20 million renovation in 2013 that restored the property to its former opulence.

MAP 7: 111 Perimeter Center West, Atlanta, 800/543-4300, www.
lemeridienatlantaperimeter.com

STANLEY HOUSE INN ⑤

The Stanley House Inn oozes romance, which may be why the eye-catching bed-and-breakfast hosts so many weddings. The 1897 mansion is fabulously appointed, with antiques in every cranny. Most of the seven rooms are named for Georgia locales (Buckhead, Dahlonega); each has distinctive personality with a taste for Victorian flourish and patriotic motifs. The inn sits five blocks north of Marietta Square, 18 miles from Downtown.

MAP 7: 236 Church St., Marietta, 770/426-1881, www.thestanleyhouse.com

Excursions

Highlights

★ **Best Way to Climb a Mountain:**
Stone Mountain Park has dozens of attractions aimed at the whole family, but none can beat the simple thrill of the **Summit Skyride,** a slow-moving cable car that lifts visitors to the peak of the granite monadnock (page 190).

★ **Best Place to Beat the Heat:** The sandy beach at **Lake Lanier Islands Resort** is a favorite getaway for land-locked, water-starved Atlantans (page 193).

★ **Most Romantic Getaway:** Modeled after a 16th-century French château, the resplendent **Château Élan Winery and Resort** features a vast vineyard and lots of chances to sample Georgia wines with the one you love (page 193).

★ **Most Colorful Downtown: Downtown Athens** is a hip and artsy destination for offbeat shopping, eclectic restaurants, and tipsy nightlife (page 195).

★ **Best Place to Frolic in the Blossoms:** With five miles of nature trails and 300 acres of forest, the **State Botanical Garden of Georgia** offers manicured plant collections, a great conservatory, and lots of raw woodlands to explore (page 196).

★ **Best Bizarre Tourist Trap:** Perhaps the term "tourist trap" is a backhanded compliment, but the tiny town of **Helen** did reinvent itself as a Bavarian village just to lure in travelers. The Alpine architecture and lederhosen make for a kitschy, quirky day trip (page 201).

★ **Best Natural Wonder: Tallulah Gorge** and its majestic waterfalls have been luring visitors to north Georgia for two centuries, and for good reason. It's the oldest natural gorge in the nation; only the Grand Canyon is deeper (page 201).

A journey outside Atlanta's Perimeter can feel like visiting a different state. The differences between the metropolitan area and the Georgia countryside are astounding. Though suburban sprawl oozes out in all directions around the city, you may be surprised by how quickly a more relaxed rural ambience settles in. It's not all peanut fields and pine forests. Stone Mountain, about 30 minutes east of the city, is a dramatic geological curiosity, a chunk of solid granite surrounded by a lively theme park and recreation area. To the northeast, Atlantans escape the summer heat with dips in Lake Lanier and weekends in the Blue Ridge Mountains, which come into view after an hour's drive. The area offers lots of lake houses and mountain cabins to rent, picturesque bed-and-breakfasts, and genuine down-home dining.

You'll find a different energy on the streets of Athens, a bohemian college town known for the indie rock bands that have risen from its manic music scene. Located 70 miles from Atlanta, Athens promises a diverse mix of fun day-trip possibilities, including primo dining, historical sightseeing, an amazing botanical garden, and a wild bar scene.

Although the destinations profiled in this chapter are some of north Georgia's best and most popular, they're by no means the only options. Travelers with time to spend exploring—and who doesn't mind lazy drives through lush farmland and country crossroads?—can discover many hidden treasures in the state's diverse landscape.

Previous: Antebellum Plantation and Farmyard at Stone Mountain; the city of Athens.

Excursions

© AVALON TRAVEL

PLANNING YOUR TIME

Many of the excursions detailed in this chapter can be completed in a day or less, though traffic on Atlanta-area interstates is notoriously unpredictable—especially on holiday weekends. For a more authentic outing, venture off the expressway and experience the small towns on their own terms. Stone Mountain and its theme park are popular for the kid-friendly activities. It's a great option for a full afternoon and easy one-hour drive back inside the Perimeter. Destinations near Lake Lanier and Athens are farther away, between 60 and 90 minutes respectively. Any trip into the mountains of the Chattahoochee National Forest will take at least two hours (probably longer).

The best way to travel to these areas is by car, though a couple of companies do provide shuttle services between Hartsfield-Jackson Atlanta International Airport and Athens. Biking is probably not a good idea anywhere other than central Athens or on the trails around Stone Mountain Park.

Georgia's temperate climate makes most any destination a year-round draw, with crowds lowest during the winter months and heaviest in July or August—despite the pervasive humidity. Spring arrives early, and autumn brings in a huge explosion of vivid foliage—the back roads around Dahlonega and Helen can be crammed with "leaf-lookers." Lake Lanier Islands puts on a magnificent display of holiday lights, which attracts throngs of visitors.

Stone Mountain

It's not only the state's most-visited tourist spot, but also one of the most-attended attractions in the nation. Stone Mountain is a giant monadnock that towers 825 feet at its highest point—the single largest piece of exposed granite on earth. The northern face of the mountain features its famous **Confederate Memorial,** a three-acre carving of three mounted generals from the Civil War. Stone Mountain Park, the 3,200-acre recreation area that surrounds the mountain, is home to a huge range of entertainment options, including a theme park, resort, antebellum plantation, museums, campsites, and hiking trails.

This is not to be confused with Stone Mountain Village, the sleepy railroad town nearby. The village's quaint tourist district is listed on the National Register of Historic Places and has a handful of souvenir shops and restaurants, but your time is better spent inside Stone Mountain Park itself. All of the sights discussed here are within park property and have various admission fees and open times, which change seasonally. Call the park at 770/498-5690 or 800/401-2407 for information about specific attractions.

Stone Mountain Park includes standard amusement park fare, like hot dogs, hamburgers, and pizza.

SIGHTS

STONE MOUNTAIN PARK

Stone Mountain Park (1000 Robert E. Lee Blvd., 770/498-5690, www.stonemountainpark.com; daily 6am-midnight; $8 per car, cash only) has numerous museums and attractions. Admission prices and hours vary among attractions, and not all sights are open year-round. A one-day **Adventure Pass** ($30 adult, $25 child) grants access to all the major attractions.

DISCOVERING STONE MOUNTAIN
MUSEUM AT MEMORIAL HALL

Any visit to Stone Mountain Park should start at the **Discovering Stone Mountain Museum at Memorial Hall,** which presents a detailed history of the mountain. The main exhibition hall explains the mountain's geology and unique natural habitat, and also features artifacts from ancient Native Americans through the Civil War era. A timeline traces Stone Mountain's fate as disputed piece of land, stone quarry, and eventual site of a major Confederate memorial. A separate exhibition details the colossal endeavor involved with the carving, a task that took almost 50 years to complete and required three subsequent teams of artisans. The finished memorial was finally dedicated in 1970.

★ SUMMIT SKYRIDE

The **Summit Skyride** ($6 one-way, $10 round-trip) transports visitors to the top of the mountain via a hanging Swiss cable car. Though the vehicle doesn't exceed 30 miles per hour, it can be a dizzying experience on windy days. The breathtaking view from the gently sloped peak reveals the vast forest of the Georgia Piedmont, with the Atlanta skyline and Kennesaw Mountain visible. Catch the Summit Skyride at Skyride Plaza, next to the Discovering Stone Mountain Museum. Lines can be long in the busiest summer months, but they tend to move quickly. Adventurous types can also choose to hike to the summit along a 1.3-mile trail.

OTHER PARK ATTRACTIONS

Beyond the majesty of Mother Nature, the park includes plenty of manmade attractions, most of them aimed at children. **Crossroads** (free with park admission) recreates a lively 1870s Southern town, where demonstrators in period costume show off craft-making skills. A short hike away, the poorly curated **Antebellum Plantation and Farmyard** ($10) preserves an actual homestead built in 1845, appointed with period furnishings.

Other park attractions include the **4-D Theater** (individual tickets not available, included with Adventure Pass) and a 19th-century-style paddleboat, *Scarlett O'Hara* (included with Adventure Pass). The boat takes guests on a 20-minute cruise around the park's 383-acre lake.

FESTIVALS AND EVENTS

Beyond Memorial Hall, the great lawn facing the Confederate monument hosts a variety of festivals, concerts, and events year-round. The most

Above: Summit Skyride at Stone Mountain. **Below:** Lasershow Spectacular at Stone Mountain.

popular is the summertime **Lasershow Spectacular** ($17-24), a 40-minute light show on the mountain's face set to music. Get there early to claim a spot on the lawn. The **Indian Festival and Pow-Wow** ($15 per car) each autumn celebrates Native American culture through dance, cooking, crafts, and storytelling. December brings a park-wide holiday celebration and **Snow Mountain** ($19-30), three football fields of fresh (artificial) snow, along with tube racing and a snow lift.

SPORTS AND RECREATION

Many visitors to Stone Mountain each year never set foot in any of the man-made attractions, focusing instead on the plethora of outdoor activity options in the serene 3,200-acre park. The area features 15 miles of hiking trails, including the six-mile **National Recreation Trail** (daily 6am-midnight), which traces the base of the mountain. Visitors can learn about park history while floating in a 1940s-era military boat at **Ride the Ducks** (Riverboat Marina Complex off Robert E. Lee Blvd.; $14 adult or child). Swimming in the lake is not permitted, but **fishing** is. The lake is stocked with bass, carp, catfish, and brim; a valid Georgia fishing license is required ($9 annual, $3.50 one-day) and sold at the Campground Grocery Store, at the campground's entrance on Stonewall Jackson Drive.

Golfers can explore the two courses at **Stone Mountain Golf Club** (770/465-3278; daily 7:30am-5pm; $29-59 for 18 holes), which wind through a forest of Georgia pines around the lake. Trained PGA professionals staff the club, which features instruction options and precision club fitting. The club includes a golf shop and full-service restaurant.

HOTELS AND CAMPING

The **Marriott Evergreen Marriott Conference Resort** (4021 Lakeview Dr., 770/879-9900, www.evergreenresort.com; $249 d) is an expansive lodge where many of the 311 rooms offer balconies with serene lakeside views. The modern hotel has beautiful grounds, well-appointed suites, and a spa.

Expect a different sort of experience at the nostalgic **Marriott Stone Mountain Inn** (1058 Robert E. Lee Dr., 770/469-3311, www.marriott.com; $149 d), a white-columned replica of a 19th-century plantation. The 92-room hotel offers easy access to the mountain, and some rooms feature sleeper sofas.

Stone Mountain Park's extensive (and heavily used) **campground** (770/498-5710, www.stonemountainpark.com; $33-139) includes 441 wooded campsites, 147 full hookups, and 247 partial hookups with water and electricity (for tents, pop-ups, and motor homes), plus another 47 primitive tent sites. Reservations can be made online. There's a two-night minimum stay on some lots.

GETTING THERE AND AROUND

Stone Mountain is about 17 miles east of Atlanta, best accessed via U.S. 78. Traffic can be cumbersome during morning or evening weekday crunch times, but an afternoon drive shouldn't take more than 20 or 30 minutes. If coming from outside the city via I-285, take exit 39B for U.S. 78 East

(Snellville/Athens). Travel 7.7 miles and take exit 8, which leads to the park's East Gate entrance. Road signs in the area will point you toward nearby Stone Mountain Village, if you're so inclined.

There's ample parking inside the park, but expect a day with lots of walking since most attractions are fairly spread out. The **Stone Mountain Railroad** (free with Adventure Pass) journeys around the mountain via a 1940s-era locomotive with open-air cars. The five-mile trek takes about half an hour, and the train can be boarded and de-boarded from Memorial Depot in Crossroads or Confederate Hall at the base of the Walk-Up Trail.

Lake Lanier and Vicinity

More than seven million visitors a year flock to Lake Sidney Lanier, the 38,000-acre reservoir that serves as one of Atlanta's primary water sources. Named for the 19th-century Georgia poet who wrote "The Song of the Chattahoochee," the lake was created in 1956 when the U.S. Army Corps of Engineers completed work on Buford Dam. Water from the Chattahoochee River slowly filled the valley between Hall and Forsyth Counties. At its normal water level, the lake's shoreline stretches for almost 700 miles and touches five counties, though lake levels occasionally reach surprising lows during times of drought. Rowing and canoeing competitions were held here during the 1996 Summer Olympics, which led to a rush of new development along the lake's northern fingers.

SIGHTS
★ LAKE LANIER ISLANDS RESORT
One unintended consequence of the filling of the reservoir was the creation of a handful of islands in the lake's southeast corner. Rather than trying to correct the problem, the state of Georgia decided to dedicate the land for recreational use. Today **Lake Lanier Islands Resort** (7000 Holiday Rd., 800/840-5253, www.lakelanierislands.com; $189-279 per night) has grown to include a luxury hotel, golf club, conference center, equestrian center, and spa. Its half-mile sandy beach and **water park** (hours vary, roughly 10am-6pm May-Sept.; $35 adult, $20 child) are packed during the summer months; the water park features Georgia's largest wave pool and several water slides. The resort also hosts a popular display of holiday lights in late November and December. The islands are accessible by car and located about a half mile from I-985. The resort includes four restaurants, though some are only open in high season.

★ CHÂTEAU ÉLAN WINERY AND RESORT
It's no Napa Valley, but Georgia has developed a small and growing wine industry, with almost a dozen vineyards and wineries popping up in the northeast corridor. The most famous is **Château Élan Winery and Resort** (100 Rue Charlemagne, 800/233-9463, www.chateauelan.com; $212-425 per night), the largest producer of premium wines in the state. The 42,000-square-foot winery is housed in a surprising 16th-century-style

French château surrounded by vineyards, with a golf club, spa, and conference center included. Located in Braselton, about 40 miles outside of the city, the winery is easily one of the area's most romantic day-trip destinations. Die-hard oenophiles can also use the château as the starting point for following the **Georgia Wine Highway** (www.georgiawine.com), a meandering itinerary of 10 wineries spread from Dahlonega to Clayton. Just be sure to pick a designated driver!

SPORTS AND RECREATION
Boating

The area around Friendship Road in Buford includes several places to rent or purchase boats and personal watercraft for use on the lake. **Harbor Landing** (7000 Holiday Rd., Buford, 770/932-7255, www.lakelanierislands.com/boating/rentals; hours vary by season; $125-490 per day), part of Lake Lanier Islands Resort, rents out ski boats, pontoon boats, houseboats, sailboats, and even some yachts.

Golf

For golfers, the resort's two courses ($45-84) are some of the most scenic in the state, with a total of 21 waterfront holes. **PineIsle Golf Club** (9000 Holiday Rd., Buford, 770/945-8787, http://lakelanier.com/pine-isle-golf-club; daily 7:30am-7pm) is a par-72 18-hole championship course, while **Legacy Golf Club** (7000 Holiday Rd., Buford, 678/318-7861; daily 8am-5pm) underwent a sweeping renovation and facelift in summer 2009.

Hiking and Biking

Closer to Gainesville, **Elachee Nature Science Center** (2125 Elachee Dr., 770/535-1976, www.elachee.org; Mon.-Fri. 10am-5pm; $5 adult, $3 child) is a serene environmental conservancy and museum located in the 1,500-acre Chicopee Woods Nature Preserve. It includes more than 12 miles of hiking trails, which are free to visit and are open daily 8am-dusk. For a somewhat bumpier forest experience, the nearby **Chicopee Woods Mountain Bike Trails** (Elachee Dr., www.mtbproject.com; daily 8am-dusk) offer 13 miles of trails for mountain bikers.

SHOPS

The tiny hamlet of Buford, Georgia, may seem like an improbable spot to plant the region's largest shopping mall, but that's exactly what happened when the **Mall of Georgia** (3333 Buford Dr., 678/482-8788, www.mallofgeorgia.com, Mon.-Sat. 10am-9pm, Sun. noon-6pm) sprouted in 1999. With more than 225 stores, the sprawling commercial megaplex has the feel of a small municipality, complete with its own town square out front. Anchor tenants include Dillard's, Macy's, and JCPenney, designer stores like Coach and Armani Exchange, and an IMAX theater.

Lake Lanier is approximately 40 miles northeast of Atlanta, best accessed via I-85. Merge onto I-985 and exit at Friendship Road, exit 8. For Château Élan, take I-85 to exit 126, Farm Market Road.

Athens

Though it's best known as a college town, there's more to Athens than the University of Georgia. The nation's oldest public research university takes up a whopping 759 acres of the city's prime real estate, with a student population of 35,000 flooding the downtown streets each academic year. The university's influence reaches beyond the classroom and informs all aspects of life in the Classic City, making this a mecca for intellectuals, bohemians, artists, and misfits of all stripes.

Since the early 1980s, Athens has also been recognized nationally for its ever-churning alternative music scene, thanks to the success of wildly popular bands like the B-52s and R.E.M. Chart-topping acts have since emerged from this important indie incubator, including Widespread Panic, Matthew Sweet, Danger Mouse, and Of Montreal—to name just a smattering of dozens.

As home to the University of Georgia Press and the *Georgia Review,* the city has a vibrant literary scene, as well as a hot arts community and a busy clique of local theaters. The luxuriant State Botanical Garden of Georgia is here, as well as a famous "Tree that Owns Itself" and enormous Stanford Stadium, home of the Georgia Bulldogs.

SIGHTS
★ DOWNTOWN ATHENS
The University of Georgia campus meets the animated downtown commercial district along Broad Street. The 20-square-block center of town is a picturesque and walkable collection of classic pre-war American buildings filled with restaurants, bars, music clubs, boutiques, bookstores, and gift shops. Any exploration of the area should start at the university's **Arch** (Broad and College Streets), the 1858 wrought-iron gate that serves as the school's symbol and mimics the design of the state seal of Georgia. The Arch once supported heavy swinging gates, but they vanished around 1885. The best of downtown's commercial district radiates outward from here to the north and tapers off around Dougherty Street.

About half a mile to the west, the **Tree that Owns Itself** stands proudly at the intersection of Dearing and Finley Streets. The large white oak is technically the offspring of the original self-owning tree, so deemed because of the final wishes of its landowner in the late 1800s.

GEORGIA MUSEUM OF ART
Located on the University of Georgia's East Campus, the **Georgia Museum of Art** (90 Carlton St., 706/542-4662, www.uga.edu/gamuseum; Tues.-Wed. and Fri.-Sat. 10am-5pm, Thurs. 10am-9pm, Sun. 1pm-5pm; free) features

a permanent collection of 9,000 objects, primarily 19th- and 20th-century American paintings, prints, and drawings. It's housed in a lovely and modern 82,000-square-foot building with 13 galleries that hosts two dozen exhibitions per year, including traveling shows.

★ STATE BOTANICAL GARDEN OF GEORGIA

Approximately three miles from downtown Athens, the splendid **State Botanical Garden of Georgia** (2450 S. Milledge Ave., 706/542-1244, www. uga.edu/botgarden; Tues.-Sat. 9am-4:30pm, Sun. 11:30am-4:30pm; free) is a serene sanctuary away from the commotion of campus. The garden's grounds spread over 300 acres, much along the Middle Oconee River, and feature more than five miles of nature trails. A gorgeous three-story conservatory hosts a permanent collection of tropical plants with an emphasis on beneficial species. Outdoors, visitors can stroll through six themed gardens, including native flora, ornamentals, and a prize-winning rhododendron collection. The grounds of the garden have longer hours than the visitors center and conservatory: October-March daily 8am-6pm, and April-September daily 8am-8pm. The garden is also popular for bird-watchers. Its nearby Whitehall Forest has been designated an Important Bird Area by the Georgia Audubon Society.

RESTAURANTS

For such a small town, Athens offers a sophisticated selection of restaurants, from much-loved dive spots to high-end eateries. **Five & Ten** (1073 S. Milledge Ave., 706/546-7300, www.fiveandten.com; Mon.-Thurs. 5:30pm-10pm, Fri.-Sat. 5:30pm-10:30pm, Sun. 10:30am-2:30pm and 5:30pm-9pm; $20-40) gets ranked not only as one of the best restaurants in Athens but as one of the best in the state. Chef-owner Hugh Acheson deserves the hype around his seasonally changing menu of New American fare with French and Southern influences.

The Grill (171 College Ave., 706/543-4770; $6) is a 1950s-style diner open 24 hours, making it a great spot to get a grease fix and enjoy some of the best late-night people-watching downtown. The menu varies from diner standards like hamburgers and hot dogs to breakfast favorites and some of the best fresh-cut french fries you'll find anywhere, served with decadent gobs of feta cheese.

Fans of R.E.M. make a point to find **Weaver D's Delicious Fine Foods** (1016 E. Broad St., 706/353-7797; Mon.-Sat. 11am-6pm; $7), the soul-food shack whose iconic sign gave the band the name for its 1992 breakthrough album *Automatic for the People*. Despite its landmark status, the humble cinder-block building just oozes authenticity, serving Southern staples like fried chicken, pork chops, and meatloaf along with sweet-potato casserole and buttermilk cornbread.

Contrary to its name, **Last Resort Grill** (174-184 W. Clayton St., 706/549-0810, www.lastresortgrill.com; Mon.-Thurs. 11am-3pm and 5pm-10pm, Fri.-Sat. 11am-3pm and 5-11pm, Sun. 10am-3pm and 5pm-10pm, $15) has been a first choice for fine dining in Athens since 1992. It's a funky little New American bistro with an atmosphere that's both comfortable and upscale. Billed as "nouvelle Southern," the menu is tinged with Southwestern influences; the signature dish is an amazing praline chicken served with a medley of cheeses. The menu also gets props for its many healthy options.

NIGHTLIFE

Bars, bars, and more bars dot the streets of downtown Athens, where noisy packs of students keep up UGA's party-school reputation most nights of the week. White-hot nightspots filled with barely legal undergrads are a dime a dozen, but you can usually find a more relaxed crowd at the **Globe** (199 N. Lumpkin St., 706/353-4721, www.classiccitybrew.com/globe.html; daily 11am-late; no cover), modeled after a classic British pub. It's a favorite gathering spot for professors and grad students, the kind of place where heated debates erupt over Chaucer or Keats. The Globe carries 70 bottled beers and 14 drafts, along with a full wine menu.

Nearby, **Georgia Theatre** (215 N. Lumpkin St., 706/549-9918, www. georgiatheatre.com; hours and cover vary with show schedule) is a music venue, watering hole, and sometime dance club, with a full and diverse calendar of acts. Formerly a movie house, the venue has hosted a Who's Who of Athens music royalty over the years, from Pylon to Widespread Panic.

Around the corner, the **40 Watt Club** (285 W. Washington St., 706/549-7871, www.40watt.com; hours and cover vary with show schedule) is a must-see temple for indie-rock pilgrims. The legendary nightspot first opened in 1979 and has moved often around town, finally settling in this gritty former furniture showroom in 1990. Countless national acts have passed through the club on their way to stardom.

Flicker Theatre and Bar (263 W. Washington St., 706/546-0039, www. flickertheatreandbar.com; Mon.-Fri. 4pm-2am, Sat. 1pm-2am; cover varies, up to $10) is, as the name suggests, both a bar and a cinema of sorts, featuring artsy screenings, live performances, puppet shows, and other eclectic ephemera.

HOTELS

Athens isn't known for a stunning selection of hotels. There are plenty of name-brand properties on the far west end of town, though discerning visitors really should aim to stay close to downtown. Filling a designer niche, **Hotel Indigo Athens University** (500 College Ave., 706/546-0430, www. indigoathens.com; $135 d) is a popular choice for visitors heading to the Classic Center, a major downtown event venue. While some other hotels in the boutique Indigo chain go for a flowery shabby-chic vibe, the key word here is sustainability, with serene wood-grain interiors and recycled materials at every turn.

Nearby, **Hilton Garden Inn** (390 E. Washington St., 706/353-6800, www. hiltongardeninn.com; $149 d) is an inviting eight-floor hotel with 185 guest rooms that include large work desks, two phones (each with two lines), and data ports. The fitness center, indoor pool, and hot tub are all better than average, but really the best aspect of this hotel is its location.

A less obvious—but highly recommended—choice for travelers is

Clockwise from top left: University of Georgia's iconic arch, Athens; a blooming orchid in the State Botanical Garden of Georgia, Athens; The Grill, Athens.

the **UGA Hotel and Conference Center** (1197 S. Lumpkin St., 800/884-1381, www.georgiacenter.uga.edu; $99 d), part of the Georgia Center for Continuing Education in the hub of campus. The hotel has 200 well-furnished rooms with a modern aesthetic that isn't necessarily reflected in some of the more traditional common areas. It also features two on-site restaurants. The UGA Hotel is convenient to the Stegeman Coliseum and Stanford Stadium, but downtown's commercial district is a 20-minute uphill walk through North Campus.

Many chain hotels can also be found in the retail sprawl west of downtown, including but not limited to **Holiday Inn Express** (513 W. Broad St., 706/546-8122, www.hiexpressathensga.com; $90 d) and **Best Western Colonial Inn** (170 N. Milledge Ave., 706/546-7311, www.bestwestern.com/colonialinnathens; $70 d).

INFORMATION

The **Athens Welcome Center** (280 E. Dougherty St., 706/353-1820, www.athenswelcomecenter.com; Mon.-Sat. 10am-5pm, Sun. noon-5pm) is an indispensable source of information about the city. It's located in the historic Church-Waddel-Brumby House, dating to 1820 and believed to be the oldest residence in town. You can also find plenty of local insights and assistance at the **University of Georgia Visitors Center** (Four Towers building, College Station Rd., 706/542-0842, www.uga.edu/visit; Mon.-Fri. 8am-5pm, selected Sat. 10am-3pm). It's housed in a former dairy barn on East Campus.

GETTING THERE AND AROUND

Athens is about 70 miles east of Atlanta, roughly 1.5 hours by car. The fastest route is via I-85 north to Highway 316. Exit at Lexington Road for destinations downtown. There is no public transportation from Atlanta to Athens.

You won't necessarily need a car to see some the best of the downtown district or the university campus, but parking can be a challenge in the Classic City. The **College Avenue Parking Deck** (265 College Ave., 706/613-1417) is a great and central place to leave your wheels while walking around town. **Athens Transit** (www.athenstransit.com) runs an extensive network of bus routes through the city and is a real bargain at only $1.75 per ride.

Blue Ridge Mountains and Vicinity

The 727,000-acre Chattahoochee National Forest caps the northeastern quadrant of Georgia like an emerald crown. This is mountain country, by and large rugged and bucolic, though sometimes surprisingly commercial. The Appalachians begin their gradual march up the Eastern Seaboard here in a range known as the Blue Ridge Mountains, named for the soothing colors the peaks take on when seen from a distance.

Several of north Georgia's most interesting tourist spots sit in the foothills of the Blue Ridge Mountains, including historic Dahlonega, site of America's first gold rush, and the southern terminus of the Appalachian Trail near Springer Mountain. There's truly no lack of outdoor adventures to be had in and around these rural hillside towns and historic Native American sites, though nature-phobic city dwellers can still have an enjoyable day trip taking in the landscape from the car window.

A thorough exploration of north Georgia's mountains could last a week or longer. Destinations covered here focus on the more popular (and easily accessed) spots located mainly along the southern edges of the Chattahoochee National Forest. Hard-core campers and hikers will probably want to push north past tourist towns like Helen or Dahlonega to discover the still-untapped pockets of Appalachian splendor.

SIGHTS
AMICALOLA FALLS
The Southeast's tallest waterfall, **Amicalola Falls** (418 Amicalola Falls State Park Rd., 706/265-4703, www.gastateparks.org/amicalolafalls; daily 7am-10pm; $5/day) rises 729 feet in a lush mountain setting near Dawsonville. The word *amicalola* is Cherokee for "tumbling water"; the tribe controlled these lands until its forced removal in 1838's Trail of Tears. The falls are surrounded by a gorgeous 829-acre park that includes four major hiking trails (including access to the Appalachian Trail).

As one of the area's most popular attractions, the trails can be packed during spring and summer months. Try to catch the park on a weekday morning for optimal viewing of the amazing waterfall. Amicalola Falls State Park is about 70 miles from Atlanta, a relatively fast drive up Georgia State Route 400, which is expressway for two-thirds of the trip.

DAHLONEGA
The town of Dahlonega is worth the drive for a visit to the **Dahlonega Gold Museum Historic Site** (1 Public Sq., 706/864-2257, www.gastateparks.org/info/dahlonega; Mon.-Sat. 9am-5pm, Sun. 10am-5pm; $7). Two decades before the 1849 discovery of gold in California, fortune-seekers flooded Dahlonega during America's first gold rush. The story of the mountain town's meteoric rise—and fall—as a mining mecca is told in the 1836 Lumpkin County Courthouse, the oldest courthouse in the state. Featured

exhibits in the museum include U.S. coins minted from Dahlonega gold and equipment used in mining.

The small downtown is a popular commercial district with folk-art galleries, restaurants, and stands where kids can pan for "gold" and gemstones. Nearby, the campus of **North Georgia College** makes for a fun photo op. The signature building, Price Memorial Hall, sits on the foundation of the former U.S. mint, and its spire is leafed in Dahlonega gold.

★ HELEN

For a town with only 420 year-round residents, the sidewalks of Helen are somehow always swarming with tourists. This sleepy mountain village decided in the 1960s to rebrand itself as an "authentic" (ahem) Bavarian village. The result is a bizarre smorgasbord of gingerbread houses, fairy-tale restaurants, cobblestone sidewalks, and vaguely German flourishes applied to everything from fast-food joints to street signs.

Scores of gift shops sell tchotchkes ranging from cuckoo clocks to decorative beer steins, though you can't go wrong with the homemade fudge—some of the best in Georgia. Alpine Helen is probably not a great destination for anyone with a low tolerance for crowds, but the town can definitely be enjoyed with a certain ironic detachment just for its sheer kitsch value. If nothing else, the kids always adore it.

Just outside of Helen's commercial district, the **Nacoochee Mound** (Highways 17 and 75) is an important Native American burial site that pre-dates even the Cherokee Nation's time in north Georgia.

ANNA RUBY FALLS

The 1,050-acre **Unicoi State Park** and scenic area is best known as the home of **Anna Ruby Falls** (1788 Hwy. 356, 706/878-4726, www.gastate-parks.org/unicoi; daily 7am-10pm; $5 per car per day), one of Georgia's finest. The rare natural wonder is actually two waterfalls in one, the site where Curtis Creek and York Creek converge in their descent off nearby Tray Mountain. It's a good hike of almost a mile from the parking lot the viewing platform at the falls, though the angle is gradual with lots of benches along the path.

The entrance to Unicoi State Park sits about two miles north of Helen's main commercial strip.

★ TALLULAH GORGE

Known as north Georgia's "first" tourist attraction, jaw-dropping Tallulah Gorge has been luring visitors to the area since the early 1800s. The two-mile gorge is second in depth only to the Grand Canyon, with rugged cliffs that climb as high as 1,000 feet. A series of waterfalls connect the gorge with nearby Tallulah Falls Lake, a manmade reservoir that was installed in 1913 with a hydroelectric plant and dam.

Any visit to Tallulah Gorge should start at the **Jane Hurt Yarn Interpretive Center** (338 Jane Hurt Yarn Dr., 706/754-7981, www.gastate-parks.org/tallulahgorge; daily 8am-dusk; $5 parking), a visitors center that includes a free exhibition detailing the history of Tallulah Gorge and its legacy of tourism. Tightrope walker Karl Wallenda crossed the gorge in 1970; artifacts from his stunt figure prominently on the site.

From the center, it's a short 10-minute walk to overlook the gorge. To descend to the bottom of the canyon, you'll need one of the 100 free permits issued daily at the Yarn Interpretative Center. Hikers are required to wear proper footwear (no sandals). The gorge floor is often closed due to weather or planned releases of water from the nearby dam.

RESTAURANTS

The Smith House (84 S. Chestatee St., Dahlonega, 706/867-7000, www. smithhouse.com; Tues.-Fri. 11am-3pm, Thurs.-Fri. 3:30pm-7:30pm, Sat. 11am-8pm, Sun. 11am-7:30pm; $18) has been cooking up classic Southern dishes in Dahlonega since at least 1946, though the property's history reaches back much further. The house dates to the late 1890s and sits over a partially completed gold mine, now viewable just outside the downstairs dining room. All meals are served family-style, so be prepared to mingle with other diners.

As the name would imply, Helen's **Hofbrauhaus** (9001 N. Main St., Helen, 706/878-2248; daily 4pm-10pm; $20) puts a premium on German authenticity. The quaint riverfront dining room and inn offers typical German favorites such as wiener schnitzel and cold potato salad. The chef actually lived for years in Bavaria, so the level of legitimacy is higher here than in many other Helen attractions.

Mully's Nacoochee Grill (7277 S. Main St., Helen, 706/878-8020, www. nacoocheegrill.com; Mon.-Thurs. 4pm-9pm, Fri. 11:30am-9pm, Sat.-Sun. 9am-9pm; $15), just on the outskirts of Helen, transformed a bare-bones 1900s farmhouse into a well-appointed dinner spot. Many dishes are prepared on the wood-fire grill; the menu is heavy with American favorites like baby-back ribs and chicken pot pie. You could definitely do worse than this wine list.

FESTIVALS AND EVENTS

Even though it's named **Oktoberfest** (www.helenchamber.com/oktoberfest.html), Helen's annual beer festival kicks off in the middle of September and runs for about six weeks. Expect bratwurst, lederhosen, and of course, beer steins galore as German bands from all over the country descend on the always-crowded Alpine village. Most of the action takes place around the **Helen Festhalle** (1074 Edelweiss St.; $7-8 admission).

Dahlonega hosts **Gold Rush Days** (www.dahlonega.org) the third week of every October. This colorful street festival commemorates the town's gold rush and brings in a crowd of over 200,000 for events that include a parade, fashion show, gold-panning contest, wheelbarrow race, hog-calling and buck-dancing contests, gospel singing, and other live acts.

RECREATION
Hiking

The **Chattahoochee National Forest** (www.fs.usda.gov/main/conf/home) stretches across 18 counties in north Georgia and encompasses around 430

Above: Dahlonega Gold Museum Historic Site. **Below:** The Smith House.

miles of hiking trails. It's no exaggeration to say an industrious hiker could spend days in this wilderness and barely encounter another backpacker. Trails range from easy afternoon strolls along trout streams to arduous climbs up treacherous rocky cliffs. Any extended expedition into the forest should start with some research and careful planning to ensure you're tackling a path of the appropriate skill level.

The **Appalachian Trail** begins its 2,100-mile trek from Georgia to Maine here in the Chattahoochee National Forest. The trail's southern terminus sits at **Springer Mountain** (www.appalachiantrail.org; daily 8am-dusk; free), roughly 20 miles northwest of Dahlonega. Hikers approaching Springer Mountain often begin their journey at **Amicalola Falls State Park** (418 Amicalola Falls State Park Rd., 706/265-4703, www.gastateparks. org/amicalolafalls; Mon.-Fri. 8am-8pm, Sat.-Sun. 9am-5pm; $5/day), where an 8.3-mile path leads to the Appalachian Trail. Another entry point is via a 1-mile segment of the **Benton MacKaye Trail** (U.S. Forest Service Rd. 42, www.bmta.org; daily 8am-dusk; free), which leads from a parking lot on a Forest Service road and then continues up Springer Mountain.

SHOPS

There were a couple of years in the early 1980s when Cabbage Patch Kids were *the* dolls every girl in America wanted. Though the fad has long since passed, its spirit lives on at **BabyLand General Hospital** (300 N.O.K. Dr., 706/865-2171, www.cabbagepatchkids.com; Mon.-Sat. 9am-5pm, Sun. 10am-5pm) near Cleveland. This hospital-themed attraction is equal parts doll shop (the "Adoption Center"), museum, and shrine to creator Xavier Roberts, the north Georgia native who first brought the toys to market in 1978.

The winding mountain roads north of Lake Lanier are dotted with makeshift produce stands selling boiled peanuts, locally made preserves, and fresh vegetables. **Jaemor Farms** (5340 Cornelia Hwy., 770/869-3999, www.jaemorfarms.com; Mon.-Sat. 7am-6pm, Sun. 1pm-6pm) near Alto borrows the concept but transfers the setting to a modern, warehouse-sized farmers market that stocks everything from ciders, honey, and candies to fresh flowers and even pottery. In the autumn (September-November) Jaemor Farms hosts a popular **Corn Maze** and hay ride.

Proving once and for all that the suburban sensibilities of metro Atlanta can flourish even as far out as tiny Dawsonville, **North Georgia Premium Outlets** (800 Hwy. 400 S, 706/216-3609, www.premiumoutlets.com/north-georgia; Mon.-Sat. 10am-9pm, Sun. 11am-7pm) offers 140 brand-name shops that are usually packed with bargain hunters. Familiar retail labels include Burberry, Ann Taylor, Gap, and J. Crew.

HOTELS, CABINS, AND CAMPING

The default accommodation for the Blue Ridge Mountains is definitely the hillside cabin. The quality and convenience of these backcountry retreats can vary greatly, as can the prices. You can locate scores of options with a simple search online, though **Georgia Mountain Rentals** (www. georgiamtnrentals.com) is one of the best sites around due mainly to its exhaustive selection. Rates go from about $75 to more than $250 per night.

Cedar House Inn & Yurts (6463 Hwy. 19 N, 706/867-9446, www.georgiamountaininn.com, $145 d) near Dahlonega gets points for originality. Not just a charming four-room bed-and-breakfast, the property also rents out two yurts behind the inn. These canvas-sided structures sit on wooden decks, sort of a cousin to a tent but a bit more stable. Guests who go for the yurt option can still enjoy meals in the main house, making this experience not all that different from the nights you spent camping out in your parents' backyard.

The vicinity around Helen is overflowing with chain motels, not bad if you want to be in the thick of the crowded commercial district. For a break from the Alpine ambience, nearby **Unicoi State Park Lodge** (1788 Hwy. 356, 800/573-9659, www.gastateparks.org/unicoi; $125 d) offers 100 guest rooms on a scenic lakeside setting. The lodge is a popular choice for travelers, though the park has a stunning assortment of other accommodations, including 30 cottages ($90-135 d), 115 campsites ($25-35 d), and 16 Squirrel's Nest shelters ($15 d)—platforms with roofs and back walls.

Finding an interesting, high-quality hotel in the vicinity of Tallulah Gorge can be a tall order. A better bet is to go for one of the 50 campsites at **Tallulah Gorge State Park** (338 Jane Hurt Yarn Dr., 706/754-7979, www.gastateparks.org/info/tallulah; $15 d). Larger groups can pay extra ($40 d) to reserve the Pioneer Campsite, which includes a three-sided shelter, pit toilet, fire ring, picnic tables, and room for three large tents. Fun for the whole pioneer family!

INFORMATION

The stately **Dahlonega-Lumpkin County Visitors Center** (13 S. Park St., 800/231-5543, www.dahlonega.org; Mon.-Sat. 9am-5:30pm, Sun. 10am-5:30pm) is a handy place to stop for maps, attraction brochures, directions, and hands-on advice from the talkative staff.

A lovely lady in traditional Bavarian dirndl will greet you at the **Alpine Helen/White County Convention & Visitors Bureau** (726 Bruckenstrasse, 800/858-8027, www.helenga.org, Mon.-Sat. 9am-5pm, Sun. 10am-4pm) and help you plan your time in the village. Ask for coupons to nearby shops and attractions.

GETTING THERE AND AROUND

Any expedition into North Georgia's mountains will require a car, preferably an SUV for destinations beyond the tourist towns. Of the sites profiled here, Amicalola Falls State Park is the closest to metro Atlanta, about 70 miles north of the city. It's theoretically possible to hit Amicalola Falls, Dahlonega, Helen, and Tallulah Gorge in one day, though the 74-mile trek across the southern edge of the Chattahoochee National Forest would best be enjoyed if broken up with overnight stays in one of the mountain towns or lodges.

Background

The Landscape

GEOGRAPHY

In his seminal 1903 essay collection *The Souls of Black Folk*, W. E. B. Du Bois wrote of Atlanta:

> South of the North, yet north of the South, lies the City of a Hundred Hills, peering out from the shadows of the past into the promise of the future. I have seen her in the morning, when the first flush of day had half-roused her; she lay gray and still on the crimson soil of Georgia; then the blue smoke began to curl from her chimneys, the tinkle of bell and scream of whistle broke the silence, the rattle and roar of busy life slowly gathered and swelled, until the seething whirl of the city seemed a strange thing in a sleepy land.

More than a century later, the "City of a Hundred Hills" might still be described as "a strange thing in a sleepy land," an audacious Southern metropolis with her eyes fixed on the future. Today the whistles, rattles, and roars have been replaced with sirens, horns, and the pervasive hum of traffic on the Downtown Connector. To say Atlanta has a hundred hills would be an exaggeration; decades of development have tamed the wild landscape, but the city's topography still features plenty of peaks and valleys, which are especially obvious in Piedmont and Freedom Parks.

Georgia's capital city lies in the foothills of the Appalachian Mountains at an elevation of 1,010 feet above sea level. It's the largest city on the vast Piedmont Plateau, which stretches from Alabama to New Jersey. The greater metropolitan area spans 8,376 square miles, comprising 28 counties and 140 municipalities. Atlanta's city limits encompass 132 square miles, most of which lie in Fulton County, with a smaller slice in DeKalb County. Of that area, less than one square mile consists of water. The city depends upon reservoirs in North Georgia for its water supply, via the Chattahoochee River. The Brevard Fault Zone runs alongside the river, but geologists consider it extinct. However, Atlantans have occasionally reported minor earthquakes, including one in 2003 measuring 4.9 on the Richter scale.

The Chattahoochee traditionally defined the northwestern border of Atlanta, but the city is otherwise in the unusual position of having no natural boundaries—which has been both a blessing and a curse to its development. Unfettered by mountains or ocean, the metro area has extended rapidly into surrounding counties over the past few decades, leading to legendary traffic congestion and making Atlanta a frequent poster child for suburban sprawl.

Previous: Georgia Tech campus; the Georgia State Capitol in Atlanta.

CLIMATE

Due to its high elevation, Atlanta enjoys four distinct seasons and is known for having a temperate climate. The average low temperature in January dips to 33°F (0.5°C). The hottest month of the year is July, with average highs around 89°F (32°C). Summers in the city are notorious for their humidity. Occasional heat waves can cause highs around 98°F (37°C), with heat indexes that reach potentially unhealthy levels.

Classified as having a humid subtropical climate, Atlanta receives an average of 47 inches of rainfall per year. The driest month here is October, which gets an average of 3.11 inches of precipitation. March ranks as the wettest, with 5.38 inches. The city sees far more sunny days than not; only 117 days of the average year experience precipitation.

Occasional ice storms sweep the metro area during the winter months, but only two inches of snow fall annually. Most years frost is experienced on 36 days. Sporadic thunderstorms are known to pass through during the warmer months. Georgia's tornado season runs March-May, with an average of six twisters per year statewide. In March 2008, a tornado swept through Atlanta's downtown business district, damaging landmarks like CNN Center, the Georgia Dome, and the Westin Peachtree Plaza Hotel. Two fatalities were reported and officials estimated that the tornado cost the city $150 million. Luckily, such extreme weather events have been rare inside the city.

History

In the family of major East Coast cities, Atlanta might qualify as the overachieving baby sister. By the time the town was incorporated in 1847, New York City had already been around for 223 years. Charleston, South Carolina, was turning 167, and even nearby Milledgeville, then Georgia's state capital, was a respectable 44-year-old. Considering the gap in years, the city's unparalleled growth and arrival as a regional power become all the more striking.

The lands of Georgia were once Creek and Cherokee Indian territories. Spanish conquistador Juan Ponce de León is sometimes cited as the first European to visit these parts, though his travels in 1513 took him farther south to coastal Florida. Contrary to local folklore, the explorer never set foot anywhere near the future site of Atlanta—even though his name would later grace one of the city's major thoroughfares.

Georgia, the last of the original 13 colonies, was established in 1733 when British general James Oglethorpe founded the port of Savannah. The coastal area was heavily disputed following the Revolutionary War of 1776, with British and Loyalist forces bearing down on Savannah and Augusta. The English recruited Georgia's Creek Indians to help them during the War of 1812, leading to the Creek War of 1813-1814. In the aftermath of those battles, the young United States rushed to build a series of defensive forts in the wilderness along the Chattahoochee River. One such fort rose close to a key Native American settlement known as Standing Peachtree, near the present-day Peachtree Creek in Buckhead. Fort Peachtree, built in 1814, became an important site for the area's incoming English, Scotch, and Irish settlers. The hilly terrain's primary Indian paths later became some of Atlanta's main roads (including present-day Peachtree Street), though the Native Americans themselves were systematically removed from the land along 1838's infamous Trail of Tears.

FROM TERMINUS TO MARTHASVILLE

By the 1830s, Georgia was prospering. As the largest state east of the Mississippi River, Georgia had become a viable center of the cotton industry, where massive plantations were worked by African American slaves. North Georgia had undergone its own boom in 1829, when America's first gold rush erupted in the tiny town of Dahlonega. A charge of newcomers to the region soon followed. State power brokers decided Georgia needed a new railroad terminus to connect fertile farmland with Tennessee, South Carolina, and the coastal ports to the south. The state sent seasoned army surveyor Stephen Long to the upcountry frontier to choose a practical site for the railroad's development. After considering several options, he selected in 1837 an untamed tract of land where several Indian trails merged. Local folklore says that Long drove a stake into the red clay close to what's now Five Points Downtown and declared the area suitable for "a tavern, a blacksmith's shop, a general store, and nothing else."

A small settlement of railroad workers arrived, and the place was given the unimaginative name of "Terminus." It quickly grew much larger than Long had predicted. By 1842, the village was booming and had attracted scores of new residents, including the wives of the railroad men. As the first train depot rose, Georgia governor Wilson Lumpkin asked that the community be renamed "Marthasville," after his small daughter. The first railroad engine rolled into town not long after. By 1846 the railroad connected Marthasville with Augusta, Macon, and Savannah.

For Richard Peters, superintendent of the Western & Atlantic Railroad, the name "Marthasville" just didn't sound like an important transportation hub. He asked his colleague J. Edgar Thompson for ideas, and the engineer supposedly began thinking aloud, "Western & Atlantic, Atlantic masculine, Atlanta feminine. Eureka! Atlanta!" The state legislature quickly approved of the change. In 1847, the incorporated community of Atlanta was born.

THE CIVIL WAR

Atlanta blossomed over the next 15 years and became known as a rough and randy frontier town with a bank, a daily newspaper, wooden sidewalks, and a problem with stray livestock blocking traffic. It also earned a reputation for lawlessness. Gamblers, drinkers, and cock-fighters ruled over Snake Nation (present-day Castleberry Hill) and Slabtown (near current Decatur Street), flouting the rule of law. In 1851, a group of Snake Nation "Rowdies" stole a cannon from neighboring Decatur and fired a load of gravel and mud at the general store owned by incoming Atlanta mayor Jonathan Norcross—a daring act of defiance. Atlanta citizens were outraged and took it upon themselves to arrest the perpetrators and burn

Peachtree: What's in a Name?

The late Celestine Sibley, a much-adored columnist for the *Atlanta Journal-Constitution* for 58 years, once wrote, "Only a lunatic would voluntarily and for any length of time leave Peachtree Street." To hear some other Atlantans tell it, only a lunatic would give every street in town the same name.

A running joke here bemoans the number of addresses in the city featuring some variation of "Peachtree," making the place darn near impossible to navigate for newcomers. It's true that "Peachtree" shows up on at least 71 street signs, including Peachtree Battle Avenue, Peachtree Place, Peachtree Circle, Peachtree Hills Avenue, and Peachtree Dunwoody Road. But confusion isn't as prevalent as the naysayers claim.

The only Peachtree Street visitors really need to know is the main one, Atlanta's central artery, which begins downtown at Spring Street and runs north through Midtown and Buckhead. (West Peachtree Street runs parallel to Peachtree Street. In 2015, its section above 14th Street was given the unexpected honorary name, Gladys Knight Highway.) In south Buckhead, Peachtree Street's name changes to Peachtree Road. It later becomes Peachtree Industrial Boulevard in Brookhaven. Simple, right? Most of the other "Peachtrees" around town are residential side streets, not easily mistaken for the grand and iconic boulevard.

So why did this town go nuts over a fruit tree almost never seen inside city limits? The phrase comes from Standing Peachtree, a prominent Creek village founded here before the Revolutionary War. Oddly enough, the "peach" is thought by some historians to be a bastardization of the word "pitch," referring to the sap that flowed from a large pine tree in the area. Had history taken a slight linguistic detour, folks might be complaining today that every street in Atlanta is called "Pitch Tree"—which just doesn't have the same sweetness.

Snake Nation to the ground. (Today's "Rowdies" tend to congregate a few blocks over on Edgewood Avenue.)

Once the American Civil War erupted in 1861, Atlanta was in a prime strategic position. Four vital railroads converged here, and the place became a center for the factories, machine shops, and foundries that would empower the Confederate Army. In three short years the city's population swelled to 23,000, and its status as a munitions and supply hub made it a target for the Union Army. In May 1864, Union general William Tecumseh Sherman began a major offensive at Chattanooga, Tennessee, with a team of 100,000 soldiers. By June his forces had reached Kennesaw Mountain near Marietta. A major battle ensued and Sherman lost an estimated 3,000 men—compared to Confederate losses of only 800. Still, the Union Army regrouped and trudged southward toward Atlanta. The Confederacy replaced Gen. Joseph E. Johnston with Gen. John B. Hood, a fiery Texan who was told to seize the offensive.

Almost 8,000 soldiers died on July 20, 1864, at the Battle of Peachtree Creek, a crushing defeat for the Confederacy (and present site of an upscale Buckhead neighborhood and Bobby Jones Golf Course). Atlanta was under siege. Residents dug out shelters from the constant shelling. Wounded soldiers were everywhere. The Union forces had targeted railroad tracks outside the city, cutting off General Hood's supply line and leading to a grisly food shortage in town. Finally, on September 1, Confederate soldiers evacuated Atlanta, taking time to blow up seven locomotives and loads of ammunition before they left. General Sherman swept in and ordered his forces to systematically torch any building that might be of future use to the Confederates. Around 5,000 homes burned, along with churches, stores, and factories. Father Thomas O'Reilly, priest at the Church of Immaculate Conception, pleaded with the Catholic soldiers among the Union Army and convinced them to spare five downtown churches and a handful of buildings. On November 16, General Sherman and his men rode out of town via Decatur Street, reportedly singing "The Battle Hymn of the Republic" as they went. Atlanta had achieved the dubious distinction of being the only large American city ever destroyed by war.

BACKGROUND HISTORY

RISE OF THE NEW SOUTH

Reconstruction reportedly began almost immediately after the dust had settled from Sherman's horses. Though their city was a smoldering wreck, with wild dogs stalking the streets and dead horses filling the ditches, battle-scarred Atlantans returned and started putting the place together again. The Union occupation actually helped hurry the process along, as Atlanta became a regional headquarters for Northern forces—a boon to its economic recovery. In 1868 the title of Georgia's state capital was transferred from Milledgeville to Atlanta, a mere four years after the inferno.

The area was flooded with so-called "carpetbaggers," Yankee entrepreneurs who saw great potential for profit in returning the crippled South to its full production potential. The city also experienced an influx of former slaves, who were seeking gainful employment for the first time in their lives. The Reconstruction Act awarded black men the right to vote.

By 1870, Atlanta's City Council included two African American men, a true sea change. Slaves had been prohibited from learning to read or write before the Civil War. The Reconstruction period saw missionaries and transplanted Northerners making a concerted effort to educate the newly free black population.

An outspoken editor of the *Atlanta Constitution* became the voice of the new era. Henry Woodfin Grady had established a name for himself at the daily newspaper in the 1870s. It was Grady who coined the phrase "the New South," envisioning a region that would prosper not just based upon its cotton and tobacco crops, but through a new epoch of industrialization. He argued for reconciliation between the North and the South, and ventured to New York in 1886 on a mission to attract investors to Georgia. There, Grady delivered what came to be known as the "New South" speech, saying, "There was a South of slavery and secession—that South is dead. There is a South of union and freedom—that South, thank God, is living, breathing, growing each hour." Tragically, the editor died in 1889 at age 38 from pneumonia.

Thanks in part to Grady's efforts, Atlanta mounted three major expositions designed to highlight the region's potential as a manufacturing center. The International Cotton Exposition of 1881, held near today's King Plow Arts Center, featured a model factory for refining cotton into cloth. The Piedmont Exposition, which took place in 1887 on the future site of Piedmont Park, was an expansive world's fair featuring artwork, lectures, and displays of textiles. It drew more than 200,000 visitors, including President Grover Cleveland. But the most lavish of the three events was 1895's Cotton States and International Exposition, a larger-than-life affair that wowed its 800,000 visitors with innovations in agriculture and technology. William "Buffalo Bill" Cody brought in his Wild West Show, and John Philip Sousa performed his new "King Cotton March" for the expo. Booker T. Washington, a former slave, delivered the legendary "Atlanta Compromise" speech, which inherently supported the "separate but equal" doctrine that became the South's legal custom of the next 60 years. The event also led to the creation of Piedmont Park.

INDUSTRY AND THE JIM CROW ERA

By the turn of the 20th century, Atlanta had become a hotbed for business—and not just cotton and textiles. A local druggist, John Pemberton, had invented a popular headache elixir in 1886, and soon sold the recipe to Asa Candler for $2,000. Candler decided the syrupy liquid might sell better if it wasn't marketed as medicine, and Coca-Cola was born. By 1919, Candler had become Atlanta's mayor, and his family sold the beverage business for $25 million to Ernest Woodruff. The Woodruff family would grow the company into an international powerhouse.

Coke wasn't the city's only success story. Downtown's M. Rich Dry Goods had grown from a small shop into one of Atlanta's largest department stores, rivaled only by nearby Davison's. The Rich's chain later expanded across the country. Both Davison's and Rich's were eventually bought by Macy's Inc. Business magnate Amos Rhodes built up a furniture empire here in the late 1800s, which paid for one of the grandest mansions on Peachtree Street, Rhodes Hall (a popular spot for Atlanta weddings today). The 1920s saw the opening of the city's first airfield, later site of Hartsfield-Jackson Atlanta International Airport, and the launch of what would later become Delta Airlines, another signature Atlanta brand.

With a population of 90,000 in 1900, Atlanta treated its residents to many modern amenities. Luxurious homes along Peachtree Street had indoor plumbing and electric lights; some even had telephones. Trolley cars carried workers from the "suburbs" (now intown neighborhoods like Grant Park) to new high-rises downtown. Life was good—at least for the white residents. African Americans found themselves living in less ideal circumstances, with all aspects of society segregated by race. After the Civil War, so-called Jim Crow Laws had stripped black Southerners of many of their rights. African American involvement in political life vanished.

Though Atlanta had a reputation for tolerance, an ugly race riot broke out in 1906. A play called *The Clansman,* which endorsed the Ku Klux Klan, had fanned the flames of racial tension the year before. Hostile headlines denigrating African Americans began appearing in the local papers, followed by a race-baiting campaign for governor. The ensuing September riot, started by Caucasians, lasted four days and left an estimated 40 black Atlantans dead.

At the same time, Atlanta was becoming a destination for blacks seeking higher learning. The city's most prominent historically black colleges—including Morehouse, Spelman, and Morris Brown—had all been established in the 1800s and helped create a new generation of educated African Americans. Atlanta University professor W. E. B. Du Bois established the National Association for the Advancement of Colored People here in 1909.

THE CITY TOO BUSY TO HATE

In 1936, Atlanta found itself once again in the national spotlight, only this time for a work of literature. Margaret Mitchell—Peggy to her friends—was a former *Atlanta Journal* reporter who was reluctant to share her rambling novel manuscript with an editor friend, but *Gone With the Wind* went on to sell more than 30 million copies. It won the Pulitzer Prize in 1937 and was made into an Academy Award-winning film. Atlanta hosted the movie premiere in 1939, though black actors from the film couldn't attend because the extravagant Loew's Grand Theatre was segregated. Critics in later years have decried the novel as racist or an apology for slavery, perhaps overlooking the fact that Mitchell used part of the fortune she amassed from the book to create substantial scholarships for medical students at Morehouse College. Mitchell was killed in 1949 after being struck by a taxi while crossing Peachtree Street at 13th Street.

As the civil rights movement gained steam across the South in the 1950s, Atlanta business leaders worked to maintain the city's reputation for tolerance. Unsightly racial incidents in Alabama and Mississippi in 1955 created fears that Atlanta would be next. But black and white community leaders worked behind the scenes to cool the rhetoric and quietly move the city forward. The city's public transit, police force, and public golf courses were all desegregated without major incident. Mayor William Hartsfield famously proclaimed that Atlanta was "the city too busy to hate."

Still, black families who challenged residential segregation by moving into white neighborhoods were met with physical confrontations and cross burnings. In 1958, a bomb exploded at Atlanta's most prominent synagogue, known locally as "the Temple." The act of terrorism was said to be a response to the U.S. Supreme Court decision *Brown v. Board of Education* and to Jewish support of the civil rights movement.

A year earlier, Martin Luther King Jr. had returned home to Atlanta and founded the Southern Christian Leadership Conference. For the next decade, King would be a pervasive national force for civil rights. Atlanta's public school system was successfully desegregated in the early 1960s. Though King died by an assassin's bullet in 1968, his message of social change transformed the nation.

The next two decades saw fundamental demographic shifts. The trend of "white flight" from inner cities led to the dramatic development of Atlanta's northern suburbs. The city elected its first black mayor, Maynard Jackson, in 1974, and the office has been held by an African American ever since.

ATLANTA TODAY

Atlanta continued to grow and prosper during the Carter and Reagan years, when several of the city's signature skyscrapers rose in Downtown and Midtown, including One Atlantic Center, Georgia Pacific Tower, and the Marriott Marquis Hotel. The city's modern preservation movement began in earnest in the early 1970s with an effort to save the Fox Theatre from the wrecking ball, though it was too late to prevent the demolition of many classic buildings. The city was on a mission to boost its credentials on the world stage.

In the late 1980s, a local lawyer named Billy Payne got the idea that Atlanta should bid on the 1996 Olympic Games. The notion was dismissed as a long shot at first, even with the backing of mayor Andrew Young. But in 1990, Payne's detractors were roundly silenced when the International Olympic Committee selected Atlanta to host the games, beating out the more likely candidate—Athens, Greece.

A massive building frenzy gripped the metro region in the next six years. The most striking changes happened downtown with the construction of Centennial Olympic Stadium (now Turner Field) and Centennial Olympic Park. By the time the summer games arrived, several parts of town had been transformed completely, and events were held in venues as far away as Athens, Georgia. A bomb exploded in the Olympic Village on July 27, 1996, killing two people, but the city refused to let the deaths overshadow the games.

The years since the 1996 Olympics have been dizzying. In the late 1990s, Atlanta was starting to seem like a victim of its own success: Inner-city neighborhoods strained with the growing pains of gentrification, while long commutes made many locals wonder where the city had gone wrong. The new millennium has seen the metropolitan area balloon to more than five million people.

The 2000s experienced a tidal wave of new residents moving back "inside the perimeter," or within the confines of I-285. Atlanta's notoriously long commutes and clogged highways have caused a greater demand for housing near the city center, with an amazing new building boom of condo towers and loft conversions. Many formerly depressed neighborhoods have become real-estate hot spots, and once-shuttered business districts now buzz with new life. The city has attracted billions of dollars in new development since 2005, including Atlantic Station, the Georgia Aquarium, and the expanded Woodruff Arts Center.

Government and Economy

GOVERNMENT

Atlanta, as Georgia's capital, is the nerve center of state government. The Georgia State Capitol building, known for its shimmering gold dome, serves as the offices of the governor, lieutenant governor, secretary of state, and the general assembly. The dome is gilded with native gold leaf extracted from Dahlonega. Nearby City Hall hosts Atlanta's city government, which is divided into legislative and executive branches. A 15-person city council serves as the legislative branch, with one representative from each of the city's 12 districts and three at-large positions. City departments, under the direction of the mayor, constitute the executive branch.

The 2002 election of Shirley Franklin was greeted by many as the dawn of a new era in local politics. For years, City Hall had been accused of being a den of corruption and backroom deals—allegations that gained traction once former mayor Bill Campbell was indicted by a federal grand jury on bribery, racketeering, and wire fraud charges in 2004. Two years later, Campbell was convicted of tax evasion and sent to prison.

Franklin, who had previously held jobs under mayors Maynard Jackson and Andrew Young, inherited a city government with a gaping $82 million budget deficit, forcing her to increase taxes and cut city staff immediately. After a campaign promise to repair potholes in city roads, Franklin made fixing Atlanta's infrastructure one of her top priorities, including a $3.2 billion overhaul of the aging sewer system. She easily won reelection in 2005 and was named one of America's five best big-city mayors by *Time* magazine.

Franklin's former campaign manager, Kasim Reed, narrowly won the 2009 mayoral election. Four years later, Reed sailed to reelection by a huge margin of victory. His time in office has been marked by an unapologetic focus on banner construction project reform. He garnered a mixed bag of praise and criticism for backing the new streetcar system and football stadium. More popular has been Reed's insistence that the city push forward with plans to complete the Atlanta BeltLine, a comprehensive urban redevelopment project that has already started to shape regional growth.

In presidential elections, the state of Georgia has gone reliably Republican since the late 1960s, except when a Southern Democrat was on the ticket. Georgians rallied behind hometown candidate Jimmy Carter in 1976 and 1980, and gave the state's electoral votes to Bill Clinton in 1992—but not in 1996. No Democratic presidential candidate has prevailed since. Regardless, Atlanta is the deep blue heart in a ruby-red state, with a line of Democratic mayors stretching back more than 60 years. In the 2008 presidential election, Fulton County voted two-to-one for Democrat Barack Obama. The split in DeKalb County was closer to four-to-one. Obama lost the state of Georgia again in the 2012 election, but he won 64 percent of the vote in Fulton County, and almost 80 percent of DeKalb County's vote.

ECONOMY

Since its founding as a railroad town, Atlanta has had a love affair with industry and transportation. Georgia was once known mainly as an agrarian state, producing cotton, corn, tobacco, soybeans, eggs, and peaches; Atlanta traditionally served as the distribution and economic center for the state's crops.

The last 50 years have seen the city rise as a home for international corporations. Atlanta ranked third in the 2014 list of cities with Fortune 500 companies. Six Fortune 100 companies are headquartered here: The Coca-Cola Company, Home Depot, United Parcel Service, Delta Airlines, AT&T Mobility, and Newell Rubbermaid.

Thanks to the efforts of Ted Turner, Atlanta has grown into a leading communications hub and cable television powerhouse. Turner Broadcasting Systems started here in the early 1970s with the launch of the "Superstation," TBS. In 1980, the company premiered the Cable News Network, aka CNN, which has become one of the world's most-watched news sources, reaching an estimated 1.5 billion people. Other members of the TBS family include Cartoon Network, Turner Classic Movies, Boomerang, and Peachtree TV. Outside the Turner empire, the Weather Channel—now owned by NBC—is located here, as well as Cox Communications, the third-largest cable provider in the nation and publisher of several daily newspapers.

EDUCATION

Atlanta's rich concentration of colleges and universities is one of the city's greatest assets. More than 50 institutes of higher learning are located here. The most prestigious of the area's private schools is Emory University, with a total enrollment of 13,893 students. Established in 1836, Emory has been named part of the "new ivy league" by *Newsweek* and consistently earns top honors from other national college ranking sources. Its 630-acre campus sits northeast of Downtown next to the U.S. Centers for Disease Control and Prevention.

Among public schools, the Georgia Institute of Technology is acknowledged as one of the best in the region. In 2014 *U.S. News & World Report* ranked Georgia Tech's undergraduate engineering program as the fourth best in the nation. In recent years, the school has been listed among the top public universities, and its engineering school is one of the largest in the nation. The 400-acre campus marks the divide between Downtown and Midtown west of the Downtown Connector.

Farther south, the historically black colleges of the Atlanta University Center have traditions dating back to the post-Civil War era, when the state saw its first flowering of African American education. Located in the historic West End neighborhood near Downtown, the group includes Clark Atlanta University, Spelman College, Morehouse College, and the Morehouse School of Medicine. Combined, the schools enroll close to 10,000 students each year. Nearby, Georgia State University has the unique distinction of being a college campus integrated into the very fiber of Downtown's business district. Known as a commuter school, Georgia State enrolls around 23,000 students and is recognized as the state's only urban research university.

Other respected institutions in the area include Agnes Scott College, a women's school near Decatur; Oglethorpe University, a liberal arts school north of Buckhead; and Clayton State University, a public school 15 minutes south of Downtown. All told, Atlanta-area colleges and universities serve an estimated 250,000 students annually.

People and Culture

DEMOGRAPHICS

With a total population of more than 5.5 million people, greater Atlanta is listed as the nation's ninth-largest metropolitan area by the U.S. Census Bureau. Of that number, just over 447,000 live inside Atlanta city limits according to estimates from 2013. In the first half of the 2000s, Atlanta experienced a major surge in new residents, with more than a third of the newcomers transplanted from other states—mostly New York and New Jersey. Regional growth began to slow due to the recession of late 2008-2009, but the population still increased by more than 6 percent from 2010-2013.

The city's exceptional growth spurt has also led to a more diverse populace. Atlanta's racial diversity is greater than America's as a whole. According to the 2010 census, the city is 54 percent black, 38.4 percent white, 5.2 percent Hispanic, and 3.1 percent Asian. Though blacks make up almost half of Atlanta's demographic, the number comes into a different focus when compared to the state of Georgia, where African Americans are 30.5 percent and whites are 59.7 percent.

The ratio of women to men here is virtually equal. The median age in Atlanta is 34—younger than the nation's average of 36. Residents over the age of 60 comprise 5.8 percent. People born in foreign countries represent 6 percent of the population, but the number of families here who speak a language other than English at home is greater than 10 percent. During the 2000s, the state's Latino population grew by a staggering 96 percent.

In the first half of the 2000s, metro Atlanta experienced a major surge in new residents, with more than a third of the newcomers transplanted from other states—mostly New York and New Jersey. Regional growth began to slow due to the recession of late 2008-2009, with population growth registering at less than 1 percent in 2009 (compared to a 4 percent increase in 2006).

Atlanta has an enviable concentration of wealth. According to the 2015 Forbes Billionaires list, the metro region is home to eight of the world's billionaires. Georgia, meanwhile, is home to more 163,000 millionaires (as of 2012). Greater Atlanta is also known for having America's largest concentration of black millionaires.

RELIGION

Atlanta is sometimes described as "the buckle of the Bible Belt," a curious distinction given the city's preponderance of strip joints. Which isn't to say Atlantans aren't religious: The metro region has more than 1,000 places of worship, and has long been a stronghold for the Southern Baptist Convention, which makes up the vast majority of the church-going populace. Methodists and Catholics are the two next largest groups, respectively. Recent years have seen the rise of "megachurches" in the nearby suburbs; for example, North Point Community Church in Alpharetta attracts roughly 24,000 members to its five campuses, making it the largest church in metro Atlanta and the second largest in the nation. America's biggest Presbyterian congregation, Peachtree Presbyterian, has a Buckhead campus that could eclipse some small towns.

The city's traditional home for black churches has long been Sweet Auburn, with the larger-than-life Ebenezer Baptist Church, Big Bethel A.M.E., and Wheat Street Baptist Church. Due to the flood of Hispanic residents, Atlanta has seen a major swelling of its Catholic population in the past decade, and many Protestant congregations here have also started Spanish-language worship services to attract the newcomers. Though many congregations in Atlanta have grown more diverse over the years, Christian churches have remained rather homogeneous groups. As Cynthia Tucker, former editorial page editor of the *Atlanta Journal-Constitution,* once noted, "Devout Christians of different races rarely attend church together; 11 o'clock on Sunday mornings remains among the most segregated hours in America."

Beyond the Christian diaspora, Atlanta also hosts a wide range of other faiths and traditions. The city ranks 11th in the nation for its Jewish population, an increase of 60 percent in just a decade. The area also has seen an increase in Muslim residents, and now supports 35 active mosques. New Thought, Unitarian Universalist, and Existentialist groups also thrive in the city.

THE ARTS
Visual Arts

As home to the High Museum of Art, Atlanta is considered a regional leader for visual art. With a history dating back to 1905, the High serves as an important center of gravity for the Southeast's cultural life. The museum experienced a major boost in 1979 when Coca-Cola tycoon Robert Woodruff promised a $7.5 million challenge grant for the construction of a new facility. The museum responded by raising $20 million, and the High unveiled its new Richard Meier building in 1983, which has since been called one of the greatest works of American architecture of the 1980s. Two decades later, the gleaming white edifice was figuratively bursting at the seams, as the High's permanent collection, attendance, and prestige had all skyrocketed. The museum responded by tapping Italian architect Renzo Piano to design three new buildings, which opened in 2005 and doubled the High's size.

With cheap rents still available and an active gallery scene, Atlanta is known to be hospitable to up-and-coming artists, with many studios operating out of lofts in still-gentrifying intown neighborhoods. The underground arts scene has long been encouraged by the Atlanta Contemporary Art Center, a multidisciplinary venue that includes studios for artists, as well as Eyedrum, a gallery and performance space famous for its experimental fare. Countless tiny fly-by-night arts collectives, galleries, and exhibitions are constantly popping up around town. The city's artistic life has benefited from the arrival of the Savannah College of Art and Design, which opened a high-profile Atlanta campus in 2005.

Commercial galleries here run the gamut from traditional painting to pop-art ephemera. Atlanta is a great place to experience photography and folk art. One of the best-known folk artists to emerge from the state in the late 20th century was Howard Finster, a north Georgia preacher who painted grand religious murals, mixing angels with the likes of Hank Williams and Elvis Presley. Though Finster passed away in 2001, many of his works are on display in the High Museum of Art, and fans can also visit his Paradise Gardens Park and Museum in Summerville. The work of local folk artist Nellie Mae Rowe has also received increasing attention in recent years. Rowe, who lived in Vinings and died in 1983, peppered her creations with African and Afro-Caribbean influences. The High Museum now owns many of her best-known works.

In print since 1980, Atlanta-based *Art Papers* magazine has emerged as a nationally read journal of art criticism. With offices in Little Five Points, the nonprofit organization also curates an array of cultural events throughout the city.

Popular Music

Although Athens gets all the credit as a launch pad for hot bands, Atlanta has played an important role in nurturing the careers of many phenomenal artists of the past 40 years. In the 1960s, the city was a must-hit spot for up-and-coming Motown and R&B stars, with Georgia natives Ray Charles, Otis Redding, and James Brown playing to packed houses. Soul legend Gladys Knight was born here and achieved one of the greatest hits of her career with "Midnight Train to Georgia," a song about coming home to the South.

In the 1970s, Atlanta helped kick-start the Southern Rock phenomenon. Lynyrd Skynyrd was discovered playing at a club here in 1972, and Macon natives the Allman Brothers Band made local fans go wild with their song "Hot 'Lanta." The Atlanta Rhythm Section developed a local following in

Atlanta Speak

Southern accents ain't what they used to be. As in other parts of the country, the regional dialect of the South has largely given way to a more universal American cadence, the result of a pervasive media machine that causes folks to sound the same no matter where they grew up. This is especially true in Atlanta, which has long felt like a separate entity from the rest of Georgia, overrun with residents from all over the world. Still, visitors here can benefit by learning the local vernacular. Here are a few examples of uniquely Atlanta words and phrases.

- **The ATL:** This popular nickname for the city is pronounced "A-T-L". Atlantans also sometimes refer to "A Town," but locals almost never use the term "Hotlanta," which is seen as déclassé and dated.

- **Buckhead Betty:** This is a sarcastic nickname for the well-to-do housewives who live in the wealthy neighborhood of Buckhead, or slang for anything that's gaudy and over-the-top.

- **The BeltLine:** A 22-mile railroad corridor encircling the city. Mentions of "the BeltLine" typically refer to specific segments of the transit route that have been renovated into trails and greenspace.

- **Coke:** Not just the brand name of the local soft-drink giant, it's also used as a broad term. Any carbonated beverage may be referred to as Coke, and occasionally as soda, but never, ever, as pop.

- **Dawg:** Shorthand for a Georgia Bulldog, aka a student from the University of Georgia.

- **Downtown Connector:** The joint section of I-75 and I-85 that runs through Downtown is also called just "the Connector."

- **Goobers:** This is a local term for peanuts.

- **Grady Curve:** Yet another road-related landmark, this is the dramatic bend

the late '70s. Singer and Atlanta native Jerry Reed capitalized on his homespun eccentricity and whittled a successful film career. Later, Atlanta rock acts like the Georgia Satellites and the Black Crowes took their Southern sound to even wider audiences.

The 1980s and '90s saw the rise of many hometown country hitmakers. Travis Tritt, a Marietta native, started churning out platinum records in 1989. Around the same time, Alan Jackson moved from Newnan to Nashville and became a honky-tonk sensation. Pop-country duo Sugarland has enjoyed breakthrough status in the past few years. The group formed in Atlanta in 2003 as part of the indie-folk scene at Decatur acoustic venue Eddie's Attic, which had previously helped launch the career of the Indigo Girls. Pop troubadour John Mayer also emerged from the Eddie's incubator and went on to win a heap of Grammy Awards.

The biggest thing to happen to Atlanta's musical standing in recent years is the blockbuster rise of Southern hip-hop. The "Dirty South" rap scene in the Downtown Connector near Grady Hospital, known for being clogged during rush hour.

- **Greater Vinings:** A snarky, or perhaps sneaky, way of describing an address that's actually in Smyrna.

- **Grits:** A traditional breakfast food of coarsely ground corn. You're more likely to spot grits on a gourmet New South dinner menu than at brunch.

- **The Highlands:** A (grammatically incorrect) term for Virginia-Highland, one that seriously irks some residents of the neighborhood.

- **Intown:** This catch-all term describes locations that are "inside the perimeter" and typically south of Buckhead.

- **ITP:** "Inside the perimeter," or within the confines of I-285. It's used as shorthand for anything intown or urban.

- **OTP:** "Outside the perimeter," or beyond I-285. Often used as a derisive term, meaning "suburban" or, even worse, "alarmingly rural."

- **Ponce de Leon Avenue:** It's pronounced "PAHNTS duh LEE-on," with no trace of a Spanish accent. It's a handy north-south dividing line, also known for its seedy street life.

- **Ramblin' Wreck:** The traditional mascot for Georgia Tech (which actually predates the more commonly used Buzz the Yellowjacket), or else a Tech student.

- **Shoot the 'Hooch:** To raft down the Chattahoochee River.

- **Spaghetti Junction:** This refers to the busy intersection of I-85 and I-285.

- **Y'all:** The second-person plural pronoun, typically used to denote a warm greeting, as in, "Y'all come back now." Never pronounced as "you all."

erupted here in the mid-1990s, thanks partly to the efforts of producer Jermaine Dupri's Atlanta-based So-So Def Recordings. East Point duo Outkast achieved fame in 1994 with their album *ATLiens* and went on to record-breaking crossover success. Ludacris, formerly a DJ for Atlanta's 107.9 FM, became an overnight hip-hop sensation who immortalized the city with his 2001 anthem "Welcome to Atlanta." Other chart-topping hip-hop acts to emerge from the prolific scene include Janelle Monáe, Cee Lo Green, India.Arie, Erykah Badu, Monica, T. I., Lil Jon, Usher, and Danger Mouse—to name just a few.

Literature

To hear some people tell it, Atlanta's literary legacy begins and ends with *Gone With the Wind,* a novel with which the city is virtually synonymous. It's true that Margaret Mitchell's Civil War romance ranks as one of the most popular works of fiction of all time, famously hyped as selling more copies than any book other than the Bible. But Atlanta and its near vicinity have produced a steady stream of best-selling authors and literary lions over the years.

Flannery O'Connor, grande dame of the mid-20th-century Southern Gothic movement, lived most of her life in nearby Milledgeville and chose Atlanta as the setting for one of her most celebrated stories, "The Artificial Nigger." Eatonton native Alice Walker attended Spelman College and later won the 1983 Pulitzer Prize for Fiction for her novel *The Color Purple.* Playwright Alfred Uhry, born in Atlanta, won a Pulitzer and two Tony Awards for his Atlanta trilogy, which started with 1987's *Driving Miss Daisy.*

James Dickey, a prolific poet and Buckhead native, saw his popularity skyrocket in the early 1970s after the release of the film version of his novel *Deliverance.* Pat Conroy, author of *The Prince of Tides,* was born in Atlanta and lived in Ansley Park for many years. Hometown author Anne Rivers Siddons (*Peachtree Road*) saw her first wide commercial success in the 1980s, and is still turning out novels today. Local columnists Celestine Sibley and Lewis Grizzard, both staffers of the *Atlanta Journal-Constitution,* also enjoyed prolific careers as authors. Another *AJC* alum, Kathy Hogan Trocheck, has filled shelves with her mystery novels and, under the pseudonym Mary Kay Andrews, breezy chick-lit comedies.

Jim Grimsley, who teaches creative writing at Emory University, has earned a pile of awards for his plays and novels, including 1995's *Dream Boy.* In 1997, West End resident Pearl Cleage became a media darling when her novel *What Looks Like Crazy on an Ordinary Day* was picked for Oprah Winfrey's book club. Cleage's former student, Tayari Jones, received critical acclaim for her gritty 2002 debut, *Leaving Atlanta.* The late E. Lynn Harris, who passed away suddenly in 2009, shed light on a rarely seen facet of African American culture with his coming-out novel, *Invisible Life,* and the dozen or so books that followed.

Hometown heroine Kathryn Stockett's debut novel *The Help* became a major bestseller and spawned an Oscar-nominated film in 2011. Prolific horror novelist Karin Slaughter has enjoyed blockbuster success since 2001 with her gritty crime novels, several of which are set in Atlanta.

Festivals and Events

SPRING
Atlanta Dogwood Festival

An Atlanta springtime tradition since 1936, the **Dogwood Festival** (Piedmont Park, www.dogwood.org, free) draws upwards of 200,000 people to Piedmont Park. Though the event is timed to coincide with April's dogwood blossoms, spectators are more likely to be caught up watching the *actual* dogs competing in the U.S. Disc Dog Southern Nationals, which stars the top Frisbee-catching canines in the country. A vibrant artists market features hundreds of vendors selling paintings, pottery, jewelry, and tchotchkes. Food and family-friendly fun abound, though the crowds can be oppressive midday Saturday.

Atlanta Film Festival

The 10-day **Atlanta Film Festival** (various locations, 404/352-4225, www.atlantafilmfestival.com, $10-50) brings indie cinema to 25,000 movie-goers every April. Festival staffers sort through more than 3,000 entries from more than 100 countries and select around 150 titles to screen; of those, 20 films compete for the festival's coveted jury prize. It's one of the few Academy Award-qualifying festivals in the country. The event features an absorbing roster of panels, screenplay readings, movie discussions, and plenty of parties. Recent years have seen festival screenings centralized into a handful of Midtown locations, with most screenings taking place at Landmark Midtown Art Center. Atlanta Film Festival 365, the non-profit group that produces the festival, hosts workshops and screenings year-round.

Decatur Arts Festival

The best thing about the **Decatur Arts Festival** (Decatur Square, Decatur, 404/371-9583, www.decaturartsfestival.com, free) may be the town itself. With vendors galore in and around Decatur Square, located six miles from downtown Atlanta, the festival has the charm and scale of a small-town street fair, but with the benefits of big-city sophistication. The annual Memorial Day weekend event features more than 160 artists selected through a competitive jury process. Kids get their own mini-festival, with events all day Saturday and even their own parade.

Georgia Renaissance Festival

Huzzah! As if by magic, the rural outskirts of Fairburn sprout a 16th-century European country faire each spring called the **Georgia Renaissance Festival** (6905 Virlyn B. Smith Rd., Fairburn, 770/964-8575, www.garenfest.com, $8-20). This sprawling 32-acre bazaar is, in a word, bizarre. The festival features a cast of nearly 1,000 costumed knights, knaves, archers, jesters, damsels, and wizards mingling with visitors—many of whom also show up in period attire. Highlights include an arts-and-crafts market, petting zoo, jousting tournament, belly dancers, and magic acts. Located eight miles south of Hartsfield Jackson International Airport, the festival runs mid-April through early June.

Inman Park Festival

Spring and summer in Atlanta are never hurting for neighborhood street festivals. The annual **Inman Park Festival** (Euclid Ave. at Elizabeth St., 770/242-4895, www.inmanparkfestival.org, free) may well be the city's most vibrant. The area's dignified Victorian architecture provides a stunning, if somewhat unexpected, backdrop for the hippie vibe of the two-day event, which delivers a labyrinthine street market, dance and musical performances, and an enjoyable tour of Inman Park homes. The boisterous street parade is always the highlight of the weekend. Finding parking on festival weekend can be a challenge: Be prepared to walk or take MARTA to the Inman Park station.

Martin Luther King Jr. Week

Kicking off with the January 15 birthday of Martin Luther King Jr., **Martin Luther King Jr. Week** (various locations, 404/526-8900, www.thekingcenter.org, ticket prices vary depending on event) usually spills over to become more of a month-long observance. King Week incorporates a range of events throughout the city, from an annual concert by the Atlanta Symphony Orchestra to lectures and workshops on many local college campuses. The King Center is the hub for most King Week activities, hosting its largest fundraiser of the year as well as a memorial service for the late civil rights leader. Some happenings are tied with programming for Black History Month in February and the Season for Nonviolence.

Sweet Auburn Springfest

The multicultural street festival called **Sweet Auburn Springfest** (Auburn Ave. and Courtland St., www.sweetauburn.com, free) has expanded its scope to include more than just the vendor tents that fill Auburn Avenue. The mid-May event dates back to 1984, but recent years have seen the Sweet Auburn Springfest tackle issues such as raising environmental awareness or hosting one of the largest outdoor health and fitness fairs in the country. The festival's primary draw remains the weekend artist market and its many international food options, along with activities aimed at kids and even a beauty pageant.

SUMMER
Decatur Book Festival

The largest independent book festival in the country, the **Decatur Book Festival** (various locations, Decatur, 404/373-2021, www.decaturbookfestival.com, free) takes place each Labor Day weekend in and around Decatur Square. Even though Atlanta has struggled over the years to maintain a successful annual literary fair, the Decatur Book Festival has found a winning formula and seems to grow larger each year. The weekend brings in more than 300 authors and offers roster of events that includes readings, lectures, a book market, cooking demonstrations, writing workshops, and activities aimed at kids and teens. Most events are free; tickets go quickly for the keynote lectures that are not.

Dragon Con Parade

No longer just Dungeons & Dragons-playing fanboys rolling 20-sided dice in hotel rooms all weekend, Atlanta's annual **Dragon Con** (downtown, 770/909-0115, www.dragoncon.org, free) has grown into one of the largest pop-culture conventions in the country. Held Labor Day weekend, the 40,000-plus member convention delivers some of the city's most outlandish people-watching of the year, best experienced at the annual street parade. Picture an army of stormtroopers invading Downtown, followed by a fleet of Spartans and a legion of superheroes. Around 1,000 costumed characters take part in the family-friendly parade, held on Saturday morning of the four-day convention. Crowds gather along Peachtree Street starting near the Westin Peachtree Plaza.

National Black Arts Festival

Founded in 1987, the **National Black Arts Festival** (various locations, 404/730-7315, www.nbaf.org, ticket prices vary depending on event) celebrates the art and culture of the African diaspora with programming in music, theater, visual arts, film, and dance. Previous years have featured appearances by Alice Walker and Gladys Knight and performances of Broadway's *The Color Purple* and *Dream Girls*. The July festival drew more then 300,000 attendees in its heyday, but recent issues within the NBAF have led to declining numbers and struggles with debt. A multi-year plan to reboot the event showed promise in 2014, leading to the selection of Wynton Marsalis as a guest curator and a new focus on the NBAF's core mission.

Peachtree Road Race

Every July 4, 60,000 runners brave the blistering Georgia heat to run 6.2 miles along Peachtree Street in the **Peachtree Road Race** (Lenox Square to Piedmont Park, 404/231-9064, www.peachtreeroadrace.org), huffing past Lenox Square Mall, the glass towers of Buckhead, and the Woodruff Arts Center to finally reach the waiting oasis of Piedmont Park in Midtown. The annual race, first run in 1970, is one of Atlanta's most talked-about local traditions, its coveted T-shirts worn by locals long after the logos have faded. The course's most challenging stretch, dubbed "Heart Attack Hill," happily coincides with Piedmont Hospital—just in case. It's fun for spectators and runners alike, but everyone should avoid driving in Midtown or Buckhead on July 4.

FALL
Art on the Atlanta BeltLine Lantern Parade

The Atlanta BeltLine Eastside Trail becomes a kinetic pageant of multicolored lights during the annual **Lantern Parade** (Atlanta BeltLine Eastside Trail, http://art.beltline.org/lantern-parade, free), held in early September.

Above: Dragon Con Parade. **Below:** Atlanta Dogwood Festival.

The all-inclusive event invites participants to create their own paper lanterns for the procession. Folks tend to reinterpret the instructions with exuberance, leading to glow-stick headgear, flashing LED parasols, giant illuminated dragons, and countless other designs. Attendance has risen quickly since the inaugural Lantern Parade in 2010, topping 20,000 by only the fifth outing.

Atlanta Celebrates Photography

Fall signals an onslaught of photography shows in the city thanks to the efforts of **Atlanta Celebrates Photography** (ACP, various locations, 404/634-8664, www.acpinfo.org, ticket prices vary depending on event). The wide-reaching "festival" feels more like a movement, with dozens of exhibitions mounted in spaces all over town, as well as parties, film screenings, and a lecture series honoring photographers. An annual gala fundraiser and photography auction helps to keep the nonprofit entity behind Atlanta Celebrates Photography afloat. You could easily visit a couple of ACP shows per day in October and still not take in the full scope of the festival.

Atlanta Pride Festival

The largest gay and lesbian pride celebration in the South is a regional affair. The three-day **Atlanta Pride Festival** (Piedmont Park, 404/382-7588, www.atlantapride.org, free) includes a parade, marketplace, full performance schedule, and mass commitment ceremony, among dozens of other unofficial events. Although it was traditionally held in June to commemorate New York's Stonewall Riots of 1969, the festival has more recently moved to October, giving events a more subdued vibe. National acts such as the B-52s and the Indigo Girls have headlined the festival over the years; the highlight of the weekend is the sprawling Sunday-afternoon parade, which winds its way from Downtown to Piedmont Park. Expect the biggest crowds to gather on 10th Street near Blake's on the Park.

East Atlanta Strut

More than 12,000 people descend upon East Atlanta Village each September for the **East Atlanta Strut** (Flat Shoals Ave. and Glenwood Ave., www.eastatlantastrut.com, free), a rambunctious affair where the crowd tends to be a bit more buzzed and grungy than at other local street festivals. The community-organized one-day event kicks off with a 5K run and includes three stages of music and comedy acts. The parade features wildly decorated art cars and floats. Younger strutters will enjoy the Kids Village, which gives a funky East Atlanta twist to face painting and wacky removable tattoos. The festival is a fundraiser for local charities.

Grant Park Mothball and Tour of Homes

The tongue-in-cheek **Grant Park Mothball and Tour of Homes** (various locations, 404/586-9999, www.themothball.com, $20-25) began in the 1970s as a potluck during the annual Tour of Homes; its name is a parody of neighboring Inman Park's formal Butterfly Ball. Now, the annual costume party and fundraiser for the neighborhood association has spread its wings to become an autumn tradition not just for Grant Park residents. The event features a silent auction, live music, and a spirited "Miss Mothball" competition. The party traditionally takes place on the Saturday evening of the Grant Park Tour of Homes (in September or October), which gives a peek inside some of the prestigious residences of Atlanta's largest historic neighborhood. The date of the event varies.

Little Five Points Halloween Festival

Most any Saturday night finds all sorts of freaks and funky characters roaming the streets of Little Five Points, so just try and imagine the place around Halloween. The alternative-minded annual **Little Five Points Halloween Festival** (Euclid Ave. and Moreland Ave., www.l5phalloween. com, free) embraces the spooky spirit of the season with rare enthusiasm, though its daytime events make this horror show a (mostly) family-friendly function. Kids and adults can enter the festival's costume contest or just sit back and enjoy the afternoon parade, featuring some of the most imaginative get-ups found this side of Dragon Con. The festival usually takes place a couple of weekends before October 31, thereby stretching Halloween into a much longer celebration.

Music Midtown Festival

After a six-year break, Atlanta's enormous outdoor **Music Midtown Festival** (Piedmont Park, www.musicmidtown.com) returned with new vigor in 2011. The two-day event has continued to grow ever since, most recently as an expansive three-stage festival spread over Piedmont Park. Past headliners have ranged from rock royalty (Greg Allman, Journey, Jack White) to hip-hop acts (Run DMC, Iggy Azalea) and indie favorites (Artic Monkeys, The Black Lips).

WINTER
Lighting of Macy's Great Tree

Since its start in 1947, the homegrown holiday tradition **Lighting of Macy's Great Tree** (Lenox Square Mall, 770/913-5639, free) has changed with the times. It was first held at the now-defunct Rich's department store downtown but has since moved to Macy's at Lenox Square Mall. More than 100,000 spectators turn out for the Thanksgiving-evening event, which includes a lot more than just throwing the switch on the store's towering 70-foot Christmas tree. Previous years have seen performances by pop and country stars and the Macy's holiday choir. Even better, the annual tree lighting signals the arrival of the **Pink Pig,** a beloved children's ride that returns each year to the mall's upper parking deck. (It's one of those things you just have to see to understand.)

New Year's Eve Peach Drop at Underground

Times Square drops a magnificent Waterford crystal ball every New Year's Eve at midnight; Atlanta drops an 800-pound fiberglass peach at the **New Year's Eve Peach Drop at Underground** (50 Upper Alabama St., 404/523-2311, www.peachdrop.com, free). The city's 16-hour New Year's celebration features a full day of live performances, family games, and fireworks leading up to the closing of the calendar. At midnight, the eight-foot-tall fruit takes less than a minute to crawl down its metal light tower as thousands of onlookers below ring in the new year. It's one of the most well-attended outdoor New Year's Eve events in the nation, but not recommended for anyone averse to rowdy crowds.

Essentials

Transportation

GETTING THERE
Air

Located 10 miles south of Downtown, **Hartsfield-Jackson Atlanta International Airport** (800/897-1910, www.atlanta-airport.com) is often cited as the busiest airport in the world, serving more than 80 million passengers per year. More than 30 major airlines and smaller carriers fly to Hartsfield-Jackson. The Atlanta Convention and Visitors Bureau notes that 80 percent of the U.S. population is within a two-hour flight from the city. The airport offers 2,700 daily flights to 231 destinations in 52 countries.

The airport is the home base and main hub for **Delta Air Lines** (800/221-1212, www.delta.com), which, along with its partner airlines, reaches more than 100 countries and six continents. Delta accounts for more than half of the annual travelers passing through Hartsfield-Jackson. Hartsfield-Jackson is also a major hub for **Southwest Airlines** (800/435-9792, www.southwest.com), a discount carrier that operates 125 daily departures from Atlanta.

Hartsfield-Jackson has more than 200 gates spread out over seven concourses (labeled T, A, B, C, D, E, and F). International flights arrive at Concourse E or F. Commuting between concourses is usually fast and painless thanks to an underground train system and moving sidewalks.

The airport has seen a flurry of construction projects in recent years that have improved the passenger experience. A significant expansion in 2006 brought the addition of a fifth runway, greatly boosting its capacity. In 2009, the airport's sleek new rental car center opened, which centralized all the rental agencies into one location accessible via train. The biggest change in recent history, though, comes with the arrival of the new Maynard H. Jackson Jr. International Terminal, a project that cost upwards of $1.4 billion. Travelers arriving from international destinations had previously gone through the tedious process of retrieving checked luggage, passing through customs, re-checking bags, and going through an additional security checkpoint before continuing to other concourses. The new international terminal eliminates the re-checking of baggage and allows international travelers to exit to ground transportation without first venturing to the distant end of the airport.

Navigating the TSA security gates at Hartsfield-Jackson can be an unpredictable ordeal. Although airlines ask passengers to arrive an hour in advance of domestic flights (and two hours ahead of international flights), it's a good idea to build in an extra half hour. There are 263 shops and restaurants in the airport—including bars, high-end gift stores, and a post office—so there's plenty to do while you wait. Also, check with an airport agent to see if you can use the North or South security checkpoints, which tend to be faster than the main TSA station. Security wait times are posted on the airport website.

Previous: Hartsfield-Jackson Atlanta International Airport; Centennial Olympic Park.

Airport Art

It's easy to get caught up in the rush of passengers hurrying through Hartsfield-Jackson Atlanta International Airport, which features the most heavily used automated people mover in the world. But art lovers with a few extra minutes to spare should make a point of sidestepping the packed underground trains and exploring the airport's unusual assortment of cultural exhibitions. The best example is the permanent exhibition of **contemporary Zimbabwean sculpture** on display in the pedestrian corridor that connects concourses T and A. This collection of striking human-sized stone figures by 12 African artists runs the gamut from playful to solemn and shouldn't be missed. Meanwhile, the airport's main atrium offers a revolving display of artwork, with exhibits that change every six weeks. The 16 wall spaces feature photography, paintings, and mixed-media works. Elsewhere, artwork by Georgia elementary and high-school students is on rotating display in concourses T, D, and E.

The airport connects to ground transportation and MARTA, Atlanta's subway system, at the main terminal. The train ride to Downtown is around 20 minutes and costs $2.50. The same taxi trip takes around a half hour, depending on traffic, and costs a flat rate of $30 for Downtown, $40 for Buckhead (with additional fees for more than one passenger). For rental cars, follow the signs to the ATL Skytrain and the rental car center.

Hartsfield-Jackson boasts the tallest air traffic control tower in North America, the fourth tallest in the world. It's the primary airport for Georgia and the region. The next nearest major commercial airport is Birmingham International in Alabama, about 150 miles west of Atlanta.

Car

Atlanta is easily accessed by car. A web of interstate freeways links the Atlanta metropolitan area with the nation. The two main arteries into the city are I-75 (running from Michigan to Florida) and I-85 (running from Virginia to Alabama), which converge in the heart of Atlanta in a 7.5-mile stretch of interstate known locally as the Downtown Connector. It's also notoriously congested and best avoided during the morning and evening rush hours (roughly 7am-9am and 4:30pm-7:30pm).

Near the main business district, the Downtown Connector intersects with I-20, which reaches from South Carolina to Texas. Another important highway for the city is Georgia State Route 400, which branches off I-85 in Buckhead and penetrates 50 miles into the northern suburbs. The metropolitan area is encircled by I-285, a 69-mile beltway that intersects with all the major interstates.

Bus

Greyhound (232 Forsyth St., 404/584-1728, www.greyhound.com) offers bus services across America. The company also features an **airport bus**

stop (6000 N. Terminal Dr., 404/765-9598). It's an inexpensive but time-consuming option for budget travelers.

Train

Atlanta's **Amtrak station** (1688 Peachtree St., 800/872-7245, www.amtrak.com) sits at the intersection of Midtown and Buckhead just north of I-85. It's part of the commuter train's Crescent line, which runs from New York to New Orleans. Although rail travel tends to be more expensive than flying, some vacationers prefer the leisurely pace of the experience.

GETTING AROUND
Public Transportation

The **Metropolitan Atlanta Rapid Transit Authority** (MARTA, 404/848-5000, www.itsmarta.com) provides rail and bus service to the city. Visitors from cities with extensive public transportation networks are often baffled by the relatively limited reach of MARTA's subway. The system loosely forms a giant X over the city, with two lines running east to west and two more running north to south. The lines intersect at the Five Points station downtown. While it's true that the subway doesn't access all parts of the city, the bus system covers a much greater area. A single one-way fare is $2.50 for either the train or the bus, and visitors who plan to use the system often should consider buying a seven-day pass ($23.75) or a one- to four-day pass ($9-19).

MARTA is a great option for anyone arriving at Hartsfield-Jackson and heading straight to a hotel in Downtown, Midtown, or Buckhead. Sadly, it's not an ideal way to explore the city once you're here, unless all your planned destinations are limited to one part of town. The trains are adequately clean and safe, but the routes are imperfect. Bus rides tend to be long and unpredictable.

In Buckhead, the **Buc** (404/812-7433, www.bucride.com) is a free shuttle that connects with MARTA rail stations and some of the area's main destinations, including Lenox Square Mall. The buses run every 8-12 minutes during the morning and evening commute hours. Check the website for routes and a detailed schedule.

Completed in 2014, the **Atlanta Streetcar** (www.theatlantastreetcar.com) runs a 2.6-mile loop around Downtown with stops at major attractions. Check the website for routes, fares, and operating hours.

Driving

Because of the abbreviated scope of MARTA, most everyone drives in Atlanta. Though some parts of town are becoming more pedestrian friendly, this is still a car city. The local love affair with automobiles has had unfortunate side effects on the region: Atlanta's commuters sit in traffic for 44 hours a year and spend an annual average of more than $5,000 per household on gas—more than anyone else in the nation.

The good news for visitors is that driving around town can be relatively easy, as long as you avoid the interstates and keep out of rush hour. Navigating the city will require a good street map or GPS system, but

Atlanta drivers tend to be far more polite than those in New York or Los Angeles. Locals are often friendly and helpful when asked for directions.

On the other hand, parking is a perennial issue here, especially in dense intown neighborhoods. Spots on the street are highly coveted and usually involve paying a meter. Rates and time restrictions vary in different parts of the city, but one factor is constant: The potential for getting a parking ticket is high almost everywhere. This has been especially true since the city outsourced its parking enforcement services to **PARKAtlanta** (www.parkatlanta.org), a private agency that has been controversial for its aggressive ticketing policies. In the worst-case scenario, cars that are parked improperly can be towed or booted. When in doubt about a parking space in Atlanta, always err on the side of caution. Fines are steep and the hassle is even worse.

Taxis

Taxis in Atlanta charge a flat rate of $8 for trips within Downtown, Buckhead, or Midtown, with a $2 fee per extra passenger. Outside of those business districts, metered rates kick in, which are typically $2.50 for the first eighth of a mile and $0.25 for each additional eighth mile. Fares from the airport range $30-40, more for points outside of I-285.

Finding a taxi can be the tricky part. Travelers accustomed to the sea of cabs seen in cities like New York or Chicago will be dismayed at the apparent lack of taxis on the streets. Your best bet is to keep a couple of cab company phone numbers handy and call about 15 minutes before you need a ride. Two services in town are **Atlanta Checker Cab** (404/351-1111, www.atlantacheckercab.com) and **Buckhead Safety Cab** (404/875-3777, www.buckheadsafetycab.com). A 10 percent tip is customary; passengers with heavy bags should tip more.

Biking

Harried Atlanta commuters have been slow to warm up to bicycling. Folks here still tend to see bikes as great for recreation but not for transportation. Sadly, cyclists who attempt to traverse some of the city's busiest streets can expect to be honked at or yelled at by passing drivers.

The good news is that the city has launched a real effort to create more bike lanes, especially in rapidly growing neighborhoods in Midtown and Downtown. The popularity of bicycling has seen a real upsurge in recent years as gas prices have increased. The **Atlanta Bicycle Coalition** (404/881-1112, www.atlantabike.org) is a grassroots group advocating safer and easier cycling options in the city.

Travel Tips

CONDUCT AND CUSTOMS

Although it sounds like a cliché, Southerners deserve their reputation for being more friendly than folks from other parts of the country. Don't be surprised if an agent at the rental car counter strikes up a leisurely conversation with you, asking detailed questions about where you're going and why you're here. This can be off-putting to impatient Northerners or guarded Midwesterners, but it's nothing to take umbrage over. Southerners also pay careful attention to rules of courtesy and look down upon pushy customers who cut in line or yell at baristas. True, Atlanta is an international city with residents from all over the world, diluting some of its regional propensity for politeness, but city dwellers will almost always stop and offer help to travelers asking questions or needing directions.

SMOKING

The rate of tobacco usage is decreasing slowly in Georgia. According to the Centers for Disease Control, smoking among adults over the age of 18 dropped from 21.2 percent in 2011 to 18.8 percent in 2013. Georgia's smoking percentage remains lower than many other Southern states. Still, Atlanta has been slow to adopt some of the clean-air laws passed in other major cities. In 2005, the state legislature enacted a ban on smoking in most enclosed public places that allow minors. Hotels are exempt from the ban, and the law still allows smoking in bars and restaurants that don't serve customers under 18. The City of Decatur went even further by banning smoking in all indoor public places.

Because of the minors clause in the state's ban, many Atlanta bars remain tolerant of smoking. Restaurants have phased out their smoking sections, and venues like Hartsfield-Jackson International Airport, Philips Arena, and Turner Field allow smoking only in designated areas.

TRAVELING WITH CHILDREN

Atlanta has long been a popular destination for parents traveling with children. The city has no lack of attractions aimed at the younger crew, from Fernbank Museum of Natural History to the Georgia Aquarium. There's also a vibrant theater scene with performances tailor-made for kids, thanks to organizations like **Young Audiences Woodruff Arts Center** (404/733-5293, www.yawac.org) and the Center for Puppetry Arts.

Many hotels are kid friendly, with the exception of a few of the swankier properties, and the same is true of restaurants. When in doubt, call ahead to see if children are allowed. In the past, neighborhoods north of the city were known for being home to more families with small kids, making the businesses there more tolerant of tykes. The past several years have seen a baby boom in more intown neighborhoods, with strollers seen on sidewalks from Midtown to Little Five Points.

TRAVELERS WITH DISABILITIES

Atlanta has made great efforts to create a city hospitable to disabled residents and visitors, with new buildings and public spaces that are wheelchair friendly and barrier free. Hartsfield-Jackson is known as one of the most accessible airports in the country.

All of MARTA's 91 bus routes are now equipped with wheelchair lifts or kneeling capabilities. Senior citizens and passengers with disabilities enjoy priority seating at the front of every bus and at one end of each rail car. All rail stations are fitted with wide fare gates for wheelchairs, as well as elevators on the train platforms.

Health and Safety

HOSPITALS AND PHARMACIES

As home to the national Centers for Disease Control and Prevention (CDC), Atlanta serves as a leading hub for medical research. Near the CDC, Emory University Hospital has been named one of the best hospitals in the country and the best in Atlanta by various rankings. Emory Healthcare also operates several clinics and medical facilities around the city.

Children's Healthcare of Atlanta is regarded as one of the leading pediatric hospitals in the country; it's the product of a 1998 merger between Egleston Children's Health Care and Scottish Rite Medical Center and operates three hospitals and 15 clinics in the metro area.

For medical emergencies and short-term care, the city has many viable options. A few of the best in Atlanta include Piedmont Hospital, St Joseph's Hospital of Atlanta, Emory University Hospital Midtown (formerly Crawford Long), and Northside Hospital. Although medical centers are located all over Atlanta, there's a particular concentration of options near the Emory campus and north of the city in Sandy Springs.

Chain pharmacies show up in strip malls and shopping centers throughout the metro area, with the most prevalent being CVS and Rite Aid. The Midtown **Walgreens** (595 Piedmont Ave., 404/685-9665) is one of the few pharmacies intown that's open 24 hours.

CRIME

Atlanta retains an unfortunate reputation for being an unsafe city, a description that perhaps is only half deserved. Some reports place the city as number nine on the list of America's 10 most dangerous cities. Defenders of Atlanta will point out that the local crime rate has been dropping steadily (if slowly) in recent years according to FBI statistics. From 2012 to 2013, violent crime in Atlanta dropped by 9.75 percent. One trend that hasn't changed: Most of the crime in Atlanta is still related to property (such as vandalism or vehicular crime), not personal injury. Robberies increased by more than 11 percent in that same time period.

The good news for visitors is that the vast majority of the city's violent crime is drug-related and isolated to metro Atlanta's most desolate neighborhoods—mainly areas far south of Downtown that tourists never come anywhere near. As in any major American city, you should take the usual precautions: Stay aware of your surroundings, leave the flashy jewelry at home, avoid dark areas at night, and travel with groups after dark whenever possible.

For years, one of the most annoying aspects of life in the city has been vehicular crime, with cars broken into even in well-lit, heavily trafficked areas. Always lock your doors and never leave any items visible in a car, even items that may not seem like they would have much value.

Information and Services

COMMUNICATIONS AND MEDIA
Phones and Area Codes

The metropolitan Atlanta area has four main area codes: 404, 470, 770, and 678. Making a local call always requires 10-digit dialing. Finding a public pay telephone in the city is a real challenge due to the rise of cell phones. Dial 1 before calling toll-free numbers (which start with 800 or 888) or long-distance area codes. Many gas stations and convenience stores sell prepaid phone cards. For directory assistance, dial 411.

Internet Services

Finding a wireless Internet hot spot here is usually no great challenge, if you're prepared to do a little digging. Although Atlanta never launched a municipal wireless Internet service like some other major cities have, most local coffee shops and many restaurants offer Internet connectivity—and in some cases it's even free. **Octane Coffee Company** (1009-B Marietta St., 404/815-9886, www.octanecoffee.com) is a popular gathering spot for laptop-wielding college students and creative professionals. The wireless Internet is complimentary for customers, so getting a good seat can be a challenge. The same is true for locally owned **Aurora Coffee** (www.auroracoffee.com), which has locations in Virginia-Highland and Little Five Points. Area chains like Starbucks and Caribou offer wireless Internet, though the service sometimes comes with a time limit.

Wireless Internet is available throughout Hartsfield-Jackson; it's provided by a handful of carriers with various fees involved. It can also be found at almost any major hotel in town, but again, isn't usually a free amenity. For a list of Atlanta businesses that offer free wireless Internet, visit **WiFi Free Spot** (www.wififreespot.com/ga.html).

Local Publications

Atlanta's largest and most-read daily newspaper, the *Atlanta Journal-Constitution* (www.ajc.com), came about through the merger of two rival publications. The *Atlanta Constitution,* first published in 1868, was traditionally a morning paper with liberal leanings. The afternoon paper, the *Atlanta Journal,* premiered in 1883 and was known for its more conservative bent. The two papers came under the same ownership in 1950 but maintained separate newsrooms until the 1980s. They merged into one publication in 2001, phasing out the afternoon edition. Today the *AJC* has a daily circulation of just over 195,000 and reaches 27 counties around metro Atlanta. Like all newspapers in America, the company has struggled to convert declining readership of its print edition into a viable revenue model online. One major push in recent years has involved promoting its popular arts and entertainment site, **AccessAtlanta** (www.accessatlanta.com).

Creative Loafing (www.clatl.com) has been Atlanta's default alternative weekly since 1972. Known for its irreverent tone, thorough arts and music coverage, and hard-hitting news stories, the "Loaf" is part of a family of weekly newspapers that includes the *Chicago Reader* and the *Washington City Paper*. While the paper's print edition has also suffered from a decline in pages in recent years, the publication has outlasted countless assaults from (now-defunct) rivals. It maintains a circulation of 90,000.

The city has several other daily, weekly, and monthly newspapers of note. The well-respected **Atlanta Business Chronicle** (www.bizjournals.com/atlanta) is a principal resource for Atlanta's corporate community. The **Atlanta Daily World** (www.atlantadailyworld.com) has served African American readers for more than 90 years. Brash and flashy **Rolling Out** (www.rollingout.com) is an opinionated guide to the world of hip-hop, fashion, and urban culture. The free monthly **Atlanta Intown** (www.atlantaintownpaper.com) puts a positive spin on community news, profiling local personalities, businesses, and charities. **The GA Voice** (www.thegavoice.com) serves as Atlanta's go-to source for gay and lesbian news.

Among the glossy titles, **Atlanta Magazine** (www.atlantamagazine.com) is still the best game in town. An authority on the city since 1961, this polite general-interest magazine has found a fresh voice in recent years as an entertaining and thorough curator of local culture. **The Atlantan** and its sister publication **Jezebel** (www.modernluxury.com) filter arts and fashion news through a polished lens of luxury.

Radio

Atlanta is the ninth-largest radio market in the country and supports a colorful—and competitive—slate of stations. As patterns of radio listening have changed across America, with the rise of Internet favorites like Pandora and Spotify as well as the continued ascendency of Sirius XM, commercial radio continues to struggle to find and hold an audience.

Long a hot spot for hip-hop, Atlanta has drifted in recent years toward more pop and R&B channels while rock and oldies stations have languished. Hip-hop powerhouse **WHTA** (107.9 FM) remains a taste-maker in the market; it's the station where chart-topping rapper Ludacris got his start as a DJ. However, the station's main competitor, **WVEE** (103.3 FM), has overtaken it in terms of ratings.

Here are some of Atlanta's noteworthy radio stations:

- talk: WGST-AM (640 AM)
- sports: WCNN-AM (680 AM)

- news: WSB-AM (750 AM)
- college radio: WRAS (88.5 FM)
- eclectic: WRFG (89.3 FM)
- NPR: WABE (90.1 FM)
- jazz: WCLK (91.9 FM)
- rock: WZGC (92.9 FM)
- top 40: WSTR (94.1 FM)
- country: WUBL (94.9 FM)
- rock: WKLS (96.1 FM)
- adult contemporary: WSB-FM (98.5 FM)
- top 40: WWWQ (99.7 FM)
- country: WKHX (101.5 FM)
- hip-hop: WVEE (103.3 FM)
- Christian: WFSH (104.7 FM)
- Spanish: WBZY (105.3 FM)
- oldies: WYAY (106.7 FM)
- R&B: WAMJ (107.5 FM)
- hip-hop: WHAT (107.9 FM)

Television

Affiliates of all the major television networks can be found in Atlanta, which is also home to the Turner Broadcasting family of cable channels.

Atlanta's primary television stations include:

- WSB (channel 2, ABC, www.wsbtv.com)
- WAGA (channel 5, Fox, www.myfoxatlanta.com)
- WGTV (channel 8, Georgia Public Broadcasting, www.gpb.org)
- WXIA (channel 11, NBC, www.11alive.com)
- WPCH (channel 17, Peachtree TV, www.peachtreetv.com)
- WATL (channel 36, My Network TV, www.myatltv.com)
- WGCL (channel 46, CBS, www.cbs46.com)
- WUPA (channel 69, The CW, www.cwatlantatv.com)

MAPS AND TOURIST INFORMATION

The best place to find brochures, maps, and tips on what to see and do in Atlanta is the **Atlanta Convention and Visitors Bureau Visitor Center** at Underground Atlanta (65 Upper Alabama St., 404/521-6600, www.at-lanta.net). The bureau also operates smaller visitors centers at **Hartsfield-Jackson Airport** (Department of Aviation, Atrium Suite 435) and inside the **Georgia World Congress Center** (285 Andrew Young International Blvd.) during major events.

Resources

Suggested Reading

HISTORY AND INFORMATION

Allen, Frederick. *Atlanta Rising: The Invention of an International City 1946-1996.* Atlanta, GA: Longstreet Press, 1996. For those lacking the patience to dig through Franklin Garrett's encyclopedic *Atlanta and Environs,* this book makes for a suitable primer on local politics, industry, and culture. Allen, who has also written a detailed history of Coca-Cola, here delivers a chronicle of Atlanta's breakneck growth in the last half of the 20th century.

Garrett, Franklin. *Atlanta and Environs: A Chronicle of Its People and Events.* Athens, GA: University of Georgia Press, 1987. The definitive story of Atlanta as recorded by its official historian is probably not ideal for a casual dip into local history. The three-volume set is roughly the size of a cinderblock and goes into meticulous detail about the city from 1820 through the 1970s. The exhaustive scope of the project boggles the mind, but makes it a standard resource for genealogy research and discovering minutiae about the city's past.

Greene, Melissa Fay. *The Temple Bombing.* Cambridge, MA: Da Capo Press, 2006. The 1958 bombing of the Reform Jewish Temple on Peachtree Street is a sometimes-overlooked footnote of the civil rights era, a seemingly isolated incident in a city that missed much of the violence of desegregation. Greene's gripping exploration of the event and its aftermath offers a thorough look at the spirit of the times and the major personalities touched by the still-unsolved crime.

Pomerantz, Gary M. *Where Peachtree Meets Sweet Auburn: A Saga of Race and Family.* New York, NY: Penguin, 1997. The author, a former reporter for the *Atlanta Journal-Constitution,* delivers a compelling narrative about the changing roles of race in local politics. He traces the family histories of two of the city's most influential politicians: Ivan Allen Jr., a white mayor of the 1960s, and Maynard Jackson, Atlanta's first African American mayor. With a reporter's talent for crafting a compelling story, Pomerantz has delivered a book that is a must-read for any student of race relations in the city.

Rose, Michael. *Atlanta: Then and Now.* Berkeley, CA: Thunder Bay Press, 2001. If every picture tells a story, then this handsome coffee-table book of classic photography might be called a nostalgic tragedy. Jaw-dropping black-and-white archival photos of the city are juxtaposed with images of the same scene today—revealing that, in most cases, the graceful, European-inspired buildings

of yesteryear were demolished and replaced by considerably less timeless
architecture.

Schmelling, Michael. *Atlanta: Hip-Hop and the South*. San Francisco, CA: Chronicle Books, 2010. The saga of Atlanta's rise as a hip-house power-house is still being written, but photographer Michael Schmelling delivers a fine examination of the key players who helped make the sound of the South an international phenomenon. The book features more than 160 photos of blockbuster artists, fledging rappers, and fans, as well as essays and interviews.

LITERATURE AND FICTION

McCall, Nathan. *Them*. New York, NY: Atria, 2007. The slippery questions surrounding gentrification take center stage in this fascinating debut novel by Nathan McCall, a former reporter for the *Washington Post*. Set in today's rapidly changing Old Fourth Ward neighborhood (an area of the city that's seen an influx of upwardly mobile white residents in recent years), the book reveals characters grappling with deeply rooted feelings of prejudice and isolation as the Atlanta they used to know morphs into a different place entirely.

Mitchell, Margaret. *Gone With the Wind*. New York, NY: Scribner, 2007. Modern Atlantans usually cringe when the city's most famous novel gets mentioned, and they're quick to point out how little the book's antebellum setting or clichéd genre-fiction conventions reflect the metropolis of today. Still, there's a reason why Margaret Mitchell's historical romance has developed such a loyal following, and it's not just due to the film (which actually departs from the novel in several key places). Mitchell's insights into the character of the post-Civil War South make for an important time capsule about Atlanta's pedigree.

Siddons, Anne Rivers. *Peachtree Road*. New York: HarperTorch, 1998. Fans of Pat Conroy and Dorothea Benton Frank will lap up Siddons's classic page-turner about Atlanta privilege. Set in Buckhead in the middle years of the 20th century, the richly drawn novel traces the life of a reluctant debutante pulling away from her wealthy family. It also features what may be the best first line of any Southern novel from the past 50 years: "The South killed Lucy Bondurant Chastain Venable on the day she was born."

Windham, Donald. *Emblems of Conduct*. Athens, GA: University of Georgia Press, 1996. Windham, a confidante of Tennessee Williams and Truman Capote, recalls his youth in Depression-era Atlanta. The emotional coming-of-age memoir details his years growing up in a stately Victorian home on Peachtree Street-followed by the family's fall to a public housing project. The writer, best known for his novel *The Dog Star,* captures a bygone era with authority and eloquence.

Wolfe, Tom. *A Man in Full.* New York, NY: Farrar Straus Giroux, 1998. The celebrated author and father of New Journalism shines an acerbic spotlight on Atlanta society. The novel relates the downfall of a good-ol'-boy real-estate tycoon on the brink of financial ruin, and offers an amusing, sometimes brutally accurate view of the city's foibles—from white revulsion over Freaknik to the complicated rules of etiquette among Buckhead bluebloods. Wolfe's agenda is no less than epic; even if the book sometimes falters, it's still an entertaining portrait of Atlanta's propensity for hubris.

Internet Resources

INFORMATION AND EVENTS

Atlanta Convention and Visitors Bureau
www.atlanta.net

The official site of the city's tourism board is a useful portal for finding events, restaurants, hotels, and insider tips to Atlanta. The site's breadth of content is impressive, with loads of information aimed at the convention market, as well as plenty of tidbits for tourists and new residents. Also offers advice for planning reunions in the city.

Atlanta Performs
www.atlantaperforms.com

The go-to guide for a comprehensive list of theater, dance, and kids' events in the city. It's the official site of the Atlanta Coalition of Performing Arts, which has more than 170 member organizations. The user-friendly show calendar lets you search by title, neighborhood, venue, or company. It's also the only place online to purchase half-price same-day theater tickets, via AtlanTix.

Central Atlanta Progress
www.atlantadowntown.com

Central Atlanta Progress, founded in 1941, is a private not-for-profit corporation dedicated to advancing Downtown's business district. The site is an exhaustive resource for local history, entertainment listings, and current city-improvement projects. The neighborhoods section delivers a helpful guide to anyone still learning their way around town.

City of Atlanta
www.atlantaga.gov

The official site of the City of Atlanta offers lots of handy information to newcomers, including a downloadable new residents' kit. From recycling questions to procedures for obtaining city permits, the site offers a user-friendly response to common concerns. Also includes links to city government offices and county agencies.

www.exploregeorgia.org

Anyone considering a day trip outside of Atlanta should first consult Explore Georgia, the state's official tourism site. With a search engine of statewide events, attractions, and accommodations, the eye-catching site makes travel planning easier. Check out the Special Offers section to get deals on hotels and tourist spots.

NEWS

Atlanta Journal-Constitution
www.ajc.com

The city's venerable daily newspaper. Its entertainment and culture coverage falls under the **AccessAtlanta** (www.accessatlanta.com) sister site.

Atlanta Magazine
www.atlantamagazine.com

One of the oldest city magazines in the country, *Atlanta* is a timely journal of local culture and personalities. The site features a couple of noteworthy blogs and easily the best restaurant listings in town.

Creative Loafing Atlanta
www.clatl.com

Creative Loafing, the city's main alternative weekly newspaper for more than three decades, delivers an independent take on local news and extensive entertainment listings.

The GA Voice
www.thegavoice.com

Atlanta's best gay and lesbian newspaper features daily updates on local and national queer happenings.

Rolling Out
www.rollingout.com

An urban culture, fashion, and entertainment guide, this is a primo resource for young African American professionals.

PARKS AND RECREATION

Atlanta Track Club
www.atlantatrackclub.org

Founded in 1964, this running group produces the annual Peachtree Road Race and a handful of other 5Ks and marathons around town.

Centennial Olympic Park
www.centennialpark.com

As one of Atlanta's busiest public spaces, Centennial Olympic Park offers programming year-round. Its official site includes complete event listings, directions, and special deals on area attractions.

PATH Foundation
www.pathfoundation.org
Outdoors lovers will want to spend some time on the official site of the
PATH Foundation, an organization devoted to developing local trails for
walkers, joggers, cyclists, and skaters. The site includes maps and thorough
trail information.

Piedmont Park Conservancy
www.piedmontpark.org
Official site of the nonprofit agency that works to preserve and promote
Piedmont Park. Includes detailed listings of events in the park and beyond.

BEST ATLANTA BLOGS AND PODCASTS

Atlanta Street Fashion
http://atlantastreetfashion.blogspot.com
Photojournalist Cameron Adams turns the camera on sidewalk couture,
offering fun and frivolous snapshots of what the natives are wearing this
week.

Live Apartment Fire
www.liveapartmentfire.com
Veteran broadcast journalist Doug Richards watches Atlanta's nightly news
programs so you don't have to. His entertaining blog supplies biting com-
mentary on local media, written with charm and precision.

Project Q Atlanta
www.projectqatlanta.com
Project Q Atlanta has an uncanny knack for covering the city's gay and lesbian scenes, offering up-to-date breaking news, witty pop culture listings,
and always-entertaining photo galleries of area events.

What Now Atlanta
http://whatnowatlanta.com
Caleb Spivak's exhaustive news site keeps tabs on changes in the city's restaurants, retail stores, and real estate. Conversational currency for days!

Index

Restaurants Index

Nightlife Index

Shops Index

Hotels Index

Photo Credits

Title page photo: © Tray Butler; page 2 (top left) © Tray Butler, (top right) © Tray Butler, (bottom) © Tray Butler; page 18 (top left) © Bdingman | Dreamstime.com, (top right) © F11photo | Dreamstime.com, (bottom) © Tray Butler; page 19 © Valery Kaczmarek /123rf.com; page 20 © Tray Butler; page 21 © Tray Butler; page 22 © Jacobzinger | Dreamstime.com; page 23 © Lpkb | Dreamstime.com; page 25 © Tray Butler; page 26 (top) © Tray Butler, (bottom) © Sframe | Dreamstime.com; page 28 © Tray Butler; page 29 (top) © Tray Butler, (bottom) © Tray Butler; page 33 (top) © Clewisleake | Dreamstime.com, (bottom) © Tray Butler; page 36 (top left) © Tray Butler, (top right) © Tray Butler, (bottom) © Tray Butler; page 38 © Tray Butler; page 41 (top left) © Tray Butler, (top right) © Tray Butler, (bottom) © Tray Butler; page 47 (top left) © Tray Butler, (top right) © Tray Butler, (bottom) © Tray Butler; page 49 (top) © Tray Butler, (bottom) © Tray Butler; page 52 © Tray Butler; page 54 (top) © Tray Butler, (bottom) © Tray Butler; page 63 (top left) © Tray Butler, (top right) © Tray Butler, (bottom) © Tray Butler; page 66 © Tray Butler; page 75 (top) © Tray Butler, (bottom) © Tray Butler; page 83 (top left) © Tray Butler, (top right) © Tray Butler, (bottom) © Tray Butler; page 89 (top) © Tray Butler, (bottom) © Tray Butler; page 91 (top) © Tray Butler, (bottom) © Tray Butler; page 102 (top) © Tray Butler, (bottom) © Tray Butler; page 105 © Tray Butler; page 110 (top) © courtesy of Center for Puppetry Arts, (bottom) © alex grichenko/123rf.com; page 115 (top left) © Tray Butler, (top right) © Tray Butler, (bottom) © Tray Butler; page 120 (top) © Tray Butler, (bottom) © Tray Butler; page 127 (top left) © Tray Butler, (top right) © Tray Butler, (bottom) © Tray Butler; page 129© Tray Butler; page 131 (top) © courtesy of the City of Marietta, (bottom) © Delta Flight Museum; page 133 (top) © Russell Ensley/123rf.com, (bottom) © Tray Butler; page 137 (top) © Andreykr | Dreamstime.com, (bottom) © Tray Butler; page 141 (top) © Tray Butler, (bottom) © Tray Butler; page 148 (top) © Tray Butler, (bottom) © Tray Butler; page 154 (top) © Tray Butler, (bottom) © Tray Butler; page 163 (top left) © Tray Butler, (top right) © Tray Butler, (bottom) © Tray Butler; page 170 (top) © Tray Butler, (bottom) © Tray Butler; page 178 (top left) © Tray Butler, (top right) © Tray Butler, (bottom) © Tray Butler; page 185 (top) © Tray Butler, (bottom) © Sepavo | Dreamstime.com; page 191 (top) © Americanspirit | Dreamstime.com, (bottom) © Lpkb | Dreamstime.com; page 198 (top left) © Tray Butler, (top right) © Karafotography | Dreamstime.com, (bottom) © Tray Butler; page 203 (top) © Tray Butler, (bottom) © Tray Butler; page 206 (top) © Tray Butler, (bottom) © Robhainer | Dreamstime.com; page 210 © Tray Butler; page 226 (top) © Tray Butler, (bottom) © Tray Butler; page 230 (top) © Pyroe79 | Dreamstime.com, (bottom) © Pyroe79 | Dreamstime.com

Acknowledgments

Huge gratitude to my assistants, John Davis and Paul Bearden, whose fact-checking skills and moral support made this book possible. I'm forever thankful for my ATL insiders who are always several steps ahead of me in exploring the city: Scott Wolfson, Lucas Miré, Suzanne Van Atten, Randy Brazee, Jonathan Huff, and Robbie Zeider. Many thanks to the multi-talented team at Avalon Travel. You make the real magic happen. Finally, much love and appreciation to my mother, Brenda Butler, who sent countless leads for new listings and joined me on some of the most fun research trips. I couldn't imagine a better traveling companion.